THE TASK OF CULTURAL CRITIQUE

TERESA L. EBERT

The Task of
Cultural Critique

UNIVERSITY OF ILLINOIS PRESS

URBANA AND CHICAGO

Library of Congress Cataloging-in-Publication Data
Ebert, Teresa L., 1951–
The task of cultural critique / Teresa L. Ebert.
p.   cm.
Includes bibliographical references and index.
ISBN 978-0-252-03434-3 (cloth : acid-free paper)
ISBN 978-0-252-07626-8 (pbk. : acid-free paper)
1. Culture—Study and teaching—History. I. Title.
HM623.E25   2009
306.07—dc22   2009009426

For
Clara Elizabeth,
Chuck, Linda,
and Paula

Contents

Preface: The Critique of Interpretive Reason ix

PART 1 ANATOMY OF CONTEMPORARY
CULTURAL CRITIQUE

1. *The Spectral Concrete* 3

2. *The Abstract of Transformative Critique* 27

3. *Desiring Surfaces* 46

PART 2 THE WORK OF CRITIQUE

4. *Affective Pedagogy and Feminist Critique* 69

5. *Chick Lit: "Not Your Mother's Romance Novels"* 97

6. *Red Love* 118

7. *Globalization, the "Multitude," and Cynical Critique* 134

8. *Reading Ideology: Marx, de Man, and Critique* 169

Coda: Reclaiming Totality 195

Bibliography 197

Index 211

Preface: The Critique
of Interpretive Reason

I argue in this book that contemporary cultural critique has
been reduced to the "interpretation" of representation, thereby translating the social world into culture and equating culture with meaning. It
then makes meaning itself an antimimetic melodrama of fragmented
letters, signs, and traces that are at odds with themselves, and therefore
the only meaning they might have is their difference from themselves.
The world that emerges from contemporary cultural critique is a world
of self-difference made of representations, which are ultimately self-rep-
resentations, because signs are seen as always pointing to themselves and
not to a reality "outside." This is a world without an outside. Contrary
to canonic theory, this missing outside is the effect not of epistemological critique but of ideological mystification. It is a cultural opacity or
"unreadability," to use Paul de Man's term (*Allegories* 245), that functions with absolute lucidity to shield capital by rendering its effects on
collective social life—from layoffs and bad schooling to poor diet and the
absence of health care—a matter of representation and the interpretation of that representation. Cultural critique, in other word, has made
it impossible to understand social injustice, class differences, and the
violent rule of capital as objective historical reality. It has turned them
into effects of oscillating signs that disrupt the formation of meaningful
words and coherent statements. By rewriting the social as representation,
canonic cultural critique obscures the underlying structures of material
social relations such as class and instead focuses on the technologies of
signs and their concrete surfaces. According to Elizabeth Grosz,

texts could, more in keeping with the thinking of Gilles Deleuze, be read and used more productively as little bombs that . . . scatter thoughts and images into different linkages or new alignments without necessarily destroying them. Ideally, they produce unexpected intensities, peculiar sites of indifference, new connections with other objects, and thus generate affective and conceptual transformations that problematize, challenge, and move beyond existing intellectual and pragmatic frameworks. (Grosz, *Architecture* 58)

Representation ("text") and not class is seen as the dynamic of the social and its only mechanism of change.

The Iraq and Afghanistan Wars and the collapse of capitalism's financial institutions have exposed the vacuity of canonic critique, yet it emphatically rejects descriptions of its interpretive practices such as the one I have just given. It claims that it has moved beyond the "old" representational modalities of the 1970s, 1980s, and 1990s ("Derrida is dead; so is Deleuze"). This formal distancing, however, has proved to be merely a discursive device for more aggressive constructions of the social world as representation, namely, as the scene of disconnected letters and vacillating signs that undercut meaning (social totality) and rewrite politics as semiotics, convert history into temporality, displace objective reality with the (Lacanian) Real, and erase the abstract via the contingent concrete.

The new, it turns out, is not all that new, and it even has a formula that is written without a hint of irony in Gary Hall and Clare Birchall's anthology *New Cultural Studies.* The marketing of the new, which is most visible in celebrity culture and the selling of commodities, is now widely deployed by the publicists of new theory to divert attention from what really matters, namely, the materialist analysis of the objective working day. The selling of what is culturally useful for capital as the new is part of the structural logic of the culture of capitalism.

This means there is more to the new-ing of cultural critique. Derrida (now the "old"), for example, conceals the underlying abstract structures of the social (class) by concluding his argument about mimesis with a meditation on "abandoning all depth" (*Dissemination* 285). The new interpretive logic—after Derrida—similarly erases depth (the abstract) but does so by means of the new object of the *digital:* depth (the abstract) is now equated with the old *analog* and relegated to the past, while concrete surfaces are seen as the reality of the new emerging regime of the digital (Hayles, *My Mother Was a Computer* 201–5). Both the old and the new, in the name of an epistemological critique, perform the task of ideology by obscuring depth and with it the structures of social relations.

The reproduction of the logic of the old in the new is not simply a matter of influence (for example, that of Derrida's writings). It is a structural feature of the culture of capital. Derrida's or Deleuze's influence, in other words, is less the effect of his writings than of that which produces those writings. Derrida's work is influential not because it contains some groundbreaking understanding of language, affect, or body but because it is the site of operation of groundbreaking linguistic, affective, or corporeal strategies by which capital legitimates itself in new ways. What Derrida, Deleuze, and other "post" theorists have said has been said many times before, each time with a new vocabulary: New Criticism, Myth Criticism, structuralism, psychoanalysis, feminism, antiracism. When capital's social contradictions exceed the interpretive command of the dominant theory of the time (for example, New Criticism), it is abandoned for a new one (for example, deconstruction) that reproduces the interpretive logic of the exhausted theory in a new, energetic language. The demand for the new is an effect of constantly rising class antagonisms and the recurring need to explain them away.

Denouncing the (recent) past as outdated and announcing the arrival of a brand new, cutting-edge reality, in other words, is part of capital's interpretive logic of self-legitimization. This becomes more clear when one considers that, in spite of all their conceptual and analytical differences, each new and different theory constructs culture by means of one synecdoche or another (such as affect, aesthetic, text, writing, letter, sign, subject, and body) as an autonomous zone free from the yoke of the "economic," that is, a zone full of playful signs, fragmented letters, nomadic meanings, differential identities, and performative singularities. This free zone is a necessity for capitalism: in culture, it gives individuals the freedom that it denies them in the working day. Culture—as an autonomous arena of wavering meanings and self-displacing identities—is the cynical response of capitalism to the limits that class relations in a wage-labor system place on individuality: "Ideologically, we see the same contradiction in the fact that the bourgeoisie endowed the individual with an unprecedented importance, but at the same time that same individuality was annihilated by the economic conditions to which it was subjected by the reification created by commodity production" (Lukács, *History and Class Consciousness* 62).

I engage and critique this interpretive logic throughout the book, because without knowing its main features and the way it is reproduced through, for example, feminism, pedagogy, desire, globalization, the displacing of materialism by materiality, the substitution of the concrete for the abstract, and their consequences, it is not possible to abandon this logic and move cultural critique in a different direction. Cultural critique needs to jettison the utopian view of culture as a free zone of singularity and begin to understand culture in materialist terms as an extension of the social relations of production.

Instead of "interpreting" the everyday in terms of the concrete "linguistic sensuality" of its representations (Barthes, *Pleasure* 54), cultural critique, I argue, needs to explain the abstract structures of daily life in terms of their material causes and produce an understanding of social totality by which the spontaneous daily consciousness of the concrete is transformed into a critique-al consciousness, which is the necessary condition for a layered class consciousness. Without it, social struggles for change (to which cultural critique claims to be contributing) are diminished, becoming an eclectic activism whose guidelines are lived experience, suffering, and hope and whose goals are set not by a thorough understanding of history but by daily events. Or they become an aggressive discursive pursuit of a "true materiality" (*true* used here as Marx used it in "'True' socialism"). This is a materiality of signs and letters: a "materiality without materialism and even perhaps without matter" (Derrida, "Typewriter Ribbon" 281). "True materiality" is the slogan of canonical cultural critique, as I indicate Part I, in my discussion of the corporeal and corporeality. As might be expected, the two—activism and true materiality—are often mixed together and turned into a hybrid that, in the name of dismantling binaries, provides an eclectic, evasive interpretive space in which critique amuses itself, for example, with meditations on "the wealth of the poor" (Hardt and Negri, *Multitude* 129–38) to further obscure class relations in the global division of labor.

The archelogic of contemporary critique—in which it articulates all its interpretations, regardless of their local differences—is the resignification of the *material* (wage labor) in terms of the immaterial (free will). This is another way of saying what I have said before: contemporary cultural critique has become a new genre of ideology. In translating the materialist world (of labor) into immaterial (meanings), it has made the world culturally safe for capital.

I therefore argue against canonic cultural critique by analyzing some of the effects of its (Nietzschean) epistemology, which has marginalized explanation in favor of interpretation and, as a result, has obscured the objective material causes of cultural practices such as representation. Explanation is an analytics of cause and effect, of which contemporary critique has become progressively more suspicious as social contradictions have increased. Without a causal analysis, social totality is pulverized into discontinuous and unrelated contingent singularities. Post-causal interpretation produces a social world in which, for example, child labor in the South is not related to the affluence of the North, and imperialism is disconnected from capitalism. This world of singularities without a material logic to relate them is, of course, the world in which capitalism thrives. Instead of explaining the material logic of culture, canonic critique instead offers the cultural logic of materiality (Jameson, *Postmodernism*).

For Nietzsche the analytics of cause and effect is the embodiment of a will to truth. In *The Will to Power*, Nietzsche writes that "we invert the chronological order of cause and effect. The fundamental fact of 'inner experience' is that the cause is imagined after the effect" (265). The representation of cause and effect as a fiction of metaphysics has had enormous consequences for both cultural theory and cultural analysis. It has suspended the base-superstructure explanation and thus, in the name of materiality, has essentially abolished the materialist understanding of culture in relation to its materialist base. The utter conceptual emptiness of indeterminate and overdeterminate analytics, which have become the interpretive logic of contemporary critique, and the necessity of base-superstructural analysis, have become more clear after 9/11 and the imperialist invasions of Iraq and Afghanistan along with the colonization of a "new" Europe. To critique the Iraq War, as many theory activists do, without explaining it in terms of its material causes—such as the falling rate of profit in global capitalism and its need for expanded and unfettered access to cheap labor and resources—is simply to produce entertaining but vacuous analyses of culture in its own terms, tautological narratives full of tropes and jokes but without any purchase on historical reality (Žižek, *Iraq*).

Canonic critique replaces causal explanation with interpretation because it regards explanation to be a foundationalist analysis that understands the everyday by appealing to Truth. Interpretation, on the other hand, is represented as a reading that is free from the metaphysics of essence (Truth), an activating of the different, the singular, and the heterogeneous corporeality. Interpretation is seen as a complex description without any determining commitment. It takes such forms as "redescription" in Rorty, "resignification" in Butler, "thick description" in Geertz, "deconstruction" in Derrida, "destruction" in Heidegger, "reparative reading" in Sedgwick, and "uncritical reading" in Warner and is, broadly, a variation in different idioms and tones of a "gray, meticulous, and patiently documentary" account (Foucault, "Nietzsche" 139).

Through interpretation, which is a version of the Kantian immanent critique in which the outside is collapsed into the inside, canonic critique reduces social structures to isolated concrete singularities and supplants critique itself by a "mid-analytics": local interpretations of "small narratives" that do not become involved in grand inquiries into origin (*arche*), end (*telos*), or what Richard Rorty calls "final vocabularies" (*Contingency* 73). Mid-analytics replaces the why (the material logic of events and their relations to social structures) with the how (the cultural logic of representations). It is a contingent story with the ironic tones of playful knowingness. Interpretation, as I show, translates the social world into a "body without organs," an absolute difference without difference. The difference that makes a material difference—class—is figured through interpretation as molecular motions on the concrete surfaces of culture.

The concrete, I argue, was a cultural weapon in the moment of the rise of a progressive bourgeoisie, used for demystifying the abstract in which the class interests of feudal owners were hidden under layers of theological and metaphysical arguments. Since Nietzsche, however, the concrete has become the sensual metaphysics of the bourgeoisie. In the name of a critique of metaphysics, it has used the singular concrete to abandon all depth and thus has shielded the deep structures of class from critique. What was a means for demystification has been turned into a device for mystification. Class and class interests are at stake here, as everywhere else. Although I have discussed class at length elsewhere, it is perhaps necessary to again say that class is the dynamic of the everyday and history itself. It is a relationship of owning the labor of others (living and past) because labor is a commodity unlike any other in that it "possesses the peculiar property of being a source of value" (Marx, *Capital* I: 270).

The task of a transformative cultural critique ineluctably involves class analysis. This is another way of saying it cannot remain an immanent critique. A critique that limits itself to an immanent analysis of culture in its own terms ends up interpreting its limits or blinds spots, its aporiae, as the result of self-division within culture, as if culture is autonomous and not an effect of a larger social and historical force. I argue that the fissures that canonic critiques finds in culture are effects of social contradictions that cannot be resolved within the existing material practices. Therefore, although transformative cultural critique often begins with an immanent critique, it must not play the game of "tarrying with the immanent" and needs to relate culture's internal economies of signification to their historical material outside. In other words, it needs to connect the inside to the social relations of production and not be seduced by the maxim "The Outside Is the Inside" (Derrida, *Grammatology* 44). In class societies the outside is always in the outside.

Transformative cultural critique should not become "genealogical," as Nietzsche recommends (*Human, All Too Human*), but instead move toward a historical and materialist understanding, as Marx argues (*Critique of Hegel's Doctrine of the State*). The aporiae in culture are not the effects of internal contradictions within culture but the outcome of the historical contradictions of class relations.

Cultural critique needs to go beyond textual activism, which produces subversive readings that give pleasure to the reader and reassure her of her discursive agency, because such agency is spectral. Rather, cultural critique needs to produce knowledge of actual material conditions, which are always matters of class. Class, of course, is deployed in contemporary critique but mostly is used as a cultural term to mean lifestyle. The culturalizing of class in canonic critique is part of the larger tendency I examine in which the material (production) is replaced by the cultural (consumption) and is often referred to as the "cultural turn" (Hall, "Centrality of Culture" 220).

The "cultural turn" is not "the same thing as saying that . . . [practices] are 'embedded' in a particular socio-cultural context, or that they are 'socially constructed'" (du Gay and Pryke, "Cultural Economy" 2). Rather, it is an argument that claims that meanings arise not from things themselves (the material) but from a cultural sign system (language) that differentiates among them and gives them meanings: "The names of things are also sobriquets. Not from the thing to the word, but from the word to the thing; the word gives birth to the thing" (Bakhtin, *Essays* 182). The cultural turn, as I have argued in *Class in Culture*, is not a new event, contrary to what many historians hold, but is a structural feature of all class societies. It becomes more prominent at times of intense class contradictions, such as early industrial capitalism (Romanticism) or the expansion of colonialism, when capitalism began to become a world regime of labor (the Victorian age), and most recently after World War II and during the 1960s. The cultural turn reduces class tension by putting lived experience (the traditional threshold of subjectivity) and language (reference and representation as the index code of "reality") at the center of social analysis. Both, I show, are circuits of ideology and converge in the concrete, which is one of the reasons for my critique of its constitution and consequence.

The Task of Cultural Critique is a contribution to overturning the cultural turn by writing materialism and class back into cultural critique and producing a transformative critique whose purpose is to be part of the social and cultural struggles for change. In order to do so, cultural critique has to move beyond the cultural turn and its poetics of the concrete. Instead of dwelling on the ad hoc, the aleatory, the excited, the playful, and the spontaneous, it needs to engage the historical and material dynamics of culture. The task of a transformative materialist cultural critique is to provide, by explanation, critique-al knowledges that can be deployed not only to fight cultural oppression but also to struggle for freedom from necessity because "the true realm of freedom, the development of human powers as an end in itself, begins beyond it" (Marx, *Capital* 3: 958). Here ideology ends because labor is no longer exchanged for wages.

Over the years, as I have struggled for social change and encountered exclusion and silence from various institutions, journals, and presses, I have received sustaining intellectual and political support from Barbara Foley and Peter McLaren, as well as from Helen Regueiro Elam.

I am also thankful for the intellectual support of Julian Markels, Bret Benjamin, Evan Watkins, Pamela McCallum, E. San Juan Jr., Deborah Peterson Kelsh, and Dave Hill.

Joan Catapano's intellectual and editorial support have been especially crucial during the completion of this project. I thank Rebecca McNulty Schreiber, Angela Burton, and Jane Zanichkowsky, who have been particularly helpful in contributing ideas and editorial advice.

As always, I have debated many of the ideas in this book with Mas'ud Zavarzadeh as part of our ongoing collective critiques.

In this book I have used various paragraphs from essays of mine that originally appeared in *Against the Current; Cultural Logic; College English;* and *Nature, Society and Thought.* I thank the editors of these journals for their intellectual support.

PART I

Anatomy of Contemporary Cultural Critique

1. *The Spectral Concrete*

The Contingent, the Material, and Stubborn Reality

The contemporary ecstasy about the concrete is commonly seen as theory's commitment to materiality or, in Eve Kosofsky Sedgwick's words, to the "heartbeat of contingency" (*Touching Feeling* 147). It shows itself especially in the pleasures that contemporary critique takes in the technologies of representation that are found in cultural texts. A contingent materiality is considered a resistance against the idealism and unbounded utopianism that have marked traditional (humanist) cultural critiques as found in the writings of John Ruskin, Walter Pater, and Matthew Arnold or, closer to our time, T. S. Eliot, Virginia Woolf, John Crowe Ransom, and Lionel Trilling, among others. Through a materiality of the concrete, contemporary theoretically oriented critique—what used to be called "postmodern" critique—puts in question the plentitude of meaning obtained by means of a conceptual closure that appeals to a final signified such as Nature (Rousseau), Reason (Kant), Spirit (Hegel), Existence (Sartre) or, most commonly, the Divine (Descartes). Not only is language treated as an untranscendable materiality in contemporary critique, but also the body is considered to be a concrete opacity whose singular materiality cannot be mastered by giving it a confining identity such as gender (Butler, *Bodies*). This contingent materiality is, I argue, neither material nor materialism. It is a new form of objective idealism—what I call a *delectable materialism*. To put it differently, it is a "materiality without materialism and even perhaps without matter" (Derrida,

3

"Typewriter Ribbon" 281). I offer a materialist theory of the concrete in chapter 2. Here, however, I would like to say that the task is not to banish the concrete but to understand it in historical and in materialist terms. In *History and Class Consciousness*, Georg Lukács writes that bourgeois historians always attempt to focus on the concrete and that

> they reproach historical materialists with violating the concrete unique-ness of historical events. Where they go wrong is in their belief that the concrete can be located in the empirical individual of history ("in-dividual" here can refer to an individual man, class, or people) and in his empirically given (and hence psychological or mass-psychological) consciousness. And just when they imagine that they have discovered the most concrete thing of all: *society as a concrete totality*, the system of production at a given point in history and the resulting division of society into classes—they are in fact at furthest remove from it. In miss-ing the mark they mistake something wholly abstract for the concrete. "These relations," Marx states, "are not those between one individual and another, but between worker and capitalist, tenant and landlord, etc. Eliminate these relations and you abolish the whole of society." (50, emphasis in original)

The concrete, I argue, means the "relation to society as a whole." But before discussing a materialist theory of the concrete, I would like to focus on the concrete as it is deployed in contemporary critique and briefly outline its genealogy, starting with early modernity.

The concrete—often in the form of representations of sensuous de-tails and the everyday—has become the main focus of contemporary cultural critique. In focusing on concrete representations, such critique has effectively obscured social totality, which, I argue, is the basis for any transformative practice. Avoiding the abstract structures of class and labor, which actually produce the everyday, cultural critique has become a subtle, witty, pleasurable, and, in the end, inconsequential teasing out of the details of technologies of representation in cultural texts. In spite of its claim to being an active agent of social and cultural change, it has been reduced to merely finding the particulars of oppositional representa-tions, tropes of resistance, and signifiers of transgressions against social equality and cultural justice.

In her reading of the film *The Full Monty*, for example, J. K. Gibson-Graham takes the striptease performed by unemployed male workers as an act of defiance of capital and as a sign of "hopeful openings to pos-sibility in line with a reparative reading of industrial change," a utopian gesture to a postcapitalist politics (*Postcapitalist* 9–10). Her interpretive ecstasy concerning the concrete of naked bodies joyously dancing quietly

obscures the abstract dark structures of unemployment and profit that
have led to these men's unemployment—an analysis of which might lead
the reader beyond the sensual pleasures of the film to a historical understanding of the work of capital and its relation with labor, specifically
its treatment of laborers as dispensable persons. In contrast, she finds
that *Brassed Off*, another British film dealing with unemployment, is
not as effective. Instead of ending with a concrete performance by men
who symbolically strip the myth of work from their identities, it ends
with a fairly long and abstract critique of capitalism by the bandmaster.
He spells out in a simple yet substantive conceptual analysis the laws
of motion of capital and its violence against the bodies of workers (he is
himself dying of a work-related illness: black lung).

The class politics of the concrete is clearly demonstrated in the way
Gibson-Graham invokes "hopeful openings," "possibilities," and becoming; in doing so, she not only lets capitalism off the hook but also subtly
affirms it by equating unemployment with liberation from exploitation.
Brassed Off's insistence on "being employed," she suggests, could only
mean a desire to be "exploited by capitalism" (13). The need to work
is, for her, the mark of a subject desiring dependency, a subject without
autonomy. Capitalism, in a strange if not perverse way, liberates workers by laying them off. The possibility of employment without exploitation is not considered (her use of the term *employment* rather than
labor is telling). According to her interpretive logic, the only way out of
capitalism is the way back into it, namely, setting up your own "free"
enterprise as the men in *The Full Monty* fantasize (16). The *jouissance*
of the utopia of their postwork lives—whose signifier is naked bodies
in a dance of defiance—is in workers' opening their own businesses so
they can have "more earning capacity" and control over their "economic
resources" (16).

Gibson-Graham reads *The Full Monty* in terms of collectivity, community, and blissful liberation. Yet she forgets that what she represents
as liberation from capitalism and a fantasy of economic independence is
still within capitalism and is subject to the same laws of profit, marketing, and commodification present in the actual performativity of capital
that underlies the film's final performance. The concrete in this case—
bodies—does not mark the independence of the desiring subject and her
resistance to capital; it denotes a liberation of desire (Gibson-Graham,
Postcapitalist 13) within the terms of capitalism and not freedom from
necessity (Marx, *Gotha Programme* 10).

Cultural critique's obsession with the concrete has marginalized
production (for example, steelworking in *The Full Monty*) in the inter-

est of consumption such as entertainment, which does not produce and acts as an event through which value is redistributed. Fetishizing the concrete has both reduced politics to a micropolitics and turned it into a form of writing—an affect with a difference (Gibson-Graham, *Postcapitalist* 53–78).

Attention to the concrete is not new; it has its origins in the rise of modernity. For early modern and Enlightenment writers, however, the concrete was a basis for critiquing the abstractions of religion and philosophy in which the class interests of feudal lords were hidden. For the contemporary, what is new is the way the concrete has become a defense of the singular, the sensuous, and the affective—a delectable materiality—and, I argue, a legitimization of prevailing social relations and market individualism. The textual activism of contemporary critique is an extension of, not an opposition (or even a resistance) to capitalism.

THE HETEROGENEOUS SINGULARITY OF THE CONCRETE

In contemporary cultural critique, the concrete is commonly assumed to be the materialization of heterogeneous reality in its resilient singularity and resistance to totality, which is regarded as the erasure of difference. Engaging the concrete is therefore seen as a test of analytical validity and critical authenticity as well as a means to bring theory and practice together in understanding the everyday and its cultural politics. The more closely a critique deals with the concrete specifics of cultural practices, the more it is considered to be thoughtful, subtle, nuanced, and free from the crudeness of abstract generalizations, which are deemed to be "gaseous theorizing" (Fish, "Theory's Hope" 376). Contemporary critique, in short, is enthralled by the concrete. The concrete—in the words of Gayatri Spivak, whose writings weave together heterogeneous tissues of concrete text without imposing any overarching arguments (abstractions) on them—affirms the "irreducible heterogeneity of the cultural" in the face of such abstractions as the "cultural dominant" (*Postcolonial* 315). Roland Barthes' description of the specificity of the text and its "linguistic sensuality" is one of the most ecstatic inscriptions of the concrete (*Pleasure* 54) and is, in a sense, an account of the underlying theory of the concrete, a theory that takes many forms in contemporary critique. The concrete as text is, for Barthes, the sublime of difference and is, therefore, "outside any imaginable finality"; it is the performative of the heterogeneous: "language in pieces; culture in pieces" (51). It is the sovereignty of pleasure where "value" (the "totality") shifts to the "sumptuous rank of the signifier" and "language" is "lined with flesh, a text where we can hear the grain of the throat, the patina of consonants, the voluptuousness of vowels, a whole carnal stereophony: the articulation of the body, of the tongue, not that of meaning, of language" (65–67).

The concrete of language is also celebrated in Avital Ronell's "Misery of Theory without Poetry," in which poetry as the insightful agent of "insurrection . . . support(s) acts of referential disobedience" (17) and becomes the allegory of the singular through which the individual is legitimated as one who resists the normative and regulated ("referential") market. The poem (concrete) and theory (abstract) stand in for a particular theory of social relations, and although Ronell states that poetry and theory are "beholden to each other" (18), "beholding" is a trope for reinstating a liberal pluralism in which the "poem" (the individual) is seen, at least in a moment of "temptation," as what theory "secretly depends on" (17–18).

Language and the body, as I discuss below, are two exemplary instances of the concrete in contemporary critique and its marginalization of the abstract, in large part as a form of totalization, which is represented as a closure imposed on the free flow of meanings by a will to "presence" (Derrida, *Grammatology* 50). I believe that the abstract provides, rather, a much more comprehensive understanding of cultural practices in their historical connections and displays their material logic, thus making the abstract a more active basis for social change. The widespread suppression of the abstract is not a purely epistemological issue, as is often suggested, nor is it done to avoid totalization, although this is the reason usually given. Contemporary critique does not hesitate to totalize a whole range of issues, including the structure of language itself, which is supposed to be the house of the concrete. Paul de Man, for example, in criticizing logocentric views of language, claims that "the figurative structure is not one linguistic mode among others but it characterizes language as such" (*Allegories* 105). Similarly, Judith Butler totalizes gender as a performative: "There is no gender identity behind the expressions of gender; that identity is performatively constituted by the very 'expressions' that are said to be its results" (*Gender Trouble* 33). This is as much a totalization as that which is often represented as a totalizing pronouncement: "It is not the consciousness of men that determines their existence, but on the contrary, their social existence that determines their consciousness" (Marx, *Critique of Political Economy* 21). That Butler totalizes contingency (of gender identity) does not make it any less of a totalization. The point is that the interest in the concrete and the war against totality do not constitute an epistemological question as it is commonly represented. It is ideological. Totalizations that legitimate existing social relations are quietly received as cultural insights and fresh ideas; those that oppose capitalism are rejected as bordering on totalitarianism.

The privileging of the concrete in contemporary critique is a subtle way of legitimating existing social relations by equating all projects for social transformation with totalization and representing any change (other than activating the play of signs) as an illusion of progress, as another act of the will to truth that disregards the difference within. The only change that is acceptable is change from within the existing structures; such change actually amounts to little more than reform. Thus What Is is kept intact, but its difference-within is given more play. Gender, for example, is resignified as a performative and thus rendered unstable, but this internal oscillation is substituted for transformation of the material social structures that produce gender in the first place. What Is, in other words, is taken as given, and all change is directed toward What Is Within, as if the inside is autonomous from the outside. The concrete is this autonomy of the inside, which protects it from history.

The debates concerning the concrete—whether they concern the work of Theodor Adorno in the *Negative Dialectic* or that of Jean-François Lyotard in *The Differend*—are, in the end, not about the specific and the universal, although that is the form they often take in Kantian and neo-Kantian, Hegelian, and existentialist discourses. Nor can they be fully understood, as I have already suggested, in terms of the more familiar arguments about totalization. The contestations about the concrete are, at root, about existing social relations and whether to legitimate them in their present form or to critique them and expose them in order to change them (Marx, *Grundrisse*).

It is necessary to critique the concrete: to question the widely held conviction that the concrete constitutes resistance to the cultural closure of heterogeneity and to challenge the way it is embraced in activist projects for change as a safeguard of openness and plurality. The concrete has, in actuality, become a means for discursively breaking up material social totality. It conceals the contradictions of capitalism by representing them as the regional differences of diverse cultural practices and depicting these as unconnected, autonomous performatives. Contemporary cultural critique deploys the concrete in order to privilege local knowledge, affect, and micropolitics, thereby limiting social change to marginal adjustments in the dominant social relations. As it produces these illusions of agency and struggles against the homogeneity brought about by capitalism, it constructs the illusion of freedom of the subject and the heterogeneity of cultural life within unfree and highly regimented social relations.

My critique of the concrete is not a call to abandon it but a call to abandon the conditions that require the illusions that the concrete is used to manufacture. The concrete, as a heterogeneous singularity marking human freedom, is obtainable, I argue, only through freedom from necessity, which requires struggles based on knowledge of social totality and not on the fantasy of a concrete that is actually a code for individualism. Individualism is a ruse of capitalism to get people to accept What Is instead of What Could Be.

MODERNITY AND THE CONCRETE

The invention of the concrete as a discursive means for cultural and social change is part of the history of modernity, the rise of capitalism, and the formation of its governing class. The roots of modernity are in the early ideological struggles against the feudal cultural order that mystified the class contradictions of feudalism through the superstitions of religion and the abstraction of (a mostly faith-based) metaphysics. The most effective weapon that modernity used in these struggles was the concrete—specifically, its appeal to the experiential, the sensuous, and the everyday empirical, which were the constituents of a new "science" used to dislodge the established feudal commonsense, with its allegiance to the supernatural and the divine.

Understanding the place of the concrete in contemporary cultural critique and its role in cultural and social transformations depends to considerable extent on understanding the rise of capitalism and its relation to feudalism. Any interpretation of the conditions that led to the emergence of capitalism also shapes interpretation of modernity and the place of the concrete in it.

The rise of capitalism is the subject of several contesting theories. Paul Sweezy (*From Feudalism to Capitalism*), Immanuel Wallerstein (*Historical Capitalism*), and, before them, Henri Pirenne (*Medieval Cities*) have all argued that capitalism is the result of profits from trade (and thus outside class struggles). Arguing against this mercantilist theory, Robert Brenner ("Agrarian Class Structure," "Agrarian Roots") and Ellen Wood (*Origins of Capitalism*) have suggested that the origins of capitalism lie in the countryside and in changes in agriculture. These changes, they contend, were brought about by the need of feudal lords for cash in order to maintain political power by means of their armies; they thus rented out their land to farmers, who in turn hired wage laborers. Feudal landlords pressured farmers to increase efficiency so that they could collect higher rents, and this in turn increased the exploitation of hired hands, leading to changes in production relations, class antagonism, and the rise of capitalism.

As Chris Harman points out, however, Brenner's theory depends on a rather eccentric theory of class struggle in which the peasants have to rebel and "free themselves from the main burden of feudal services and dues" but the lords have to "retain enough power to prevent peasants getting control of the land themselves." As a result, he says, "history, it seems, is made by those exploited classes who fight but don't fight to the end" (Harman, "Feudalism to Capitalism" 67; also see Harman and Brenner, "Origins of Capitalism"). Brenner's theory, in other words, essentially understands the dynamics of history to be political rather than economic. Both the trade and the agricultural theories regard the rise of capitalism as having taken place outside the new forces of production and the class struggles they bring about. The superstructure of capitalism, according to these accounts, is largely seen as an expansion and continuation of feudal culture.

The roots of capitalism, however, are in the class struggles between feudal lords and peasants concerning the increase of surplus labor that resulted from the use of new forces of production (for example, the iron-tipped plough, the crank, which expanded the uses of water mills, and use of the three-field system for crop rotation). "The economic structure of capitalist society," Marx argues, "grows out of the economic structure of feudal society" (Marx, *Capital*, 1: 875). This material base was the ground for the social struggles led by large-scale farmers who generalized their own class interests as the interests of all peasants and thus recruited other peasants in the fight against the feudal lords. As in all social transformations, the new forces of production changed the old ways of using labor and the social relations supporting them, and in doing so, formed new classes and class relations. Consequently, some farmers and burghers reorganized production practices by turning free laborers into wage laborers. As a result, new production units were set up mostly, but not exclusively, in towns, where the focus was on the production of commodities for market. In these new workshops, the direct producers did not have control over the material and means of production. All they had was their labor, which had itself become a commodity (Harman, "Feudalism to Capitalism"; Harman and Brenner, "Origins of Capitalism").

Modernity as the cultural superstructure of capitalism is not simply an expansion and reform of feudal ideology (as is implied in the trade and the agriculture theories of capitalism with their evolutionary views of balanced classes). It is a revolutionary transformation caused by the material triumph of a new bourgeois class, which shifted culture from its theological orientation in feudalism to the scientific culture of industrial capitalism.

The modernist superstructure legitimated the new bourgeoisie and its economic order by emphasizing the individual and her concrete experiences. In contrast to paternal and abstract authority, individualism was posited as part of the freedom of consciousness and worldliness, as an arena of civil society in which not only "civil life" but also the "commercial arts" thrived (Ferguson, *Civil Society* 172–93) and whose goal, in John Locke's words, was mostly "the preservation of property" ("Second Treatise," ch. 7, p. 141). Modernism sought authority for the concrete in science by questioning the abstractions of speculative natural philosophy and normalized the ideas and ideals of the new class. In the Renaissance, for example, the revival of the arts naturalized the sovereignty of the senses, the tangible concrete, and sensuality as parts of the free expression of the new aesthetic subject. The Reformation granted the new burgher freedom from official interpretations of the sacred by focusing on the concrete, everyday experiences of the individual, and the Enlightenment recoded the subject as one of practical reason and knowledge in order to overcome the ignorance of the individual.

These ideals were given material support by new scientific developments, which were enabled by new production practices that made more surplus labor available and thus opened up space for scientific work. (On the socioeconomic roots of modern science, see Hessen, *Newton's Principia*; Zilsel, *Social Origins*; Lefevre, "Science as Labor.") The new science put in question Aristotelian natural philosophy and its generalizations by making the concrete and singular the subject of its inquiry, and in doing so, it put aside the abstractions of the old deductive logic in favor of inductive arguments based on examination of specific issues.

The change from the old manorial "working day" to the wage labor "working day" produced a new cultural superstructure that constructed the concrete as a new threshold of reality and used it to normalize the individual and the specific. In doing so, it valorized the activities of individual entrepreneurs and asserted the formal equality of individuals (which actually meant equality in trading).

The concrete was perhaps the most effective weapon of the new bourgeoisie in its fight against the old order because it used the concrete to mark the authenticity of the new and to discredit the old as nothing but mystified abstractions with no basis in actual, sensual, tangible, and verifiable (that is, concrete) reality. David Hume, for instance, questioned the legitimacy of the old regime in his "On Miracles" (*Human Understanding* 109–31) by criticizing all that was supernatural, otherworldly, and lacking a basis in the empirical. Hume's themes of anticlericalism, rationalism, and materialism were echoed in different ways and with different emphases in the writings of Hobbes, Spinoza, Diderot, Helvetus, Montesque, d'Alembert, Voltaire, and others. In a sense the underlying logic of these critiques was outlined by Kant in his manifesto concerning reason, "What Is Enlightenment?" Enlightenment, for Kant, "is man's release from his self-incurred tutelage. Tutelage is man's inability to make use of his understanding without direction from another. Self-incurred is this tutelage when its cause lies not in lack of reason but in lack of resolution and courage to use it without direction from another" (85).

The marginalization of experience in traditional metaphysics was Kant's primary concern in the *Critique of Pure Reason.* He took the middle ground, however, in the contestation about the concrete by stating that "all knowledge begins with experience" (41), but it does not follow that it "arises out of experience" (41–42). This middle ground— which is actually an allegory for the class truce for which his philosophy strived—is sustained by a series of differences that are embedded in each other: intuition and understanding, concept and experiment, phenomena and noumena. According to Kant, "thoughts without content are empty, intuitions without concepts are blind. It is, therefore, just as necessary to make our concepts sensible, that is, to add the object to them in intuition, as to make our intuitions intelligible, that is, to bring them under concepts. These two powers or capacities cannot exchange their functions. The understanding can intuit nothing, the senses can think nothing. Only through their union can knowledge arise" (93).

Francis Bacon, in *The New Organon,* had, of course, already advanced the "inductive" mode of analysis and set it in opposition to the dominant "deductive" procedures that, following the Aristotelian syllogistic methodologies, had privileged the abstract and abstraction as the indicators of a truly reliable knowledge. "The syllogism," Bacon wrote, "consists of propositions, propositions consist of words, words are symbols of notions. Therefore if the notions themselves (which is the root of the matter) are confused and overhastily abstracted from facts, there can be no firmness in the superstructure. Our only hope therefore lies in a true induction" (*New Organon* 41).

Bacon's inductive method gave "nature" a radically different status in scientific investigations, and he argued that beyond nature, man "neither knows anything nor can do anything" (*New Organon* 39). He thus turned nature into the foundation for the scientific "concrete," which made the concrete itself exemplary of reality. In the name of this natural concrete, many of the ideological battles of the philosophes and the Enlightenment, in general, were fought against the old cultural order.

Hume's theory of ideas and causation, which were based on present impressions (the empirical), made the concrete the ground of a new paradigm of skeptical ("scientific") understanding that was a critical weapon against the faith-based knowledge of the abstract: the "creative power of the mind," he wrote, "amounts to no more than the faculty of compounding, transposing, augmenting, or diminishing the material afforded by senses and experience" (*Human Understanding* 19). Cause and effect, for Hume, is not an abstract law but, rather, the outcome of concrete, sensuous connections among ideas, which are themselves configurations of the sensuous and the concrete. "Causes and effects," Hume argued, "are discoverable, not by reason but by experience" (28).

The concrete, in other words, became the foundation for critiquing the old order and all that was not open to independent testing and democratic interrogation. Religion—and what religion represented as knowledge through its hermeneutical exegesis—became the targets of the "new" natural concrete (Diderot, *Pensées sur l'interpretation de la nature*) and were critiqued as abstractions that mystified the dominant power. The contestations over the abstract and the concrete, such as those between Berkeley (*Principles of Human Knowledge*) and his contemporaries, further complicated the status of the abstract. It became the source of imprecision and mistakes, leading "those great masters of abstraction" with "their doctrine of abstract natures and notions" into "inextricable labyrinths of error and dispute" (55). Berkeley does not dispute that knowledge consists of "universal notions" but contends that they are not "formed by abstraction in the manner premised—*universality*, so far as I can comprehend, not consisting in the absolute, positive nature or conception of anything, but in the relation it bears to the particulars signified or represented by it; by virtue whereof it is that things, names, or notions, being in their own nature *particular*, are *rendered universal* (53, emphasis in original).

Locke, on the other hand, turned abstraction into a first principle in his philosophy and wrote that abstraction is what separates man from animals: "The power of abstracting is not at all in them" (*Human Understanding* 129). Yet he made his case for abstraction by means of the concrete semiotics of the sign by appealing to the particular and sensuous textuality of words as "sensible marks" (259) that signify ideas in their arbitrary relations (that is, contingent and not formulated as necessary abstract relations [262]).

Even Hegel, who argued for the priority of the abstract, nonetheless considered the concrete to be the threshold for the truth of the abstract. According to Hegel, "in itself the Idea is really concrete, for it is the union of different determinations. . . . The truth or the Idea does not consist in empty generalities, but in a universal, and that is in itself the particular and the determined. If the truth is abstract it must be untrue.

. . . Philosophy is what is most antagonistic to abstraction. And it leads back to the concrete" (*On Art* 231–32).

TRANSVALUATION OF THE CONCRETE

The radical social inversion of the concrete—from a critique of the instituted to a subtle legitimization of the institutional—occurred with the waning of the Enlightenment and found its most passionate advocate in Nietzsche as he broke with modernity. His radical transvaluation of the concrete was a response to the increasing class contradictions of capitalism. By the time *Birth of Tragedy* was published in 1872, capitalism had moved beyond its early liberal phase to become a monopoly capitalism in its imperialist stage and was thus facing growing class antagonisms domestically and globally. The East India Company had completely taken over India (Oudh was annexed in 1856) and was confronting increasing resistance against its rule and its exploitation and appropriation of the subcontinent's resources (for example, the Sepoy Rebellion of 1857–58).

It might be helpful to briefly examine the treatment of the concrete by Rousseau, who, like Nietzsche, not only had quarrels with the Enlightenment but also entertained anarchist tendencies. Rousseau used the concrete—as experience in nature—to argue that "[m]an is born free, and everywhere he is in chains" (*Social Contract* 85). The chains were the abstractions that justified forming society and with it injustices and inequalities.

For Rousseau the concrete was a collectivity, or what he called a "general will," that "always tends toward the conservation and welfare of the whole and of each part" and ultimately is the source of "what is just and unjust" ("Discourse on Political Economy" 61). Through the specific concrete, he made the general will the counter of individualism and the basis of political legitimacy. He believed that through the general will, man, who is "everywhere in chains," could attain a just society and "civil liberty," freeing himself from the uses of force and from "impulsion by appetite" (96). The concrete was a form of resistance to scheming and slyness; the general will (concrete as collectivity) was the ground of "peace, unity, and equality," which "are the enemies of political subtleties" (*Social Contract* 139).

In Nietzsche's writings the concrete, as the banner of progressive critical modernity, was turned into a critique of modernity itself and was no longer a discursive weapon in the fight against the governing class. The concrete was used instead as a space of sensuous aesthetics in which to denounce all projects that aimed at social change because Nietzsche regarded any such project as a concealed will to truth—a violence that justified itself by appealing to metaphysics. The abstract was no longer equated with the established economic and political regime but was considered the instrument of modern culture and its Enlightenment ideal of equality, democracy, and freedom: "The lie of the ideal has so far been the curse on reality" (*Ecce Homo* 218). Instead of changing the world, he advocated "philosophizing with a hammer," destroying the "idols" of reason (*Twilight of the Idols* 21–22).

The subject of Nietzsche's critique—by way of the concrete—was no longer class despotism but rather conceptual totalization. He supported capitalism by denouncing socialism, which he regarded as the real despotism of people, outdoing "everything in the past" by "striving for the downright destruction of the individual" (*Human, All Too Human* 226) and also by legitimating class differences as the conditions for an "aristocratic society" (*Beyond Good and Evil* 173). Real justice, according to Nietzsche, could be brought to society "only within the ruling class," which "practices justice by its sacrifices and renunciations. On the other hand, to demand equality of rights, as do the socialists of the subjugated caste, never results from justice but rather from covetousness" (*Human, All Too Human* 216). His criticism of the capitalists was not that their practices were exploitative of other people but that their actions lacked cultural nobility and thus had unpleasant political consequences: "The manufacturers and entrepreneurs of business probably have been too deficient so far in all those forms and signs of a higher race that alone make a person interesting. If the nobility of birth showed in their eyes and gestures, there might not be any socialism of the masses" (*Gay Science* 107).

Nietzsche did not deploy the concrete sensuous in order to wage a war against the abstractions of religion and metaphysics through which economic aristocracy creates social inequalities and hides its class interest in going against the general will. Rather, he used the concrete to legitimate the "private will," namely, the individual and his singularity. Nietzsche's uses of the concrete are actually part of the ongoing discourses of a cultural aristocracy that regards itself as different and therefore special because of its cultural radicalism. His "revaluation of all values" (*Anti-Christ* 187) aimed at a critique not of what was politically repressive but of bad taste and crude generalizations that violated the singular. It was from the perspective of this aristocracy that he found religious beliefs vulgar and naïve: "'God,' 'Immortality of the soul,' 'redemption,' 'beyond'—without exception, concepts to which I never devoted any attention, or time, not even when I was a child. Perhaps I have never been child-like enough for them?" (*Ecce Homo* 236). In the end, his main objection to metaphysics was that it was an annoying obsession with truth that got in the way of "play." Play was an aristocratic value because it questioned the utilitarian cast of mind of the bourgeois and its instrumental approach to culture: "I do not know any other way of associating with great tasks than *play:* as a sign of greatness, this is an essential presupposition" (*Ecce Homo* 258). Play is also the condition for the transvaluation of all values. The fixation on truth is the expression of the ordinary person's fear of deceiving and being deceived. The question for the playful aristocrat, on the other hand, is "But why not deceive? But why not allow oneself to be deceived?" (*Gay Science* 281). For Nietzsche truth is the name of totality, which is shattered into fragments by play. The concrete is the truth in ruins; it is the singular part without totality and the restrictions of the whole. It acts as the allegory of freedom from the will to truth, which is all that is coherent, logical, and linear.

Nietzsche's transvaluation of the concrete is perhaps nowhere more clear than in his rewriting of the law of cause and effect. In classical science, cause and effect was a means by which the world was explained by the worldly. In other words, it was a weapon in the battle against attributing supernatural causes to natural events and thus conflating empirical reality with the divine. In classical interpretation, the first event was the cause followed by the second event as its effect. The first always explained the second.

Hume, in a mode not radically different from Nietzsche's, had questioned the role of reason in the formulation of cause and effect in order to foreground the concrete of the senses (*Human Understanding* 25–39, 42–47). He nevertheless argued that the first event always explains the occurrence of the second (74–79). Nietzsche not only denied that cause and effect was the law of the objective world inferred by reason, but he also reversed the order of causality and, in a sense, overturned Hume's rejection of "miracles" (109–31), in which the supernatural explains the empirical. Nietzsche's reading of causality replaced the scientific with the poetic and returned to an interpretation with a religious aroma; although it used post-modern idioms, it restored a faith-based pre-modern social critique affirming existing social relations by privileging the ineffable, the mystical, and the religious.

In *Beyond Good and Evil,* Nietzsche wrote that one should not follow scientists in using cause and effect for rational "explanations" but simply as "conventional fictions for the purpose of designation and communication" (29). In *The Will to Power,* he called the law of cause and effect the result of the "crudest and clumsiest observation" and argued that it is essentially a fiction invented by a "chronological inversion"

(265) to satisfy a metaphysical need for order. For example, he noted, we first perceive pain in a part of our body and then find a cause: "cause is imagined after the effect" (265).

The crucial point is not that there is a linear connection between cause and effect but that all processes, practices, and phenomena are, to use Nietzsche's words, "completely atomistic" (*Will to Power* 265): the everyday has no material logic that connects all its seemingly disparate parts but is a constellation of autonomous entities, each with its own singularity. The concrete singular in Nietzsche—and in the cultural critique called postmodernism in the late twentieth century—becomes constitutive of the social in such a way that fissures, limits, and differences cannot be sutured into a totality. "Society," in what might be called a Nietzschean social theory, "never manages to be fully society, because everything in it is penetrated by its limits, which prevents it from constituting itself as an objective reality" (Laclau and Mouffe, *Hegemony* 127).

Foucault translates Nietzsche's thought into a cultural critique for what followed (postmodernism, poststructuralism, postmarxism, and so on). He makes the concrete singular the basis of an ethics for a new micropolitics and its agent—the "specific intellectual" (*Power/Knowledge* 125–33). Similarly, for Lyotard the concrete grounds a new aesthetic politics aimed at "a war on totality" and at activating "differences" (*Postmodern Condition* 82). Lyotard radicalizes his singularism in *The Differend* and in *Just Gaming*, which echoes Nietzsche's notion of play, and argues for the incommensurability of the concrete singular and the lack of any "common measure" for different games (50). One of the significant consequences of this lack of common ground is that justice becomes a concrete pragmatic action and not a grand truth, which Lyotard thinks is simply a matter of conformity with the law (a form of ontological closure). His antifoundationalist idea of justice as a pragmatic obligation that cannot be grounded in truth breaks with the idea of justice as an imitation of the nature of being coded in laws and is a powerful critique of mimesis (65).

The most influential arguments for valorizing the concrete in contemporary cultural critique, however, are found in the works of Jacques Derrida, even though he is formally opposed to the valorization of any term or practice because he sees it as quest for presence. He puts in play all the terms of analysis, but the playfulness clears out all abstractions and their implied totalities: the apparatus by which he attempts to establish an equality of power between opposites (abstract/concrete :: presence/absence :: speech/writing) is itself a technology that privileges the concrete and the singular. Although I focus on one of his early texts, the valorization of the concrete singular is in fact the main object of later works such as *A Taste for the Secret,* in which Derrida writes, for example, "I am not part of any group. . . . I do not identify myself with a linguistic community, a national community, a political party, or with any group or clique whatsoever, with any philosophical or literary school. . . . I want to keep my freedom, always: this for me is the condition not only for being singular and other, but for entering into relation with the singularity and alterity of others" (Derrida and Ferraris 27). Not only is the subject singular, but all subjects are singularities, whereas abstractions (such as party, nation, and language) form the machinery of totalization. This is the core of the contemporary neoliberal ethics of capitalism, which is the main reason for privileging the concrete, as I explain below. In contemporary cultural critique, then, the concrete becomes the discursive means for legitimating the status quo, largely with the excuse of resisting totality, and any project for substantive change is dismissed as an exercise in the will to truth, a totality that is indifferent to difference.

Derrida's early and widely read essay "Structure, Sign and Play in the Discourse of the Human Sciences" (*Writing and Difference* 278–93) deeply affected cultural critique. Here Derrida argues that traditional critique is based on a centered structure whose goal is to produce presence through totality, as Lévi-Strauss does in *The Raw and the Cooked.* Lévi-Strauss contends that achieving totality is an impossibility because the empirical is inexhaustible and therefore "totality is never complete" (*Raw and the Cooked* 7). In other words, totality cannot be mastered. He further argues that totality is not necessary for systematic knowledge of a subject: a linguist does not know all the words added to a language since it was first spoken, nor does she have knowledge of words and structures that may emerge in the future. Nonetheless, she is able to write the grammar of that language. Totality is both impossible and unnecessary. Derrida critiques such a view, arguing that Lévi-Strauss's analytical relation to totality (the fact that data are infinite and therefore cannot be completely assembled and analyzed) is not a critique of totality (its presence and logocentrism) but a recognition that it is difficult to achieve. For Derrida, Lévi-Strauss's concerns about totality are themselves a totalization—a centered structure in search of presence.

Totality, Derrida argues, cannot be mastered, not because the empirical is infinite but because language, which is deployed in totalizing, is always in play. "If totalization no longer has any meaning," he writes, "it is not because the infiniteness of a field cannot be covered by a finite glance or a finite discourse, but because the nature of the field—that is, language and a finite language—excludes totalization. This field is in effect that of *play*, that is to say, a field of infinite substitutions only because it is finite, that is to say, because instead of being an inexhaustible field, as in the classical hypothesis, instead of being too large, there is something missing from it: a center which arrests and grounds the play of substitutions" (*Writing and Difference* 289).

The concrete cannot be totalized, not because it is infinite but because it exceeds the structure of totality, and its excess cannot be brought to an end because whatever is used to end it is itself an excess in play. Derrida replaces totalization with supplementarity, which recognizes the absence of totality within a seeming presence, because supplementarity is the "strange cohabitation" of two significations: it is an addition that fills the missing in the plenitude, a "plenitude enriching another plenitude" (*Grammatology* 146), which is an acknowledgment of the absence in presence. The concrete, in other words, is not reducible to totality (Derrida, *Margins* 11).

Derrida's notion of the concrete singular (variously articulated as "*différance*," "hymen," "writing," "trace," "dissemination," "democracy-to-come," and "specter") is a resistance to abstraction (totality). In this sense it shares certain features with modern uses of the concrete to fight the abstract, but epistemologically, it is an entirely different order. Derrida's notion is antiessentialist. This means that unlike the modernist idea of the concrete (found in the writings of, for example, Bacon, Hume, or Berkeley), in Derrida's theory the concrete cannot become the foundation for a theory (totalization). These ideas of the concrete have radically different onto-epistemologies and play different political roles in relation to the social relations of the time. Modern critics deployed the concrete to battle the abstractions of religion and metaphysics in which the power of the old regime was legitimated. The concrete was the ground for a different social organization.

Contemporary theory deconstructs the modern idea of the concrete as essentialist and deploys the concrete as a threshold of différance by which it resists all totalization, including what it regards as the totalization of a "new" society with a different social organization. Consequently, the contemporary concrete, following Nietzsche's practices-in-fragments, detotalizes the social into autonomous singularities and thus renders knowledge of social totality a fiction of presence. In doing so, I argue, contemporary critiques—whether by Bataille, Foucault, Derrida, Lyotard, Agamben, Žižek, or Badiou—all affirm the actually existing social relations, in spite of their radical language of resistance to power. They help undermine social change aimed not simply at cultural freedom but at freedom from necessity.

The concrete becomes the essence of a new antiessentialism for dealing with what is popularly represented as cutting-edge reality: a reality that is considered to be contingent and whose contingency is taken as a sign of its radical concreteness—its singularity. The condition of contingency is even extended to science (abstraction). In *The Savage Mind* Lévi-Strauss draws a distinction between the *bricoleur* (a person who uses "whatever is at hand" [17], the concrete, the different, and the practical) and the engineer (or scientist), who works according to an abstract model of truth, a method. Derrida argues, however, that the engineer or scientist, as a person who "supposedly breaks with all forms of *bricolage*," is a "theological idea"; he, too, does not "construct the totality of his language, syntax, and lexicon" but, like the bricoleur, "borrows" his concepts from the text of a "heritage which is more or less coherent or ruined" (*Writing and Difference* 285). Science, far from being an instance of absolute rationality, is, like bricolage, a contingent practice, and it shares the conditions of bricolage as textual play, as difference. In contemporary critique, the most effective mode of knowing is no longer science but is assumed to be textuality, or science as a form of writing. (for example, Lenoir, *Inscribing Science*; Ross, *Science Wars*).

Textuality is valorized because its rhetorical constitution is antiessentialist, or as Derrida puts it, "It deconstructs it-self" ("Letter to a Japanese Friend" 274). But the very idea of antiessentialism is itself essentialist, as I have already suggested. In contemporary cultural critique, the text is assumed to deploy its own rhetorical strategies to undo all totalization—including its own—through the specificity of its tropics, which simultaneously assert and deny the authority of the text (de Man, *Allegories* 3–19). In the new order of knowledge, the concept (totality as abstraction), which is the basis of all scientific knowledge, is considered to be a linguistic construct, and like all such constructs, it is perceived as a tropic structure. The trope, in the new order of the concrete, is not simply an ornamental margin of language but "characterizes language as such" (105). The concrete, which in early modernity was deployed as a weapon of science used against the abstraction of superstition, has now become a weapon against science.

THE CONCRETE AND THE MATERIAL LOGIC OF CULTURE

Nietzsche's transvaluation of the concrete turned it into a means for containing equality and safeguarding the aristocracy by shifting the object of critique from class to culture. The tendency to focus on culture as differences and singularities that resist totalization is more active in what used to be called postmodern critique but is not limited to it. This is because the privileging of the concrete is a cultural response to the material logic that shapes all cultural products.

Cultural practices are shaped by the material base of culture in ways that normalize and validate its economic dynamic. Culture, in the words of Marx and Engels, is the "expression of the dominant material relationships" as ideas, values, acts, attitudes, and affects (*German Ideology* 59). But once culture emerges from its material conditions, it plays an important role in the way people understand and produce meanings in their lives, find purpose, and act. Culture, to put it differently, exercises "influence upon the course of historical struggles" (Engels, "Letter to Joseph Bloch" 395). However, and this is where my views differ from the dominant theories, culture is not autonomous. Culture is not, as Stuart Hall suggests, "primary and constitutive, determining its own shape and character as well as its inner life" ("Centrality of Culture" 215). Rather, through various formations and subtle articulations, the material conditions of culture always assert themselves as necessary, no matter how thick and opaque these meditations might be.

Although contemporary cultural critique has, at times, acknowledged the crucial importance of materialism in cultural formations, it has been preoccupied mainly with the materiality of technologies of representation in cultural mediations (see, for examples, works of Jameson and of Ronell cited in the bibliography). In contrast, I argue that a transformative cultural critique should not be too distracted by these mediations and their seductive, subtle, and delectable textual play in representations. A transformative critique needs to focus primarily on the ways in which culture, in its concrete practices, is ultimately the articulation of the abstract: the material structures that actually shape the concrete. If appearance and the real were identical, there would be no need for critique. Contemporary theory, however, has discredited as essentialist any recognition of the alienation of appearance from the real. It has kept critique on the surface, the appearance of the real and, furthermore, argued that the real is itself a construct of representational events. The complications of representation—and the pleasures of engaging them—have obscured the depth of the alienation of contemporary reality. This alienation and its causes should be the object of transformative critique.

Existing social relations use the concrete for cultural legitimization because these relations are fraught with fundamental class contradictions that have to be obscured in order for these social relations to have ethical authority and cultural confidence. The concrete occludes antagonisms that cannot be solved within the governing class structures. To be clear, the existing social relations are based on the appropriation of the surplus (unpaid) labor of the working majority by a small owning minority. This contradiction—the exploitation of the many by the few in a democracy that declares itself to be for the equality of all—is constitutive of capitalism and is structured in the unequal exchange between labor and capital.

This structured inequality is a social relation. Understanding it therefore requires a knowledge of social totality, a grasp of the underlying material logic that relates all parts of social life and culture and shapes their specificities. This logic shows, for instance, the relation of class and heath care (Navaro, *Dangerous to Your Health* 53–70) and points to the ways in which one's education is determined primarily by class standing but also by race and gender. Focusing on the concrete and analyzing the everyday in terms of particular aspects of individual practices, while treating each as autonomous, conceals the working of this structure and makes it more difficult, if not impossible, to comprehend the underlying relations of social life and their material logic. The uses of the concrete, in other words, disperse social totality into endless singularities and attribute to each its own internal "cultural logic." Consequently, the organizing contradiction of capitalism—the exchange of wages for labor power—is portrayed as an individual act, namely, a "contract" between "free persons" (Marx, *Capital* 1: 280), and the fact that this exchange is structural and takes place under the "silent compulsion of economic relations" (1: 899) is made invisible. The portrayal of social life as a set of unrelated practices, as autonomous fragments and events, that are free from any regulatory determination (Foucault, *Language, Counter-Memory* 139–64, 205–17) makes the exchange of wages for labor power seem as if they were

> the exclusive realm of Freedom, Equality, Property and Bentham. Freedom, because both buyer and seller of a commodity, let us say of labour-power, are determined only by their own free will. They contract as free persons, who are equal before the law. Their contract is the final result in which their joint will finds a common legal expression. Equality, because each enters into relation with the other, as with a simple owner of commodities, and they exchange equivalent for equivalent. Property, because each disposes only of what is his own. And Bentham, because each looks only to his own advantage. The only force bringing them together, and putting them into relation with each other, is the selfishness, the gain and the private interest of each. Each pays heed to himself only, and no one worries about the others. (Marx, *Capital*, 1: 280)

By normalizing this logic of the singular "as the way things are," the concrete conceals the structural inequality and, as Marx says, "provides the 'free-trader *vulgaris*' with his views, his concepts and the standard by which he judges the society of capital and wage-labour," obscuring the reality of the worker, who is "like someone who has brought his own hide to market and now has nothing else to expect but—a tanning" (1: 280).

The concrete is thus the primary object of interpretive interest not only in theoretical critiques but also in other forms of contemporary cultural writings. In traditional (antitheory) cultural criticism, for example, the concrete is treated as the aesthetic basis for the work of art and as a sign of its moral commitment. The main focus of interpretation is on the details—not so much as parts of the text's apparatuses of representation (and thus shared by other works) but more as marks of artistic uniqueness and the sincerity of the artist. The concrete is seen as a matter of aesthetics and of ethics (for example, Dickstein, *Mirror in the Roadway*; Donoghue, *Speaking of Beauty*; Abrams, *Doing Things*).

The concrete is also the centering object of interpretation in the theoretically antitheory writings of such authors as Stanley Fish and Richard Rorty, who, from a pragmatist perspective, oppose dealing with the "big (and stupefyingly dull)" questions of "gaseous theorizing," to quote Fish again ("Theory's Hope" 376), because these avoid the detailed contexts of the everyday. Rorty regards all abstractions (such as "true," "good, and "right") as elements of what he calls a "final vocabulary" and contends that they are put in question by the "ironist," who is a thinker of the concrete (*Contingency* 73–95).

Similarly, cultural activists, both in their writings and in their interventions, take the concrete to be the object of struggles for social change. Engaging the concrete is seen as a test of seriousness and commitment to social transformation (for example, Gitlin). Commenting on "Deconstruction and the Other," in which Derrida writes that he "would hesitate to use such terms as liberation" (121), David McNally argues that such a view of language is the outcome of an idealism that believes that "we may play with words, but we can never hope to liberate ourselves from immutable structures of oppression rooted in language itself." The "new idealism," he concludes, "and the politics it entails are not simply harmless curiosities; they are an abdication of political responsibility, especially at a time of ferocious capitalist restructuring, of widening gaps between rich and poor, of ruling class offensives against social programs. They are also an obstacle to the rebuilding of mass movements of protest and resistance" ("Language, History, and Class Struggle" 27).

The irony is that contemporary theory is itself profoundly antitheoretical because it regards theory as totalizing the self-difference of the texts of culture (de Man, *Resistance to Theory* 3–20). On an ideological level, they are all—activists, antitheorists and theorists—allied in their opposition to any knowledge of social totality (theory). The alliance has its most effective moments in such books as Gibson-Graham's *Postcapitalist Politics*. Activists as well as contemporary theorists are practitioners of a micropolitics that they consider to be a politics of difference and, therefore, an effective politics (for example, Sanbonmatsu and Foucault) as opposed to theories and politics that aim at providing a total view of society. The differences between activists and cultural theorists lie in the way they understand such issues as experience. Activist cultural critique grounds itself in the immediacy of experience—the concreteness of the senses and the tangibility of oppression (Yates). On the other hand, post-theory (poststructuralism, for example) questions the reliability of experience—whether as the immediate ground of concreteness or as the basis of knowledge—because, in its interpretation, both are essentialist. The activist, according to post-theory, places the concrete outside language and its textual representation and assumes that it is a truth in itself and, as such, an embodiment of presence.

The new concrete in post-theory cultural critique (which is my primary interest) is an antiessentialist concrete or, to use Derrida's term, the concrete of the "différance" of the writerly text (*Margins* 1–27)—the site of ecstatic knowing and the space of pleasure and bliss segregated from social totality. The concrete, which had intervened in existing social relations, is now used in the contemporary as a justification for the ruling order. Paradoxically, the concrete has become an abstract closure.

MATERIALISM AND THE CONCRETE

The concrete is valorized because it is said to be the dense materiality of culture as exemplified in language or in the body. But such a materiality, as I have already noted, is more an objective idealism than it is materialism. Before I examine how the body and language become sites of delectable materialism in contemporary critique, it may be useful to say a few words about matter, materiality, and materialism, a subject that I have discussed at length elsewhere (Ebert, *Ludic Feminism*).

Materialism is the worldliness of human practices that, in constantly revolutionizing (the relations of) production, make human history, specifically, progress toward freedom from necessity. Materialism consists of the objective productive activities of humans that involve them in social relations under definite historical conditions that are independent of their will and are shaped by the struggles between contesting classes over the surplus produced by social labor. Materiality, on the other hand, is in the speculative tradition of Feuerbach; it produces what I call a form of spiritualism and what Derrida calls a "materiality without materialism" and "without matter" ("Typewriter Ribbon" 281). It is the contemplative corporeality of difference—which is the effect of the textual sensuality of language, the body, and their affective resistance to conceptuality and determinate meanings. In the linguistic turn of contemporary critique, materiality becomes a performativity, a species of meaning, and an effect of archives, of memories. It becomes, in short, the effect of "matter as a sign" (Butler, *Bodies*, 49).

Delectable materialism is the theory of materiality without materialism. Its concrete is the sensuous surfaces of the everyday. But the concrete is not an autonomous particularity; it is the effect of an abstract generality. The concrete, to put it differently, is the effect of the historical development of human labor. It is, therefore, understood in a radically different way by historical materialism, which deploys the concrete not in order to retreat into the sensuous and avoid the abstract structures that make the sensuous but in order to historicize it, as Marx ("Theses on Feuerbach") does: "Feuerbach, not satisfied with *abstract thinking*, appeals to *sensuous contemplation*; but he does not conceive sensuousness as practical, human-sensuous activity" (7, emphasis in original). "Human-sensuous activity" is fundamentally human labor.

The idealism of the concrete in contemporary critique is not limited to poststructuralist theorists but encompasses nearly all writings concerning culture, including those by such a thoughtful Marxist as Fredric Jameson. Jameson begins his rhapsody on the "greatness" of Deleuze—in particular the "transcodings" of Marxism—by invoking Marx with regard to the concrete. "Marx," Jameson writes, "had a better formula: bourgeois thought, he said (which we may also read as Greek philosophy), sought to rise from the particular to the universal; our task is now to rise (note the persistence of the verb)—to rise from the universal to the concrete" ("Marxism and Dualism" 394). Jameson, in short, is invoking Marx as a benediction in the pursuit of the concrete rather than the universal, but by a different relay. Yet Marx never proclaimed that this was the task. Jameson seems to be referring to the passage concerning the concrete in the *Grundrisse*. Not only is this not a careful paraphrase; it is, in fact, a rather astounding misinterpretation of Marx for such a sophisticated reader—a reading that is particularly telling of the "post" condition and the way it has affected contemporary thought.

In representing Marx's text in this way. Jameson reifies a binary (concrete/universal) that Marx himself subjects to a materialist critique and dialectical overturning. The binary, however, is central to both the old bourgeois and new theoretical distortions of Marx: it is the binary of concrete particularities and reified, abstract universals. By attributing such a binary to Marx's theorization of the concrete and the abstract, Jameson is turning Marx's materialist intervention into the ideology of the concrete upside down. What is even more telling is that Jameson does so in order to fit Marx into an analogy to Hegel—a gesture to re-Hegelize Marx. In order to do so, Jameson also instructs us to read "bourgeois thought" in a quite ahistorical way as "Greek philosophy" ("Marxism and Dualism" 394) when the bourgeois thought that Marx is critiquing is political economy: Adam Smith, not Aristotle (Marx, *Grundrisse* 100–108). Marx turned Hegel's dialectic on its head in order to render it materialist (Marx, *Capital* 1: 102–1), but now Jameson is overturning Marx's materialist notion of the concrete, occluding it, and turning it into an idealist theory. The concrete in Marx is not the "self-evidence" of common sense, nor is it the bodily sensual, the epistemologically empirical, the textually tropic, or the daily consumable. This is an "imagined concrete" (1: 100). The actuality of the concrete for Marx, as I discuss more fully below, is in the complexity of social relations.

But contemporary critique uses the concrete to invert these social relations, in particular, production's relation to consumption, thus making the market the dynamic of history. I want to examine some of the relays by which the concrete is deployed to obscure the social relations of production and focus on two major concerns of contemporary cultural theory: language and the body. I analyze the mimetic(ological) concrete of language in chapter 2 and take up the surfacing of the body concrete in chapter 3.

2. The Abstract of Transformative Critique

Critique, Mimesis, and the Crisis of Details

Different modes of cultural critique are articulated according to the underlying logic of their interpretation, which is basically a theory about the relation of language to reality. At the focal point of all these theories, whether explicit or, more often, implicit, is the matter of mimesis. Mimesis, of course, is not a purely literary or cultural issue. The reason such a seemingly innocuous issue is the subject of ongoing contestations and conflicts in contemporary cultural theory is that it is ultimately a question of class.

De Man, however, argues that mimesis is "the figure of a figure," "one trope among others"; it is "language choosing to imitate a nonverbal entity just as paronomasis 'imitates' a sound without any claim to identity (or reflection on difference) between the verbal and non-verbal elements" (*Resistance to Theory* 48, 10). De Man's reading of mimesis is grounded in his understanding of deconstruction as a negative knowledge, a knowledge that replaces mimesis as a site of presence—as do all totalizations—"by the knowledge of its figural and epistemologically unreliable structure" (*Allegories* 187). Mimesis, in other words, is a representation of a representation, something that Derrida calls "mimetological" (*Positions* 70). It is a text whose signifiers, contrary to the text's claims, do not transcend themselves to become a determined signified (truth) that precedes them but, rather, remain in play. Mimesis, like all writing, is a textual difference.

The same self-inspection of the concrete textuality of imitation—rather than the abstract truth that is said to be imitated—shapes Derrida's understanding of mimesis. His reading of Mallarmé's *Mimique* foregrounds mimesis as an imitation without the imitated, mimetology without presence (*Dissemination* 173–285). Following his usual protocol for reading, Derrida, of course, does not reject or deny mimesis: to deny it on the ground that it makes literature secondary to an original reality outside itself is as problematic for him as is the quest for a pure literarity sought by Russian Formalists, Copenhagen School theorists, and others to make literature primary (*Grammatology* 59). Both mimesis and pure literature are, in the end, parts of a metaphysics of presence, and both therefore limit the play of the signifier. For Derrida, the mimetological is fundamentally a matter of différance, a "determined interpretation of mimesis" (*Positions* 70), and as such a problem that affects all representations. Writing, according to Derrida, is always mimetic, but with a difference: its referents are never used up by its referentiality; its signifiers never cease their playfulness and settle on any particular truth outside themselves. "The referent is lifted, but reference remains" (*Dissemination* 211). Mimesis, then, is an instance of "differences without any central presence" (210).

Within this context, mimesis is received in the dominant cultural critique as the sublime of spectrality. What a mimetic critique assumes to be the objective cultural reality of its analysis is now believed to be actually constructed through the analyses themselves without any objectivity outside the texts—there is no "ontology" or even "dialectic" to which they can refer back (Derrida, *Dissemination* 207). Cultural critique has therefore become largely a self-reflexive critique of representation, and it cultivates considerable uncertainty about mimesis and its truth.

In epistemological terms, mainstream cultural critique finds mimesis to be an idealist view of the relation between language and reality based on a correspondence theory of language that undoes difference (de Saussure, *General Linguistics* 111–22). In aesthetic terms, it regards mimesis to be an instrumentalist writing that negates its own materiality and imposes a totalizing closure on the play of signs by substituting the phenomenal for the linguistic. Mimesis, in other words, is a form of "aesthetic ideology" (de Man, *Aesthetic Ideology*). On the social and political levels, contemporary critique takes for granted that mimesis and realism are obstacles to social change because it assumes that in order to change What Is, one has to change its representations, which requires going beyond the mimetic reflectionism that stabilizes existing cultural practices. (This view informs works as varied as Lacoue-Labarthe, *Typography*; Lyotard, *Differend*; Coward and Ellis, *Language and Materialism*; and MacCabe, *Tracking the Signifier*). Antimimetic representation is valorized in contemporary critique because it is seen as opening up a cultural space for the marginal and the repressed, thus bringing about change through the practices of the other (for example, Haraway, *Simians*; Hayles, *How We Became Posthuman*).

Although the criticisms made by post-theory are for the most part directed against mimetologism and realism, these quarrels are basically family quarrels. Both antimimetic theories and realism consist of writings about the irreducible sensuousness of concrete surfaces— the grain of language, in the case of the antimimetic (Barthes, *Pleasure*), and delight in the textures of objects in the world, where "things themselves speak" in the "serious treatment of everyday reality" in the case of the realistic (Auerbach, *Mimesis* 491). The theorists who engage mimesis in what is theoretically the radical middle, for example, Adorno, Horkheimer, and Taussig, travel on the tickling surfaces of the "real and the really made up" (Taussig, *Mimesis and Alterity* xvii).

If realism is a spectral writing, a reference without a referent, then contemporary antimimesis can be read as a marionette textuality in which the absent referent does not in any way negate its active presence in the superstructure of the culture of capital because both the mimetic and the nonmimetological are effects of the social relations of production. Capitalism, not a metaphysics of presence, produces both the referential and the nonreferential, the missing presence and the present absence, because it needs them both in order to address different class fractions and persuade them of its own ethical authority and democratic plurality.

Realists and antimimetic cultural critics, in other words, are ideologically united in opposing interrogative writing that goes beyond textual surfaces and brings to the fore the many materialist determinations of which the concrete surfaces are made. Following different formal strategies, antimimetic and realist writings focus on the mechanics of the signifier, whether it corresponds with or slides away from the signified. Their main focus is representation (and/as verisimilitude), not the represented and the historical constitution of reality. The self-gazing sentences in a Raymond Carver story would be quite at home in the pages of Derrida's *Post Card*; in both cases they are trapped within the bourgeois relations of production and the class melancholy of bourgeois language.

In contrast, the language of transformative writing is much more concerned with understanding the represented than with scrutinizing the technologies of representation of reality. Language is not a meditation on the fate of its own meaning, nor is it a portrayal of the details of individual experience and its objects. Rather, it is an investigation of the material structures that make language and daily experiences historically possible. This root critique is necessary because the contemporary everyday, contrary to the claims made by de Certeau and others, is not a spontaneous space of resistance to capital but a reified construct of wage labor.

Transformative cultural critique is a de-reification of the everyday. It is grounded in Marx's argument that "all science would be superfluous if the form of appearance of things directly coincided with their essence" (*Capital* 3: 956)—thus the necessity of interrogating the surface and not being enchanted by intricate and seductive details. I call this mode of writing *proletarian realism*, a realism that is not objectist; it does not replace social totality with fragments that dismember that totality by means of the lush surfaces and sensuous textures of the world, as canonic bourgeois realism does. What is traditionally called realism is actually what Georg Lukács calls "naturalism" (*European Realism* 1–19); it is a fetishizing of surfaces, and it needs to be distinguished from realism. Lukács actually deploys this difference to point out the dissimilarities between Flaubert and Balzac.

Through an increasingly subtle and complex style, Flaubert avoids the class contradictions of the time and simply disperses them in the complex textualities of his writing. Balzac, on the other hand, confronts questions of class and labor and shows, in Marx's words, "a profound grasp of real conditions" (*Capital* 3: 130). Unlike Flaubert, whose novels are saturated with false objectivity, Balzac, "by stripping the social institutions of their apparent objectivity and seemingly dissolving them into personal relationships," according to Lukács, "contrives to express what is truly objective in them, what is really their social *raison d'être:* their functions as bearers of class interests and as the instruments of enforcing them" (*European Realism* 41–42).

By *proletarian realism,* then, I mean a realism that de-reifies reality by grasping the essence of its specific stage of historical development and by examining the relations of the subject to the totality of social relations that situate the subject in the social division of labor. Such realism goes beyond everyday consciousness to show how consciousness is a class construct and how that which is designated unconsciousness—that last retreat of the bourgeois from daily social conflicts, whether depicted in terms of Freudian spectrality or in the linguistic vocabularies of Lacan—is the residue of the unresolvable class contradictions in which the subject is trapped in class societies. Realism (mimesis) is not simply a technology for representing a missing truth as plenitude (Lacoue-Labarthe), nor is it an aesthetic of verisimilitude. Rather, realism is a social relation, a historical analysis of existing social reality that can provide the knowledge needed to remake it. To put it another way, proletarian realism is a radical experimentalism that theorizes writing not, as in Derrida's terms, as a "dangerous supplement" (*Grammatology* 141–64), nor as a utopian space (Jameson, *Archaeologies*), but as texts that "grasp [the real] by the root" (Marx, "Critique of Hegel's Philosophy of Right" 251).

In the discourses of cultural critique as well as in mainstream aesthetics, *experimental writing* is code for antirealism. The assumption is that realism is a form of writing that denies its own textuality, thereby closing upon itself to form a coherent totality that claims to correspond with objective reality in a quest for determinate meanings. In other words, realism is equated with the epistemology of presence and closure derived from an Aristotelian theory of truth as correspondence (*Metaphysics* IV.v.1011, pp. 746–47). Because contemporary critique takes it as given that there is no direct access to reality (to which discourse could correspond), realism is regarded as a logocentric pursuit of presence and plenitude: not so much a realism as a spectralism.

Experimental writing, on the other hand, is considered to be an acknowledgment of the textuality of writing and its difference and, therefore, a resistance to determinism and certainty. Consequently, it is seen as an affirmation of the ethic of undecidability. Although mimesis is seen as the other of experimental writing, the antimimesis of contemporary critique is never outside mimesis but is a rewriting of it as a self-reflexive miming of its own textuality. The question is not one of mimesis in opposition to antimimesis but of modes of mimesis. The issue of mimesis is not a formal or an epistemological issue. It is ultimately a class question, and the contestations about the mimetic and the postmimetic are ultimately class conflicts over the referent of labor and its appropriation by capital or by the direct producers.

The unavoidability of mimesis and, therefore, the inevitability of the struggles over the referent are most lucidly shown in Derrida's reading of Mallarmé in "The Double Session" (*Dissemination* 174–286). Derrida reads Mallarmé's story "Mimique" as a text about mimesis that "preserves the differential structure of mimicry or *mimēsis*, but without its Platonic or metaphysical interpretation, which implies that somewhere the being of something that *is*, is being imitated" (206)—miming, the miming of another mime without origin ("presence"), a "textual labyrinth paneled with mirrors" (195). Miming as writing resists the adequation of signifier and signified. It is a gestural performance that represents nothing but difference and thus "imitates nothing" (205); it "plays out a difference without reference, or rather without a referent; without any absolute exteriority the Mime mimes reference . . . he mimes imitation . . . a copy of a copy" without the original (219). In tracing out this mimetological circulation of simulacra, writing produces "the very movement of truth" (205)—not truth as "adequation between the represented and the present of the thing itself" but "truth as the present unveiling of the present[;] . . . the mime produces, . . . makes appear *in praesentia*, manifests the very meaning of what he is presently writing: of what he *performs*" (206). In Derrida's poetics, mimesis does not "reflect" an anterior truth but is a mimesis of its own language, which mimes its own indeterminacy. It is a mimetic without mimesis in which language demonstrates its own productivity by foregrounding its rhetorical details, which display the materiality of its signifiers and the impossibility of their being dissolved into the abstract truth of a signified. The concrete "materiality of an inscription," as de Man describes it (*Resistance to Theory*, 51), the facticity of signifiers themselves, put all concepts (Truth) under suspicion.

Realism, too, is a representational regime of signifiers without signifieds, appearance without essence, and representation without truth. In "Reality Effect" Roland Barthes argues that modern realism consists of a succession of fragmented, intersecting notations that "denote what is ordinarily called 'concrete reality' (insignificant gestures, transitory attitudes, insignificant objects, redundant words)" (146). The "realism" of "realistic literature," Barthes writes, is one that "is only fragmentary, erratic, confined to 'details'" (147). In bourgeois realism the "concrete detail" is "semiotically . . . constituted by the direct collusion of a referent and a signifier; the signified is expelled from the sign" (147), a referential feature shared with Derrida's nonmimetic mimesis. By expelling the signified, realism, like nonmimetic mimetology, banishes conceptuality. Bourgeois realism, then, again like Derridean antimimesis, is a referential discourse without referents, one that denotes "concrete reality" as the "real" referent of the sign. It is "any discourse which accepts 'speech-acts' justified by their referent alone" (Barthes 147).

The difference between mimetic mimesis (Auerbach, *Mimesis*) and nonmimetic mimesis (de Man, *Allegories*) is more a matter of which kinds of details are valorized: the concrete experiential (for example, Auerbach's reading of Proust, *Mimesis* 541–44) or the concrete textual-rhetorical (as in de Man's reading of Proust in *Allegories*) because they both, in different ways, reduce historical reality to concrete surfaces.

Nonmimetic writing is *"a miming of appearance* without concealed reality" (Derrida, *Dissemination* 211, emphasis in original), whereas the mimetic becomes a site where "things themselves speak" (Auerbach, *Mimesis* 491). In both, critique becomes an account of the particular without particularity, details without detailing, and the concept without conceptuality. This is the final result of the specific concrete: the concept is reduced to concrete tropic signifiers without explanatory authority and is thus unable to critique the class dynamics of social relations, of which language's relation to reality ("mimesis") is an effect.

Detailism—the practice of writing in which the "signifier [has] in the last instance no signified" (Derrida, *Dissemination* 207)—fetishizes singularity and contingency and reduces history to a "concrete" actuality. Bourgeois writing is heavily saturated with a thickly textured, sensuous vertigo of details that provides an illusion of dense reality—whether as a profusion of verisimilitude or as the excesses of the signifier (Schor, *Reading in Detail*).This vertigo of details is all-encompassing and diverting, and its ideological role is to locate the subject entirely on the surface of reality. It occludes the deep structure of reality, namely, the relations of production and divisions of labor, and substitutes a depthless surface for root reality itself. Depthlessness is itself canonized as the cutting-edge "cultural logic" of the contemporary and is celebrated as transgressing the Truth ("conceptuality") of modernity (Jameson, *Postmodernism* 1–54). Details, as proof of the real, are legitimated not only in aesthetics but also in analytical discourses. Clifford Geertz, for instance, valorizes details as "thick descriptions" of culture, and Michel Foucault privileges details as "genealogy."

The question of details, however, has to be placed in historical context. Details, as Ian Watt argues in *The Rise of the Novel*, are what make the novel a new literary genre distinguished from, for example, romance. The rise of the novel, of course, was part of the rise of industrial capitalism, and the attention to details was necessary for the working of administrative reason. This is another way of saying that detail is not simply a matter of experience or textuality but one of history and political economy. Mainstream realism and contemporary experimentalism strip details of their history (the material conditions that produce them) and reduce them to a language effect or a testament to experience. In short, the contestation about details is part of the social struggle over social reality. Does reality reside in its details? Or is it the effect of the abstract structures of the social relations of production?

Two Critiques: Tropology, Class Consciousness, and the Reading of Culture

Proust's *Swann's Way* contains a fairly long section on the act of read-ing that Paul de Man reads as a discourse on the relation of language to reality and its implications for critique (*Allegories* 57–78). In his read-ing of Proust, de Man normalizes the fragmentary concrete through the trope of metonymy, in which relations are constructed on the basis of the material singularity of the specific parts and their objective relations ("In the sweat of thy face shalt thou eat bread"). As a consequence, the specific piece does not disappear in a totalizing structure of meaning, a state of consciousness ("Annihilating all that's made / To a green thought in a green shade," Andrew Marvell, "The Garden" 101). Metonymy is an insistence on the sensible (concrete), whereas metaphor absorbs the sensible into the intangible (abstraction). This is one of my main points. Contemporary cultural critique is metonymic, but the difference between metonymy and metaphor—fragment and totality—is not simply a formal matter but a class question: metonymy (the singular) is the trope of the class in power by which it always undermines the metaphor (totality).

De Man's specific strategies of reading have lost their immediacy not because they have been found wanting but, on the contrary, because they have been completely absorbed by contemporary cultural theory and are no longer recognizable as his contributions. They now form the interpretive unconsciousness of normal cultural critique, in which it is self-evident, for example, that "binaries" are effects of the will to truth (power); that cultural texts are opaque and unreadable in the sense that they produce "a set of assertions that radically exclude each other" and thus destroy the foundation for any single interpretive choice; that con-cepts are tropes, and therefore cultural texts are void of epistemological authority (truth) and should thus be read as language effects; that all cul-tural texts deconstruct themselves, which means that cultural practices contain within themselves a counter practice, a resistance to the closure of their own meanings; that ideology is a misreading of the linguistic as phenomenal reality; that representation is never identical with the repre-sented and is therefore a tracing of difference; that cultural texts include within themselves a theory of their own reading, which means that in order to understand culture one has to read it immanently and honor the self-reflexivity of its language; that cultural practices are political and their politics should be read in terms of their representations, in terms, that is, of the relationship "between the referential and the figural se-mantic field"; that culture in the end is not a plenitude through which

the constitutive undecidability of language can be resolved but is itself
a language effect, a representation without presence; culture, in other
words, exists in bits, disjointed and fragmentary (metonymic), and not
an organic whole in totality (metaphor). These and many other reading
practices are either developed by de Man or are further theorized and made
useable by him in posthumanist cultural critique. His impact on cultural
critique, especially for the purpose of reading ideology, is so significant
that I discuss it at length in a separate chapter. Within the assumptions
of normative critique, the concrete is regarded as the working of culture
in its irreplaceable singularity, when it is stripped of its metaphysics
and read not phenomenally but as a language performativity. Reading
de Man's reading of Proust's scene of reading will bring to the fore the
dynamics of the concrete in normal cultural critique.

De Man begins his reading by theoretically broadening the subject
into the query whether "a literary text is *about* that which it describes,
represents, or states" (*Allegories* 57, emphasis in original). Can we learn
about reading by reading a text's discourse on reading? For the text's
statement to have epistemological validity, it has to coincide with itself
and become representational. De Man's argument is that a tropic fissure
always prevents the text from becoming identical with itself and "meaning" what it "says." The only referent of a literary text is itself—the
concrete of its own signifiers.

There is, in other words, a nonconvergence between an "aesthetically
responsive" reading of the text and a "rhetorically aware" reading. The
two readings are mutually exclusive and assert the "impossibility of a true
understanding on the level of figuration as well as of the themes" (*Allegories* 72). In reading Proust's discourse on reading, de Man explains how
that which writing represents or states is textualized (that is, undone as
conceptual knowledge) by the tropic structure of its own language, which
resists covering the gap between the linguistic and the phenomenal. Writing, for de Man, is always already about its own processes of signification
and has almost nothing reliable to say about what it states.

De Man first analyzes the way the scene of reading is framed in the
text within a set of irreconcilable binaries: "Two apparently incompatible
chains of connotations have . . . been set up: one, engendered by the idea
of 'inside' space and governed by 'imagination,' possesses the qualities
of coolness, tranquility, darkness as well as totality, whereas the other,
linked to the 'outside' and dependent on the 'senses,' is marked by the
opposite qualities of warmth, activity, light, and fragmentation" (60).

In the novel, these polarities are transcended, and a world of lucidity
and coherence is produced in "reading," which is enabled by a textual

regime based on the "priority of metaphor" and its opposition to "metonymy" (62). The novel privileges metaphor, which it regards to be the trope of inwardness, intelligibility, and imagination, and marginalizes metonymy, which it considers to be the figure of the everyday contingent reality and its dullness. Metaphor provides the coherence of the inner world and its complex self-reflexivity; metonymy merely displays actual links that are dependent on a commonplace empirical logic. It inscribes predictability and is the marker of contingency, fragmentation, and difference. In the poetics of the novel, de Man writes, metonymy is by definition "unable to create genuine links" (63). Metaphor, on the other hand, is the trope of organic relations that erase differences, totalizing opposites and "compelling coherence" (63).

Reading, for Proust, becomes a sublime pleasure of solitude far superior to the mundane and almost vulgar enjoyment of the outdoors. As de Man describes it: "The inner world is unambiguously valorized as preferable to the outside, and a consistent series of attractive attributes are associated with the well-being of the enclosed space: *coolness*, the most desirable of qualities in this novel of the 'solar myth' in which the barometer so often indicates fine weather, itself linked to the restorative *darkness* of shaded light . . . and finally tranquility, without which no time would be available for contemplation" (*Allegories* 59, emphasis in original).

Marcel, however, cannot simply rest in the sedentary solitude. "The mental process of reading," de Man argues, "extends the function of consciousness beyond that of mere passive perception; it must acquire a wider dimension and become an action" (63). This is, of course, part of what de Man calls "aesthetic ideology." Solitude, the lack of activity in Proust's text, is not only passive but also unethical because it is produced by retreating from the activities of the real word and indulging in the guilty pleasures of reading. The task of reading is, therefore, to turn the "confinement to the obscure, private existence of inward retreat" into "a highly effective strategy for the retrieval of all that seemed to have been sacrificed" (59–60). In an exuberant act of imagination, therefore, reading recuperates all that is lost because of Marcel's restful immobility—"the *warmth* of the sun, its *light* and every *activity*" (60, emphasis in original)—are all recaptured. Reading, through metaphor, confers on the inside the qualities of the outside: "Miraculously," de Man writes, not only does the "'dark coolness' of the room . . . acquire the light without which no reading would be possible" but also "the 'unmediated, actual, and persistent presence' of the summer warmth and finally even . . . the shock and animation of a flood of activity" (60) permeate the inactive quiet of the room.

Through reading, in other words, Marcel is able to stay in his room and still have access to "the total spectacle of summer" as well as to the "attractions of direct physical actions." The telling point is that through reading, Marcel is able to realize all his experiences as an organic totality with a compelling coherence. Had he actually been involved in the outside world's activities, on the other hand, he could only have known them "by bits and pieces." The logic of imagination is the logic of metaphor, while the actual world is ruled by the order of the metonymical.

De Man analyzes at length the mechanics of the operation of tropes in Proust's theory of reading. For example, he shows the use of visual metaphors in the text to represent the sun by its "reflection of light which . . . succeeded in making its yellow wings appear [behind the blinds], and remain motionless . . . poised like a butterfly." Similarly, the qualities of the "outside" are sutured to the "inside" by the "buzzing of the flies, generalized into 'the chamber music of summer'" (62). Reading ties the sensory to the imaginative and constructs a seamless experience that arches over the ontological gap between the two. But this transcendence—the union of the imaginative and the sensory, the linguistic and the phenomenal—which is represented in the novel as identical with reading, is, de Man argues, an illusion constructed by the "hidden system of relay" (60) that privileges metaphor rather than metonymy.

The unity is an illusion because, de Man argues, it is grounded in the tropological sleight of hand that conceals the fact that the working of metaphor is enabled by metonymy; metaphor is actually a form of metonymy. What the text states as the truth of reading is resisted by its own rhetorical operation, which textualizes that truth and displays it as the effect of "aesthetic ideology." The necessity and coherence of reading (seemingly achieved by metaphor) is the effect of the contingency and incoherence (of metonymy). He demonstrates this by analyzing a section of the text beginning with the words "like a hand reposing motionless in a stream of running water, the shock and animation of a torrent of activity and life" (Proust, *Swann's Way* 63). He writes that its rhetorical structure, which is typical of the tropological system of the novel, is "not simply metaphorical" (de Man, *Allegories* 66) but "doubly metonymic" because "torrent of activity" ("torrent d'activité") is a cliché and not a living metaphor, and its two terms are related not because of any "necessary link" (the logic of metaphor) but by "mere habit of proximity," which is the logic of metonymy (66). He goes on to say that the cliché ("torrent of activity") is "the reanimation of the numbed figure [by] means of a statement ('running brook') which happens to be close to it, without however this proximity being determined by necessity that would exist on the level of transcendental meaning" (66).

De Man concludes that "in a passage that abounds in successful and seductive metaphors and which, moreover, explicitly asserts the superior efficacy of metaphor over that of metonymy, persuasion is achieved by a figural play in which contingent figures of chance masquerade deceptively as figures of necessity" (*Allegories* 67). A literal and aesthetic reading of the text that "takes the assertions of the text at their word" would be "put in question if one takes the rhetorical structure of the text into account" (67). The "aesthetically responsive" and the "rhetorically aware" reading are at odds, and the disjunction between the two "undoes the pseudo-synthesis of inside and outside, time and space, container and content, part and whole, motion and stasis, self and understanding, writer and reader, metaphor and metonymy, that the text has constructed" (72).

It is, however, tempting to read the text aesthetically, teach it aesthetically, and turn it into an aesthetic pedagogy because "the desire for a secluded reading that satisfies the ethical demands of action" (*Allegories* 67) is fulfilled in such a reading. This temptation grounds "aesthetic ideology." In *The Resistance to Theory*, de Man describes ideology as "precisely the confusion of linguistic with natural reality, of reference with phenomenalism" (11). Proust's discourse on reading is an instance of aesthetic ideology, in which reading ties the sensory to the imaginative and constructs a seamless experience that spans the ontological gap between the two. Transcendence, de Man insists, is a metaphorical residue of a romantic poetics that privileges the aesthetic rather than the rhetorical, organic coherence rather than aleatory connection, and necessity rather than contingency.

Resisting aesthetic ideology, de Man writes that the incompatibility of the two readings "asserts the impossibility of a true understanding" of the text on any level (*Allegories* 72). The text is an allegory of reading, and "such an allegory will deflect from the act of reading and block access to its understanding. The allegory of reading narrates the impossibility of reading. But this impossibility necessarily extends to the word 'reading,' which is thus deprived of any referential meaning whatsoever" (77). What the novel says about reading is undone by its rhetorical work. What seems to be a coherent lesson about reading in Proust's text is actually the product of tropes of incoherence and fragmentation. The novel describes and represents reading, but what it says about reading is not reliable because it is grounded in a tropic illusion that conceals the fact that the novel is always already about its own rhetorical work. De Man's argument is that Proust's lesson about reading is an abstraction enabled by the concrete. Its totalizations of reading are effects of metaphors that actually are produced by the concrete singularities of metonymies. This means that its seemingly coherent theory about reading is the result of language in bits. Writing is the spacing of concrete signifiers in difference. All texts, in other words, are scenes of textual self-difference (their language is at odds with their conceptual conclusions), and because this self-difference is transgeneric, its immediate region—a novel, a poem, a play, or a critique—is irrelevant. All writings consist of writing as difference. In fact, several of the objects of de Man's inquiry in *Allegories of Reading* are not novels or poems but rather discursive critiques (for example, Rousseau's *Social Contract* and Nietzsche's "On Truth and Lie in an Extra-Moral Sense" and *Will to Power*). Cultural critique, accordingly, is language in bits and in difference. Its claim to explain cultural practices, like the claim of Proust's text to explain reading, is undone by its own textuality. Critique cannot explain anything; all it does is describe its own unreadable textuality and the opacity of its own writings. Cultural critique, at its most effective moments, according to such narratives about the self-referentiality of language, is an anticritique that emancipates critique from reason and educates the reader in the workings of language and its obliqueness, which are necessary for an antiessentialist understanding of the everyday.

Before turning to Lukács' reading of Balzac, which provides a radical counterpoint to de Manian reading, I would like to pause to examine the implications, conditions, and consequences of a few of de Man's assumptions about critique as a form of writing and writing as the concrete of difference. Cultural critique, like all writing, is a linguistic construct, and as such it is a discourse of irony, catachresis, and highly involved mediations. It is not a transparency whose message can be read directly. But this does not mean that language is a formal system, as de Man argues, nor that meaning is the outcome of the immanent working of its semiotics and rhetoric (*Allegories* 3–10; *Resistance to Theory* 115–21). Instead, the opacity of language is an effect of social relations and class contradictions. What de Man and others see as the subtle indirections and self-reflexivity of language are the effects of class contradictions. What capitalism cannot solve in its actual daily practices, it resolves discursively through the ironic and self-canceling language of cultural texts that, it claims, are ultimately not about an "outside" (class) but an "inside": an allegorical narrative of their own signification. To put it differently, language is opaque—but what produces opacity? The immanent working of a self-inspecting textuality? Or the class contradictions that arise in the struggle over the appropriation of surplus labor and are obscured in the relays of language, which are then read as its subtle self-deconstruction (de Man, *Resistance to Theory* 118)? Is it the materialism of labor (Marx, *Capital*, 1: 340–416)? Or the "materiality of the letter" (de Man, *Resistance to Theory* 89)? Depending on how it approaches this issue, contemporary cultural critique takes radically different shapes and moves along different analytical paths.

Meaning is the effect of abstract social relations of production expressed in the concrete signs of language. The medium of meaning is language, but the meaning of meaning is *social*. The view that the medium makes meaning was popularized by Marshall McLuhan (*Understanding Media*) and later Jean Baudrillard (*Simulacra and Simulation*) in response to capitalism's transition from Fordism to post-Fordism and was developed in more sophisticated theoretical arguments by Derrida, Lyotard, de Man, and Lacoue-Labarthe when post-Fordism merged with neoliberal economics. To say that the medium makes meaning is an ideological move depicted as epistemology; the purpose is to conceal the social relations of labor (which structure signification at any specific historical moment) under the concrete of linguistic signs, whose nomadic meanings can never be settled. Consequently, all the material conflicts over resources are depicted as cultural differences concerning interpretations of the meanings of texts of culture—from labor contracts to images, from understanding Abu Ghraib to understanding Carl Schmitt's theory of parliamentary democracy. Depicting language as independent of social relations is an act based on class, not a philosophical issue. Or, rather, it is a philosophical issue that represents class interests as the work of language—"language speaks" (Heidegger, *Poetry, Language, Thought* 190)—and thus reduces class agency to an interpretive subjectivity with regard to what the language has said. "Language," according to Marx and Engels, "is the immediate actuality of thought. Just as philosophers have given thought an independent existence, so they were bound to make language into an independent realm. . . . The problem of descending from the world of thoughts to the actual world is turned into the problem of descending from language to life" (Marx and Engels, *German Ideology* 446).

The fact that language is the medium of meaning does not mean that meaning is linguistic. Meaning consists of the material relations of production grasped as the performativity of language. Meaning, to put it differently, is always the surface articulation of deep economic conflicts among classes: "in an age and a country where royal power, aristocracy and bourgeoisie are contending for domination and where, therefore, domination is shared, the doctrine of separation of powers proves to be the dominant idea and is expressed as an 'eternal law'" (Marx and Engels, *German Ideology* 59). Democracy and democracy-to-come, in other words, are effects not of language, as Derrida seems to suggest—"no democracy without deconstruction" (*Politics of Friendship* 105)—but of capital in its relation to labor. Meaning is the abstraction of the social relations of production, expressed in sensuous signs.

For cultural critique to have any serious transformative impact, it needs to go beyond the obvious fact that it is a form of writing, and as such a complex construct of differences, to produce knowledge of the abstract social relations that make differences and produce the material everyday (including writing). My point is not that cultural critique should deny its own linguistic makeup or rhetorical composition. Rather, I argue that critique should recognize its own referential opacity and textual complexity and realize that these are historical. Critique thus needs to act within such understanding of itself in order to produce knowledge not simply of its own unreadability, as de Man suggests (*Allegories* 77, 245), but also of social totality and the material social relations within which its own unreadability becomes a condition of meaning. What are the social conditions that require meaning to be interpreted as the unreadability of meaning? Such a materialist cultural critique does not simply open up textual and cultural fissures in order to question the relation of language to reality and its own status as an analytical work; more important, this critique teases out the material cause of these fissures, namely, the fundamental contradictions in the social relations that produce it and the subject of its inquiry.

The difference between critique as the *concrete* of language, which de Man maps out in his reading of Proust, and materialist critique as knowledge of the *abstract* structures that make social life is clear in Marx's reading of Balzac's *Peasants* and its elaboration by Lukács. Marx writes:

> In a social order dominated by capitalist production even the non-capitalist producer is dominated by capitalist ways of thinking. Balzac, a novelist who is in general distinguished by his profound grasp of real conditions, accurately portrays in his last novel, *Les Paysans* (*The Peasants*), how the small peasant eager to retain the good-will of the money-lender performs all kinds of services for him unpaid, yet does not see himself as giving something for nothing, as his own labour does not cost him any cash expenditure. The money-lender for his part kills two birds with one stone. He spares the cash expenditure on wages and, as the peasant is gradually ruined by depriving his own fields of labour, he enmeshes him ever deeper in the web of usury. (*Capital*, 3: 130)

Lukács calls *The Peasants* the "most important" novel of Balzac's maturity. It is a powerful work about the advance of capitalism and the disintegration of the old aristocratic culture. In describing it Balzac says:

"In eight years I laid aside a hundred times and then took on hand again this most important book I want to write" (Quoted in Lukács, *European Realism*, 21). Marx's reading of Balzac is a lesson in a different cultural critique, one focused not on the concrete particular as embodied reality but on the abstract social relations that shape the working day under capitalism. He focuses on the text itself as a cultural product of social contradictions and shows how these determine the operation of the text in spite of Balzac's counterrevolutionary politics. In other words, for Marx, writing is a historical effect of social conditions as these conditions develop. Lukács elaborates on Marx's critique and writes that in spite of Balzac's "painstaking preparation and careful planning, what Balzac really did in this novel was exactly the opposite of what he had set out to do: what he depicted was not the tragedy of the aristocratic estate but of the peasant smallholding. It is precisely this discrepancy between intention and performance, between Balzac the political thinker and Balzac the author of *The Human Comedy* (*La Comedie Humaine*), that constitutes Balzac's historical greatness" (Lukács, *European Realism*, 21). The difference, in other words, is not determined by language, as de Man would claim, but by the social division of labor, by class relations.

The Peasants, according to Marx's reading, is the ironic dramatization of "false consciousness," which is, of course, a taboo concept in mainstream cultural critique because, after Althusser's critique (*Lenin and Philosophy* 127–86), it has been regarded as essentially an epistemological claim based on the binary of true/false. In Marx, "false consciousness is not about epistemology, or, rather, it is about epistemology only insofar as epistemology is part of class relations. False consciousness is about the exchange of wages for labor power and the way this exchange is represented as fair and equal (*Capital*, 1: 270–80): it is, in the first instance, a socioeconomic relation in which labor is obscured as the source of wealth.

In Balzac's novel the small peasant does not realize that his labor is the source of value and therefore gives his labor to the banker for free because he has been persuaded that money is the producer of wealth: the sign of wealth (discourse) is confused with the source of wealth (labor). Marx's reading moves in exactly the opposite direction from an idealist reading such as the one de Man offers. For de Man, ideology mistakes the concrete sign (language) for phenomenal reality (labor); the sign is the limit of the real (*Resistance to Theory* 11). For Marx, as he makes clear in *Capital* (1: 280), it is the phenomenal (labor) that is concealed by the sign (language); critique needs to go beyond the concrete sign to unconceal the concealed by making the underlying abstract social relations intelligible.

The Peasants demonstrates this fundamental contradiction of capital and, in doing so, also shows one of its most effective ideological operations. The peasants give their labor for free so that they can have good relations with the bankers. Marx shows how Balzac dramatizes the ideological practice by which the economic exploitation inherent in capitalism is mystified through cultural practices (in this case, affect in the form of friendly relations), the way capitalism exploits compassionately, with a smile. In other words, the economic always lurks in cultural values; cultural values are economic relations in disguise.

Balzac's novel is a critique of values and their second-order mystification (Nietzschean "transvaluation"); it is an ideological demystification of material contradictions that shows how they are depicted as spiritual. Thus it transforms the spontaneous consciousness of the reader into a critical consciousness as a step toward class consciousness. This transformation, for Marx, is the fundamental task of literature. As his reading of various literary and artistic texts shows, Marx does not deny the local density and opacity of the work of art. In his description of Greek art in the *Grundrisse* (109–11), for example, he writes about what seems to be an uneven development between material and cultural relations, how Greek art produced under specific social conditions has had a seemingly eternal value. Addressing the issue, Frederic Jameson writes that what seems to be a contradiction in Marx's theory of aesthetics is actually a confirmation of it, since

> precapitalist art, and particularly the art of ancient Greece, reflects a world in which the division of labor has not yet taken place, in which the market and commodity system has not yet made an abstraction of human experience. So it is scarcely surprising that out of the alienating structures of nineteenth-and twentieth-century capitalism we should look back with a (not necessarily unrevolutionary) nostalgia at such moments in which life, and form, are still relatively whole, and which seem at the same time to afford a glimpse into the nature of some future nonalienated existence as well. (Jameson, "Introduction" xvi–xvii)

For de Man, however, language is an excess of signification that cannot be reduced to fixed meanings. It is a self-reflexive performativity, and critique-as-writing is the sublime of this semiotic excess: an overflow of meanings that makes nonsense of any explanation that critique might offer. De Man's view of language and his interpretation of Proust's writing about reading, as well as his theory of the literary, are based on a hermeneutics that seeks the meaning of a text in the text itself and regards any attempt to read the text in relation to its "outside" as reductionist.

Some critics, such as J. Hillis Miller, have suggested that any reading—such as that by Marx or Lukács—might be unethical because it does not honor the singularity of the text's own concrete terms. But those terms are not immanent in the text; they are historical, and, as such, they are terms of class relations.

In reading Proust on reading, de Man never asks how Marcel can spend so much time reading and contemplating. Who provides this time? The time for reading is part of Marcel's class relation because it is the time produced by the surplus labor of others and relayed to him by his immediate family. De Man removes class from his reading by two inter-connected strategies—the local and the global.

On the local level, he displaces class with ethics. "The ethical in-vestment in this seemingly innocent narrative," he writes, "is in fact considerable." Proust's "passage on reading," he argues, "has to attempt the reconciliation between imagination and action and to resolve the ethical conflict that exists between them" (64). Ethical reading—which both resolves the text's discursive conflicts and is seen as honoring its singularity—is, in the final analysis, an ideological act. In the name of respecting the text, it erases the very conditions of its production, which are the effects of human labor and its relation to capital. Privileging the "ethics of reading" is, I believe, part of an individualistic liberalism that substitutes ethics—individual relations—for politics—collective praxis.

On the global level, de Man theorizes ideology as a confusion of sign and reality. He demystifies Proust's theory of reading and shows its metaphysics, but in the same move, he remystifies it with his theory of ideology.

Proust teaches reading as a practice by which one withdraws from the social and yet benefits from it. In *The Peasants*, on the other hand, the reader is educated about the labor theory of value: labor, not money, is the source of wealth because capital is not money; it is a social rela-tion. The novel, in spite of the author's counterrevolutionay politics, is devoted to transforming social relations.

In "Critique of Hegel's Philosophy of Right," Marx acknowledges that "the weapon of criticism cannot replace the criticism of weapons, and material force must be overthrown by material force" and goes on to say, "but theory also becomes a material force once it has gripped the masses" (251). Marx's reading of Balzac is an attempt to turn theory into a material force and show how theoretical analysis paves the way for social transformation. This is a point that Lenin states more directly. "Without revolutionary theory there can be no revolutionary movement. This idea cannot be insisted upon too strongly at a time when the fashionable preaching of opportunism goes hand in hand with an infatuation for the narrowest forms of practical activity" (*What Is to Be Done?* 369). In his reading of Hegel and his critique of Kant, Lenin writes in the *Philosophical Notebooks* that "abstraction reflects nature more deeply, truly and c o m p l e t e l y" ("Conspectus of Hegel's Book *The Science of Logic*" 171). This, I argue, is the logic of a transformative materialist critique, or as Lenin further elaborates, "From living perception to abstract thought, *and from this to practice*—such is the dialectical path of the cognition of *truth*, of the cognition of objective reality" (171, emphasis in original). Materialist cultural critique historicizes the concrete as the alienated reality of capitalism and seeks the roots of this alienation in the estrangement of labor under capital.

3. *Desiring Surfaces*

The Delectable Materiality of the Everyday Concrete

Although the concrete in contemporary feminist theory as practiced by Judith Butler, Diana Fuss, Elspeth Probyn, Elizabeth Grosz, and others is taken as a mark of materiality, it is actually the surface of a new spirituality. The association of feminism with materiality is based on the body's "own weighty materiality" (Grosz, *Volatile Bodies* 21), but this "weighty materiality" is more an objective idealism than it is materialism. The alienated concrete that grounds this idealism is the imaginary of what I call *delectable materialism*—a "materiality without materialism and even perhaps without matter," to recall Derrida ("Typewriter Ribbon" 281). This neomateriality has critiqued *historical materialism* in contemporary theory on the ground that its commitment to objectivity and to the truth of history is a reductive essentialism that is indifferent to difference and forms a totalizing analytics. Using the language of the market wherein the label "new" is the device for rebranding commodities to increase their sales, it labels historical materialism "outdated" (that is, nonmarketable). Instead, delectable materialism claims to offer, by means of the concrete, an up-to-date account of the specificity, differences, and singularity of the subject and events of the everyday.

Delectable materialism is the ecstasy concerning the concrete in its most exuberant moment. It reads the details of everyday life as blissful singularities and in doing so segregates them from their historical conditions and severs them from the social totality whose generality actually

46

makes singularity possible. The alienated concrete of delectable materialism becomes the space of the unrepresentable, a desire that defies all explanations.

In "The Professor Wore Prada," Elaine Showalter turns the details of everyday shopping into "closets" of pleasure that defy the normative and, in doing so, assert a de-centered singularity: people, she writes, "expect me to dress more like Susan B. Anthony than Diane Sawyer, but I just can't seem to adjust" (80). The concrete of clothing, for Showalter, performs a freedom to be maladjusted and acts out an identity based not on her work (as a scholar of reason) but rather on her consumption (as a subject of desire). Consumption, in her daily desire, is the language of her self-fashioning. Yet what she represents as the autonomous concrete details of the everyday and regards to be the effects of her singular desire are, in fact, constructed by the logic of capital, which uses popular culture to valorize consumption as the proof of individual sovereignty. The celebration of the concrete, in other words, is itself part of the political economy of production. "I'm a woman," Showalter continues, "whose idea of bliss is an afternoon in the makeup department at Saks" (80). Her consumption, which she is careful to represent as a rebellious act against institutional normativity ("I was once so desperate for a shopping fix at a Salzburg seminar on gender that I visited a dirndl factory," 80), is, in the end, an act of installing consumption as the norm of the a-normal. The political in the concrete, for Showalter and for mainstream contemporary cultural critique, is an excuse for retreat rather than a means of intervention. The conceptual (the seminar on gender), in other words, is overwhelmed by the concrete of consuming, which is, in her language, an addiction, a "fix." Addiction, in contemporary critique, is itself the trope of desire that can never be cured by reason (Ronell, *Crack Wars*). The everyday is the addiction of the postmodern. In consuming the concrete, Showalter claims she is trying to put the "femme" back into "feminism" in order to "make the life of the mind coexist with the day at the mall" (80). In her actual practice, however, the femme displaces the feminist "for those of us sisters hiding *Welcome to Your Facelift* inside *The Second Sex*" (80). The political becomes only a vehicle for consumption. The norm of the everyday is set by "catalogs" (92), which display, to use Eve Kosofsky Sedgwick's words, "luscious-looking clothes" (80).

Showalter's bliss of shopping as a text of autonomy is, of course, not very autonomous. It is authorized by other texts, among them Michel de Certeau's *Practice of Everyday Life*, which has become a canonic text for rebellion by means of consumption. The everyday, for de Certeau, is "a science of singularity," that is, "a science of relationship that links everyday pursuits to particular circumstances" (ix). These circumstances, however, as I argue more fully below, are isolated from the material conditions that make them circumstances. Consequently, for him, as for Showalter, the seeming density and layeredness of the concrete becomes a mystification of the concrete. De Certeau cleanses the everyday of its historical conditions of existence by turning it into a formal structure of language (in negotiation with the writings of Wittgenstein, Benveniste, Saussure, and others). "Language," he writes, "is indeed the privileged terrain on which to discern the formal rules proper to such practices" (32). He thus obscures the class relations that construct the everyday by turning it into a Deleuzian assemblage of cultural techniques operating by means of "strategies" and "tactics" (34–39), which, he argues, both constitute "procedures of consumption" and subvert and transform consumption itself. Through strategies the subject of consumption engages in the "calculation (or manipulation) of power relationships" in a delimited location, and tactics constitute "a calculated action determined by the absence of proper locus" (35, 37). With these techniques, the act of consumption is reconstituted into a dynamic, "producerly" act (Fiske, *Reading the Popular*, 107). In contemporary cultural critique, then, the everyday is constructed as the space of a "producerly" consumption—as the arena of a delectable materialism of sensuous, concrete pleasures.

Refiguring (Feminist) Spirituality on the Surfaces of the Body

"Materiality without materialism" moves cultural critique away from the objective structures of the everyday (labor) to the specific flows of meanings (affect). It redefines materialism as consisting of the sensualities that exceed conceptuality, as a resistance to all fixed meanings and to the norms implied by them. For feminist critics such as Grosz, the body is the exemplary site of the materiality of the concrete. "The focus on bodies, bodies in their concrete specificities, has the added bonus of inevitably raising the question of sexual difference in a way that mind does not. Questions of sexual specificity, questions about which kinds of bodies, what their differences are, and what their products and consequences might be can . . . more readily demonstrate, problematize, and transform women's social subordination to men" (*Volatile Bodies* vii–viii).

The concentration on the body leads Grosz to propose a cultural critique based on what she calls "corporeal feminism," which is a form of cultural theosophy based on a neovitalism that is grounded in Bergson's *élan vital* (*Creative Evolution*) and the flows and intensities of postmodern mysticism evolving around the trope-concept of "body without organs" (Deleuze and Guattari, *Anti-Oedipus, Thousand Plateaus*). Grosz's corporeal feminism grounds women's subjectivity on the body's concrete surfaces and claims to be "nondualist" and "committed to both a . . . nonphysicalist materialism and an acknowledgment of sexual difference" (viii). It is an epistemology of the concrete as the sensuousness that defies all abstractions and conceptuality.

Her cultural critique focuses on the sexed body as "inscriptive surface" (138–59), and although she acknowledges that "the specificity of bodies must be understood in its historical rather than simply its biological concreteness" (19), her own analysis is anything but historical. History, in her readings, is a form of Nietzschean genealogy that is a project of immanent tracing of descent (not "origins") of forces, identities, and concepts. In practice, however, contemporary genealogy evolves around the circulation of power, which it sees as moving through all social relations. By making power omnipresent and available to all through discourse, it discursively equalizes the materially unequal. Genealogy, in other words, is a class project that substitutes speculation about the discourses of knowledge and their relation to power for a materialist analysis of power. Power, I argue, is the effect not of discourse formations but of private property—accumulated surplus labor. Owning the means of producing wealth causes power to become powerful. This is exactly what genealogy mystifies. It does so with two interrelated reading strategies: by dismantling the relation of cause and effect and by destratifying all social relations and consequently erasing the binary relations between the powerful and the powerless.

Genealogy's rejection of cause and effect is rooted in Nietzsche's theory that it is a fiction of chronology invented to satisfy the will to truth because in actuality, Nietzsche contends, effect always comes before cause (we first fall, then we find the cause of the fall), but we reverse the concrete order of the empirical occurrence of events in order to produce a metaphysical truth (*Beyond Good and Evil* 33). The entire project of genealogy and its master concepts, such as discursive formation, discontinuity, effective history, series, and events, are aimed at dismantling cause-and-effect relations in history and showing that effects do not bear a resemblance to their causes. Consequently, "the forces operating in history are not controlled by destiny or regulative mechanisms, but respond to haphazard conflicts" (Foucault, "Nietzsche" 154). Power is, therefore, isolated from its material cause (or any cause, for that matter) and turned into an all-encompassing relation that corresponds to all social relations because it is said to be a "multiplicity of force relations immanent in the sphere in which they operate and which constitute their own organizations" (Foucault, *History of Sexuality* 92). This view of power obscures its cause and eliminates the binary of powerful and powerless (which is caused by the class binary of capital and labor/owners and workers): "There is no binary and all-encompassing opposition between rulers and ruled at the root of power relations" (94).

For Grosz, following Foucault, genealogy turns history into a series of autonomous "events" without any depth (causal relations). She defines events as "discrete, disparate, often randomly connected material conjunctions of things or processes" (*Volatile Bodies* 145). The meaning of events is said to lie on their "surfaces," which is another way of banishing the "deep" abstract causes of history to the diaspora of metaphysics. According to Foucault,

> the event—a wound, a victory-defeat, death—is always an effect produced by bodies colliding, mingling, or separating, but this effect is never of a corporeal nature; it is the intangible, inaccessible. . . . Physics concerns causes, but events, which arise as its effects, no longer belong to it. . . . As bodies collide, mingle, and suffer they create events on their surfaces, events that are without thickness, mixture, or passion; for this reason they can no longer be causes. . . . An event is not a state of things, something that could serve as a referent for a proposition. (*Language, Counter-Memory* 173)

To treat an event as a material effect, Foucault argues in his review of Deleuze's writings, is "in a schizoid fashion" to reduce "surfaces into depth" (*Language, Counter-Memory* 175). An event, then, is the nonmaterial material, an incorporeal corporeality, that obliterates the materialism of history. "Event" is essentially an abstraction such as "dying" that "can never verify anything" (173). It annihilates the materialism of the "dead," which threatens to become a "referent for a proposition" and thus reduce an event to a depth. Unlike abstraction in Foucault's account of dying-dead, which annihilates the materialism of history, abstraction in Lenin leads to a materialist knowledge of history that paves the path to critical practice. In his conversation with Foucault, Deleuze rejects Lenin's model and states that "theory and practice" are nonidentical: "For us . . . the relationships between theory and practice are far more partial and fragmentary" (205).

Although genealogical projects side with the oppositional and discontinuous knowledge that aims at questioning hegemonic practices, they are not emancipatory and regard emancipation as part of a metaphysics of freedom from repression (Foucault, *History of Sexuality,* 17–35). Foucault opens his introduction to *Herculine Barbin* by asking: "Do we *truly* need a *true* sex?" (vii, emphasis in original).For genealogy, freedom is not freedom from necessity but freedom from categories and concepts: how what is constituted conceptually as a discourse (for example, as "class") can be deconstituted and released from the discourses that have formed it. The goal is to show that behind the social practices there is "not a timeless and essential secret, but the secret that they have no essence or that their essence was fabricated in a piecemeal fashion from alien forms" and that history is born "from chance" (Foucault, "Nietzsche" 142). Thus exploitation is not systematically caused by capital's practice of extracting surplus labor from workers, but rather is seen as an event without regulatory mechanism, as a contingent matter.

Like the event without material cause, the body is, for Grosz, a corporeality that is noncorporeal: what she calls, in an ever-expanding eclectic middleness, a "psychical corporeality" (*Volatile Bodies* 22). The body is an assemblage of "intensities and flows" (160–83) that are, in the end, spiritual, even though she formally erases the binary of mind/body. The spiritualism of her analytics is not a local matter related to particular issues but an encircling faith-based approach to social practices. In her reading of Deleuze and Guattari, for example, she advises the reader to put aside reason, suspend "criticism," and simply "trust" them: "this trust is required in order to grasp, to be moved, and to be able to utilize their works" (166). The body concrete is a generalized trust in surfaces and a mistrust of all deep structures that explain the concrete and reveal trust to be an effect of the ideology of capital.

Grosz's theory of the body is grounded in a new flat-ism devoted to the destratification of cultural practices; it argues that questions of consciousness, subjectivity, affects, and agency can more effectively be grasped by refiguring them on the surfaces of the body (*Volatile Bodies* viii). As part of her analytics, the "body is seen as a purely surface phenomenon, a complex, multifaceted surface folded back on itself, exhibiting a certain torsion but nevertheless a flat plane whose incision or inscription produces the (illusion or effects of) depth and interiority" (116). The focus on the surface, as Grosz makes clear, is not simply a reversal of the conventional depth model: it does not mean that she is abandoning concepts associated with depth, psyche, agency, consciousness, or the interior (viii). Rather, the flattening of the body is a way of moving away from binaries of mind/body through remapping and refiguring these issues "in terms of models and paradigms which conceive of subjectivity in terms of the primacy of corporeality . . . on the model not of latency or depth but of surface" (viii).

The refiguring of consciousness, depth, and subjectivity on the body is not going beyond them. The writings of Derrida, Deleuze, Lyotard, and others have argued that any going beyond is a promise of proximity to Truth and thus part of a metaphysics of presence. The rearticulation of interiority on surfaces is part of a new material interiorism or spiritual materiality. Modernist interiorism has lost all believability in the contemporary culture of hyperconsumption, in which all cultural practices must have some relation to the body of the commodity and everyday appearances. The cultural imaginary has passed the historical moment in which it could grasp spirituality as an absolute unwordliness. The unworldly must now be grounded in the worldly yet never be identical with the world. In other words, it must always remain a materiality without materialism. Grosz's remapping of consciousness on surfaces gives the interior a material exteriority that makes it at home in the everyday of hypercommodities. It is, of course, not an isolated move: it is theoretically related through a Deleuzian-Guattarian neo-theosophy to Bergson's élan vital and is also part of a generic social movement based on spiritual materiality whose most recent manifestation is the green spiritualism of (Right-wing religious) Evangelicals, who are refiguring faith on the materiality of God's earth.

The flat-ist theory of culture (a spiritualism of surfaces) is ostensibly a project for removing all strata of privilege by flat-ing practices, mapping them onto their exteriority and reinscribing them as assemblages free from ranks, levels, and stages, thereby producing new post-hierarchical objects and practices. In actuality, it is a discursive means for equating appearance with essence and obscuring the invisible material structures that actually produce and, therefore, can explain the seemingly autonomous objects and practices. In the name of freeing culture from the metaphysics of depth (presence), it puts in question the binary of essence and appearance and represents the alienated surface as the real itself.

The analytics of the flat in the writings of such different thinkers as Fredric Jameson, Gilles Deleuze, and Thomas Friedman, to name three of its prominent exponents and annotators, is popular because it is fundamental to the cultural representations of recent capitalism. It shrinks contemporary reality to the visible surfaces and thus limits social knowledge of everyday appearances, which are the spheres of lived experience. Capitalism depicts the lived everyday experience as reality, but "this 'lived' experience is not a *given*, given by a pure 'reality,' but the spontaneous 'lived experience' of ideology in its peculiar relationship to the real" (Althusser, *Lenin and Philosophy* 223).

In his *Postmodernism* (1–54), Jameson argues that in late capitalism "depth is replaced by surface or multiple surfaces" (12). In contemporary cultural critique, the depth/surface binary is theorized in terms of the hermeneutics of inside/outside, which is critiqued as part of a logocentric will to truth. Jameson seems to relate this new surfacism to emerging technological changes and writes that it has put an end to such "old" projects as (ideology) critique (46), which relied on depth models in social theory. In the destratified culture of the media, there is no critical distance left for cultural critique (46, 399). Friedman, on the other end of the ideological spectrum, widens the scope of inquiry to geopolitical issues and theorizes that the world has become flat, by which he means that in global trade "the playing field is being leveled" (*World Is Flat* 7). Moreover, flat analytics has been given theoretical density and intellectual excitement in the writings of Deleuze and Guattari, especially in their concept of the "body without organs."

The flat-ing of global culture and economic relations is a component of a rather new politico-epistemological project that provides concepts for the way in which capitalism is remaking the global economy in terms of traveling capital. Flat theory dismantles as "outdated" essentialist depth models all the concepts—such as the labor theory of value, base/superstructure, and periphery/metropole—that offer a critique-al understanding of capitalism. It replaces them with "new" concepts (for example, immaterial labor, assemblage, and borderlessness). The flattening of cultural practices is based on Derrida's trope-concept of différance and the analytics of "The Outside and the Inside" (*Grammatology* 30–64). By arguing that the outside is the inside (44), he deconstructs the determining role of material practices (depth/inside) in shaping culture (outside/surface) and, consequently, dismantles, among other things, the concept of base/superstructure, as well as the dialectical relations of opposites and the notion of false consciousness. Derrida substitutes an idealist understanding of culture as hospitality for materialist analysis; he uses hospitality to replace a labor theory of value with affect and turn the immigrant worker into the generic foreigner (*Hospitality* 3). "For if I practice hospitality '*out of* duty' (and not only '*in conforming with* duty'), this hospitality of paying up is no longer an absolute hospitality, it is no longer graciously offered beyond debt and economy, offered to the other, a hospitality invented for the singularity of the new arrival, of the unexpected visitor" (83, emphasis in original). Doing so abolishes social collectivity and supplants it with interpersonal affective relationships. The culture of capital is regrounded in affective relations. Although these relations are represented as ethics, they are actually the logic of business relationships and deal making. Affective ethics is the basis of market networking, which embodies capital's will to deregulation of the market. Friedman's flattening of the world is an interpretive device for concealing the transfer of labor (wealth) from the peripheries to the metropole (580–604).

Grosz's theory of the body is a version of the analytics of the flat. She starts her theory of the body by rejecting materialist theory as a depth analysis based on the centrality of "relations of production" (165). Materialist theory, according to Grosz, is a barrier to developing "powerful weapons of analysis," such as those offered by Deleuze and Guattari, for a new feminist theory of intensities and flows. She thus rejects the base/superstructure model of cultural analysis and dismisses dialectics (as a logocentric totalization of difference). Her criticism of base/superstructure is a generic argument based on the assumption that it is a "model in which biology provides a self-contained 'natural' base and ideology provides a dependent parasitic 'second story'" (17). In other words, she reads base/superstructure as a binary analysis (23) that situates body and mind, depth and surface as opposites. As such, it is, according to her, a version of a metaphysics of truth based on a determinism that denies women's agency. Such a representation is, of course, quite common today. Yet the relations of base and superstructure, as Engels has argued, are not about subjugating superstructural practices to the base or depriving them from having an impact on the world. Once particular cultural practices emerge from the social relations of production, they "exercise their influence upon the course of the historical struggles and in many cases determine their form" ("Letter to Joseph Bloch" 395). Grosz's mechanical interpretation of base/superstructure is in part the effect of her eradicating dialectics (21), which is the logic of the relation of base and superstructure. For Grosz, dialectics is a metaphysical fiction aimed at securing plenitude as an identity of truth. But "dialectical logic," according to Lenin,

> demands that . . . in order really to know an object we must embrace, study, all its sides, all connections and "mediations." . . . Secondly, dialectical logic demands that we take an object in its development, its "self-movement" . . . in its changes. In relation to a glass this is not clear at once, but even a glass does not remain unchanged, particularly the purpose of the glass, its uses, its *connections* with the surrounding world. Thirdly, the whole of human experience should enter the full "definition" of an object as a criterion of the truth and as a practical index of the object's connection with what [humans] require. Fourthly,

dialectical logic teaches that "there is no abstract truth, truth is always concrete." ("On the Trade Unions" 94)

For Lenin, the concrete is not the singular but, rather, a collectivity of relations.

At the center of Grosz's feminist analytics of the flat is the body itself, which she remaps on its surfaces by means of two interrelated reading strategies: (a) she rewrites what she calls the binary of the mind and body through difference, and (b) she destratifies the body as a nonhierarchical assemblage of heterogeneous links, flows, and intensities.

She suspends the binary of mind/body through a feminist reading of Nietzsche (*Volatile Bodies* 115–37) and Foucault (145–59) and argues for a new corporeal epistemology that is free from essentialism. Her reading of Nietzsche and Foucault is based on the belief that "bodies have all the explanatory power of minds" (vii). By focusing on the "concrete specificities" of bodies, corporeal epistemology has "the added bonus of inevitably raising the question of sexual difference in a way that mind does not" (vii). Refiguring the body on the surface, in other words, produces knowledge of the singular, which is the aim of the analytics of the flat. It moves the focus of cultural critique away from the collective and abstract to the concrete and individual and thus blocks any knowledge of social totality. Knowledge of social totality is a dangerous knowledge for her project because any critique that makes sense of the material logic of culture—showing how all the seemingly disparate practices are connected to the logic of production—will unmask corporeal epistemology as an ideological project aimed at normalizing the logic of the market through an inversion of depth and surface (essence and appearance). Such an inversion represents the reality of the market—its concrete everyday—as the real, when it is, in actuality, an inversion of what takes place at the point of production. In the more specific terms of Grosz's project, her analytics of the flat represents knowledge of social totality as outdated depth and instead depicts disconnected, nonexplanatory and purely descriptive understandings of the surface as cutting-edge knowledge. Disconnected knowledge cuts off relations of cause and effect (production and corporeality) and thus obscures the logic of the exchange of wages for labor power by portraying it on the surface of the working day as a contract between two equal persons (capitalist and worker), when in fact it is the invisible, underlying material structure—the "silent compulsion of economic relations" (Marx, *Capital*, 1: 899)—that forces the worker to sell her labor power for wages. The analytics of the flat hides the *co-*

ercion exerted by the deep structure and represents it as *consent* on the surface corporeality of the working day.

In erasing the binary of mind/body, Grosz relies mostly on Nietzsche's writings because she reads Foucault's theory as situating the body as passive raw material manipulated by various networks of power-knowledge and other social processes (122). In Nietzsche, on the other hand, the body is an active source of the will to power and site of the movement of forces. The Nietzschean body does not yield "truth or knowledge" but through the will to power drives toward "self-expansion, the movement of becoming" and increases the "body's quantity and quality of forces and energies" that lead it toward "vigorous, free, joyful activity" (Nietzsche, *Genealogy of Morals* 33, quoted in Grosz 122–23). Nietzsche's theory of the body, in other words, provides the concept-tropes and the language for refiguring the interior onto the exterior. "Instead of seeing the body in terms of the mind/body distinction or regarding it as a substance to which various attributes, such as consciousness, can be added," he sees the body as a "kind of chaos of whirling forces, defined in terms of their quantities and intensities" (123).

By suspending the binaries of inside/outside by way of Nietzsche, Grosz produces the body mystical, a body that is driven by a Bergsonian life force and, as such, is beyond all calculatory reason. It is a postrational body moved by desire without any preordained direction. It is an anarchic body in rebellion against all regulations and norms. It is the body of capital itself. In other words, the body that is refigured on its surfaces in order to overcome the binarism of mind/body is an allegory of the anarchic chaos of the capitalist market, in which the logic of production is inverted and only "quantities" and "intensities" of the market shape its links and flows. The corporeal body is an allegory through which the deregulated market is normalized as an assemblage of heterogeneous forces and desires. The suspension of the binary, it seems, is more an inversion of the relation between production and market. In her *Architecture from the Outside,* in which a corporeal epistemology is deployed in order to read the body architectural, Grosz describes the postbinary corporeal body as the site of "excess of any representation, and indeed, of all representations" (27). Body, in its Nietzschean reconfiguration, becomes ineffable, and its corporeality turns out to be a spiritual materiality, a soft religiosity of postmodern latter days.

The deregulation of the body is further intensified by its destratification, which Grosz undertakes in a reading of Deleuze and Guattari (*Volatile Bodies* 160–83), especially their centering trope-concept of the "body without organs," which first appears in Deleuze's *The Logic of*

Sense but receives more and more elaboration in *Anti-Oedipus* and *A Thousand Plateaus*. For Deleuze and Guattari the body is first and foremost a complex of relations, relations of various parts to each other and also to other bodies that produce joy or melancholy. As such it is most effectively understood without a hierarchy of organs ("organism") that regulate the body by arranging its parts in relation to a center ("organization"). What matters in the body is its intensity: "The BwO causes intensities to pass; it produces and distributes them in a *spatium* that is itself intensive, lacking extension" (*Thousand Plateaus* 153). Destratification of the body, suspending its hierarchy, increases its intensity: "It is non-stratified, unformed, intense matter, the matrix of intensity, intensity=0; but there is nothing negative about that zero, there [are] no negative or opposite intensities" (153). Their notion of a body without organs (which is narrated in Artaud's *To Have Done with the Judgment of God* but has its tropic roots in the "unorganized bodies" of Bergson's *Creative Evolution)* is an assemblage, relations (of organs) without relationship ("organism"), because a hierarchy of organs dissipates intensity by diffusing it through various orders of organs. The body without organs—unlike the Lacanian body, which is a body whose desire is lack—is the body of open relations, and its desire is productive. The body without organs is "full of gaiety, ecstasy, and dance" (*Thousand Plateaus* 150). It is the virtual body, the space of potentialities; "How Do You Make Yourself a Body without Organs?" (149–66).

The body without organs is the field of absolute intensity and as such the figure of subversion and emancipation from rules, norms, and hierarchies. As an allegory of a market freed from the State, it is, like all liberal-anarchic, antistate subversions, also an extremely conservative and containing figure. Its destratification is always partial. Like Derridan deconstruction, it never breaks with the system but always works within it: "You have to keep enough of the organism for it to reform" (*Thousand Plateaus* 160).

It is the trope of a market that opposes the State to the extent that the State regulates it, but it relies on the same State for legal protection of private property. The body without organs, in other words, is not an organless body but a bourgeois fantasy of subversion. It cannot free itself from the very condition that it criticizes in psychoanalysis, namely, that psychoanalysis converts "everything into phantasies" (151). It is not the "opposite of organs" (158) but is opposite the structure that organizes them; it is a trope valorizing the concrete (organs) but obscuring the abstract (structure) that actually turns an organ into an organ because outside the structure, singular entities are not organs in any meaningful sense of the word. The body without organs is pure matter in the sense that "Matter equals energy" (153), and matter-as-energy is the theosophical life force that turns the concrete singular into the threshold of the real. This is one of the reasons why, for example, Alain Badiou argues that Deleuze is a metaphysician of the "One" (*Deleuze* 44–48). His "One" is the flowing concrete, which makes it the ideal trope not only of the body as lines of connections and intensities but also of the streaming tropics of digital capitalism. "The BwO is desire; it is that which one desires and by which one desires" (*Thousand Plateaus* 165). It is the body of "new" capital which, unlike the old Fordist capital of mass homogeneity, is the body heterogeneous (assemblage) of links of difference; it is the body in différance.

It is the difference (organ) without differentiations (organism) that Grosz finds most productive for a feminist theory of the body concrete. For her the body without organs is, in other words, a strategy for dismantling the "molar" organization of sexualities and identities (172–73) and arriving at a singular network of links and relations of difference by means of molecular motion and energies figured on the surfaces of the body—a body without hierarchies that is the field of plurality, of molecular desires instead of molar consciousness. The molar is all that establishes unities by an arboreal logic and, in doing so, eclipses difference. Grosz privileges Deleuze's approach to the body precisely because it goes beyond these unities that she sees as effects of historical materialism, which evolves around the arboreal logic of the "centrality of relations of production" in social analysis (165). It thus leads to such molar categories as class, which is directly threatening to sexual difference: "whatever class and race differences may divide women," their sexual differences remain intact and cannot be "overcome" since they are "ineradicable" (18). Whereas sexual difference is, in Deleuze and Guattari's theory, "molecular" and marks the difference within, thus bringing out the "man in the woman and the woman in the man" (172), class is "molar": it stabilizes identities and is thus an obstruction to change. I leave aside the point that she formally argues against essentialism (for example, that of class), but she actually practices it as an essentialism of sexuality and its difference. Her indifference to labor and her effort to transfer its materialism to the materiality of surfaces of the body leads to her sustained attack on such concepts of historical materialism as base/superstructure and dialectics.

The body without organs creates enormous political and theoretical problems for feminism. To begin with, it situates woman as a stage ("becoming woman") in the transformation of fixed subjectivities of men and women into minoritarian identities and, in doing so, erases the very feature that Grosz argues for throughout her book, namely, women's ineradicable difference (18). "Becoming woman" for a woman, Grosz acknowledges, remains "disturbingly unclear" (177). In part this is because such a concept subjugates women to the larger project of minoritarianism and molecularism. It is telling that while Grosz objects to Marxism on the ground that it "subordinat[es] women's struggle to the class struggle" (179), she defends Deleuze and Guattari (with a tone that is more tinged with a panic of materialism than an argument) for reproducing, according to her own narrative, a very similar structure of relations. She claims that "Deleuze and Guattari fit less easily into this category than it seems on first reading" (180). It is clear that what is at stake here is not woman but a particular theory of woman that is more acceptable to the culture of capital, a theory that has all the marks of difference but is, in the end, the same. By flattening the body, Deleuze and Guattari provide the idioms and arguments for this transformation without transforming.

The body without organs is an ideological combination of surfaces and intensities that turns the real into flowing concretes and serves as the authorizing trope for Grosz to produce a feminism that normalizes the logic of a new corporeal capitalism as the molecular world order, which has put behind it the molar logic of class.

The new corporeal order of capitalism represented as molecular feminism "insists on the flattening out of relations between the social and the psychical so that there is neither a relation of causation (one- or two-way) nor hierarchies, levels, grounds, or foundations" (*Volatile Bodies* 180). The social is no longer privileged with respect to the psychical (as she claims to be the case in Marxism), nor is the psychical enlarged at the expense of the social. The two "run into, as, and through each other" (180). This means that there will be no mediations of "systems of ideology or representation, not through the central organization of an apparatus like the state or the economic order" (180). This is the core logic of postnational capital: it is an order in which capital is not the cause of the devastation of the environment, unemployment, collapsing schools, or the widening gap between capital and labor. There is no cause and effect; the prosperity of the few is not caused by the misery of the many. It is a spontaneous state of being. In this order, capital "runs into as, and through" the labor of the other without the regulations of the nation-state or even resistance through ideology. Corporeal capitalism, depicted as a Deleuzian subject of feminism, is the final stage of direct exploitation—without the State regulating labor, wages, the environment, or health. It is what Bill Gates calls "friction-free capitalism" (*Road Ahead* 180–207).

Michael Hardt and Antonio Negri invert it and celebrate it as a form of democracy without mediations (*Multitude* 231–358). Instead of organized struggles (by the party, trade unions, and other so-called molar unities), there will be spontaneous molecular "systems of compliance and resistance" (*Volatile Bodies* 180).

The surface-ing of depth in the new corporeal world order eliminates not only cause and effect and the mediations of ideology (which could be a space of resistance) but also the State. The State, of course, has always been the protector of capital, but in protecting it, it also has had to enforce laws that minimally protect workers in order to maintain a ready workforce and, in ideological terms, hold on to its claim of ethical legitimacy. Postmolar capitalism no longer needs State protection: it directly exploits the workers, and it does this through an order of subjectivity that, "eschewing psychical depth," abandons the "necessity of interpretation, the order of signification based on the latency of signified in the signifier" (*Volatile Bodies* 180). The corporeal order of the real refuses to "duplicate the world, to create a world and its reflection, whether that reflection appears on the psychical interior in the form of ideas, wishes, and hopes or on the social and signifying exterior as meanings, latencies, representation" because the relations in the molecular order are "direct and unmediated" (180–81). The new order, it turns out, is the old one, in which spontaneous experience—renamed as intensities—is the embodiment of the real. The body without organs is a corporeal evangelism of experience and direct contact: "There is no ideology and never has been" (*Thousand Plateaus* 4). The way things seem is the way thing are and ought to be.

Through a liberal logic of "both-and-relations" (*Volatile Bodies* 181), corporeal capitalism, masquerading as feminism, suspends binaries that are reproductions of class relations, namely, the rise of private property (Ebert and Zavarzadeh, *Class in Culture*). It attributes a binary (two-tiered and oppositional) economy not to property relations but to the metaphysics of truth and obscures its material relations through the lines of energy and links of desire of the heterogeneous body without organs.

The corporeal logic becomes more clearly identical with the entrepreneurial logic of the market in its insistence that nothing be explained in terms of its underlying structure, that "events and impulses" should not be read "as being about something else." Everything is itself and thus should be read in its own terms, "what they do, what they make" (181). But what is done and made is always done and made within the existing system of production, and to measure the real in terms of its immanent features and pragmatic consequences is to affirm the system, the existing, as concrete.

As I mentioned above, Grosz is aware of some of these problems, but her critique remains innocuously immanent: she criticizes Deleuze and Guattari for doing that which they critique, but at the same time she erases her critique by saying that "all critiques succumb to what it is that they criticize" (*Volatile Bodies* 182). So even though they deterritorialize woman only to reterritorialize her in their universalist project of becoming woman, Grosz argues, Deleuze and Guattari "have a lot to offer to feminists" (182).

The Digital Concrete and the Posthuman

In cybertheory the processes that erase social totality and obscure the understructure of the everyday are going through a radical change. As is common in the knowledge market of capitalism, new and "improved" cutting-edge theories are supplanting current cutting-edge theory. For example, Grosz, in *Architecture from the Outside*, discusses corporeality in the digital age (74–89), but her arguments concerning this matter (like Deleuze and Guattari's discussion of the digital in *A Thousand Plateaus*) are more a transcoding of predigital thinking than a digital conceptualization of surfaces. In contemporary cybertheory appearance is severed from its essence in the name of a radical shift not only in human knowledge but in human evolution (to posthuman), in the relation of *Homo sapiens* to *Robo sapiens* (Menzel and D'Aluisio, *Robo Sapiens*). Reality and subjectivity are being transformed into two different modalities, and the question of the concrete is no longer an epistemological one but an ontological one.

Reality that is perceived as having a dimension of latency—an invisible dimension that has to be analyzed in order to attain full understanding—is considered to be an old "analog" reality. Analog reality is that in which the "complex surfaces are matched analogically with equally complex interiors" (Hayles, *Mother Was a Computer* 204). This is the reality of depth on which, for example, the traditional notions of subject, (un)conscious, ideology, and human rights are based and in which depth implies "meaningful interiority" (203).

On the other hand, reality freed from the "legacy" attributes of depth and interiority is thought of as "digital" reality—a reality without depth. "A relatively simple program" creates "an impression of complexity that contrasts with the simplicity of the underlying rules" (Hayles, *Mother Was a Computer* 204). The digital subject is the subject of fragmentation and segmentation. It is the subject without totality, an assemblage of links and connections that has simple underlying rules. "The complex emergence bears no analogical resemblance to the mind-numbing simplicity of ones and zeros" (203). There is a fissure between the interior and the surface.

In the Deleuzian model, which is influenced by cybertheory, as well as in cultural cybertheory, depth and interiority are conceptualized in their bourgeois sense as immanent interiority—within the subject. Interiority, however, is not simply the depth within, consciousness or unconsciousness, but the underlying structure that produces the subject. Only in formal terms is the interiority of the digital subject the "mind-numbing simplicity of ones and zeros." The interior needs to be understood historically and within the social totality. What has made the digital and the analog possible is not a particular technology or a metaphysics but human labor. It is the surplus labor of humans that provides the time within which the analog subject acquires depth or the digital subject is constructed on surfaces. It is the materialism of labor, in other words, that is the underlying structure of the analog and the digital: the interior is always the outside. There is no interior in the inside, and the outside is the abstract structure of class relations.

This is why critics who have obscured the underlying structures of the real and have refigured the real on surfaces (whether corporeal, analog, or digital subjectivity) have found it necessary to jettison the very idea of materiality or rewrite it as an innocuous mode of, for example, signification. It is equally important to note that in all these postmaterial ideas of materiality, the material is isolated from the physical. Deleuze (and especially Grosz), for example, seem to equate the physical with the natural and suspect both of being codes for essentialism (Deleuze and Guattari, *Thousand Plateaus* 254; Grosz, *Volatile Bodies* 18). They both deny the fact that it is nature that, in the dialectics of labor, produces the digital, the analog, and the corporeal. For Grosz materiality is "pure difference" (sexual specificity). She therefore calls for a "subject [that] is no longer seen as an entity—whether psychical or corporeal—but fundamentally as an effect of the pure difference that constitutes all modes of materiality" (208). Materiality, in other words, is (sexual) difference as a "difference that is originary and constitutive" and that "occupies a preontological—certainly a preepistemological—terrain insofar as it makes possible what things or entities, what beings, exist . . . and insofar as it must preexist and condition what we can know." (209).

Hayles abandons the quasi-mystical categories of Deleuze and Guattari and rewrites materialism as the materiality in an embodied entity resulting from the interaction of its physical characteristics and its signifying strategies (3, 103). In effect, she substitutes matterism for materialism. She first rewrites materialism as materiality and then theorizes it in cultural terms as signification. She thus reproduces the idealism that dominates the writings of such theorists as Judith Butler, for whom the material is simply a sign (*Bodies* 49). Yet materiality, I argue, is a culturalization of materialism, which is the effect not of the meaning, sign, or physical properties of an embedded object but of humans in their social and political relations as they, by their sensuous labor, produce material life within the conflicts of classes. Interiority is not in the interior but in the material structures that produce the interior.

Inverting the Real through the Concrete

In claiming that the concrete is embodied reality free from the metaphysics of interiority, contemporary cultural critique has instituted what Lenin, in his reading of Berkeley, calls an "objective idealism" (*Materialism and Empirio-Criticism*, 32). In other words, the concrete—masquerading as the material—has become the new corporeal metaphysics of cultural critique.

Reality under capitalism initially appears to be directly available to the senses as "experience," which is assumed to be immediately intelligible. Its concrete details seem to testify to its irreducible facticity. But actually it is very much like the (capitalist) "commodity," which, as Marx writes, "appears, at first sight, an extremely obvious . . . thing. But its analysis brings out that it is a very strange thing, abounding in metaphysical subtleties and theological niceties" (*Capital* 1: 163). Like the commodity, the concrete is "a very strange thing." Not only is it highly fetishized, but it is also inverted.

In *Marxism and Ideology*, Jorge Larrain argues that reality under capitalism is characterized by a "basic inversion at the level of production [that] is . . . concealed at the level of circulation" (126–27). In other words, "the appearances of the circulation process are the reverse of the inner reality of the productive process. But this is so because the very essential relations at the productive level are, in their turn, twisted and inverted" (126). Concretism mis-takes this inverted reality for reality itself by saturating it with details.

Larrain identifies three kinds of inversions. The first is "alienation or the basic inversion of subject and object whereby live labor is subordinated to dead labor." In other words, the process of production for commodity exchange converts "man as a producer . . . [into] a product and his products take the form of producers" (*Marxism and Ideology* 127). Or as Marx writes in *Capital*, the social relation between people assumes "the fantastic form of a relation between things" (1: 165). In the second kind, this inversion is itself reversed in "the market and the process of circulation . . . which presents [the reversal] as a natural process of objectification realizing freedom and equality; and [third is] ideology, which reproduces the level of appearances in the mind, thus inverting the inner 'twisted' relations" (Larrain, *Marxism and Ideology* 127). What this means is that "inverted appearances" and ideology are not effects of a reversal of consciousness but, rather, form an "inverted objective reality . . . that generates an inverted consciousness," in short, ideology (124). As Marx and Engels write in *The German Ideology*, "If in all ideology men and their circumstance appear upside-down as in a camera obscura, this phenomenon arises . . . from their historical life-process" (36). In *Capital* Marx describes what he calls the "working day":

> In the market, as owner of the commodity "labour-power," [the laborer] stood face to face with other owners of commodities, one owner against another owner. The contract by which he sold his labour-power to the capitalist proved in black and white, so to speak, that he was free to dispose of himself. But when the transaction was concluded, it was discovered that he was no "free agent," that the period of time for which he is free to sell his labour-power is the period of time for which he is forced to sell it, that in fact the vampire will not let go "while there remains a single muscle, sinew or drop of blood to be exploited." (1: 415–16)

The individual, in other words, is forced to sell her labor power in a transaction that on the surface appears free but in the very structure of its labor relations follows, as Marx says, the "silent compulsion of economic relations" (*Capital* 1: 899). The individual is no 'free agent' but is herself a "commodity" sold into the "slavery" of wage labor under capitalism. Although it appears to be a free and fair exchange of labor for a wage, this is both an inversion and an occlusion of the real relations.

The cultural critique of the concrete bypasses the logic of the real and simply plays with its texture. Some Marxist critics, such as Jameson, are overwhelmed by the layered and complex texture of daily reality under capitalism, mistaking this enormous inversion of reality for the real. In *Postmodernism* Jameson gives such priority to the proliferation of commodity exchange that he claims that there is "an explosion: a prodigious expansion of culture throughout the social realm, to the point at which everything in our social life—from economic value and state power to practices and the very structure of the psyche itself—can be said to have become 'cultural'" (48). So much so, he seems to think, that in postindustrial societies "traditional production has disappeared and . . . social classes of the classical type no longer exist" (53). We are left, in the writings of these postmodern Marxist critics, with Max Weber's notion of class as lifestyle, as "life-chances in the market-place" ("Class, Status, Party" 182). Like Žižek, Jameson substitutes a Lacanian notion of the ineffable "Real" (*Sublime Object* 50–51) for the concealed, inverted structural reality of the relations of production. Jameson so fetishizes the "depthlessness" of the arena of circulation in capital that he abandons as "outmoded" such fundamental practices of historical materialism as "critique," "opposition," and "reflexivity" because we have lost, he says, our "critical distance" and are now "submerged" in the "new space of postmodernism" and thus "incapable of distantiation," of positioning ourselves "outside the massive Being of capital" (48). Instead he advocates an "aesthetic of cognitive mapping" as a description of daily details in the "depthless" spatial arena of the global circulation of commodity exchange (51).

The pleasures and seductions of details saturate daily life and every aspect of culture in bourgeois capitalism. Yet one should avoid mistaking the vertigo of details at the level of commodity circulation for the reality of capitalism at the level of production. Instead of fetishizing depthlessness, in other words, cultural critique needs to produce a "deep knowledge" of reality and understand reality and its concreteness in its materialism and historical relations.

In "The Method of Political Economy" (*Grundrisse*, 100–111), Marx writes that, for example, in the study of population, "it seems to be correct to begin with the real and the concrete. . . . However, on closer examination this proves false" because the concrete is "an imagined concrete" (100). Its "individual moment" is "an abstraction" achieved only by leaving out its connections to the root relations that shape it, notably "classes" and "the division of labor." The "concrete is concrete," according to Marx, "because it is the concentration of many determinations" (101), and it is only through analysis—in other words, through conceptuality—that one is able to discover these root determinations and "move towards ever more simple [that is, fundamental] concepts (*Begriff*), from the imagined concrete towards ever thinner abstractions until I had arrived at the simplest [root] determinations. From there the journey would have to be retraced until I had finally arrived at the [concept, for example,] population again, but this time not as the chaotic conception of a whole, but as a rich totality of many determinations and relations" (100–101).

This is the project of transformative cultural critique: to unpack the "imagined concrete" of bourgeois detailism and its seductive sensualities and instead develop a critique-al and dialectical conceptuality that unveils the "rich totality of many determinations and relations" constituting the concrete.

An effective cultural critique is grounded not in the concrete but in the many determinations that make the concrete and that are situated, through material relays, in production practices because "production predominates not only over itself . . . but over the other moments as well. . . . A definite production thus determines a definite consumption, distribution and exchange as well as *definite relations between these different moments*" (Marx, *Grundrisse* 99, emphasis in original). Contemporary critique is located in the inversion of this relation. Turning it upside down, it gives primacy to consumption and the market, and it is this inversion of the market—putting consumption over production—that bourgeois ideology seeks to secure through the proliferation of the concrete.

PART 2

The Work of Critique

4. *Affective Pedagogy and Feminist Critique*

Like all cultural practices, pedagogy is structured by class relations. In pedagogical critique, however, nothing is more aggressively excluded from the scene of teaching than class. In more traditional critique, class is declared completely irrelevant to learning. According to these narratives, teaching should go beyond all social and ideological limits and teach the "truth" of the subject, and class is viewed as the most limiting of all limits. In much recent contemporary critique, class is bypassed altogether by stating that the main task of pedagogy is to teach the impossibility of teaching. What needs to be taught, these pedagogies maintain, cannot be taught because it is beyond all normative representations. What is teachable is that which is unable to act as a transgressive intervention in cultural practices because it is merely an affirmation of existing representations.

The ontologies of the impossible produce different forms of unrepresentability in pedagogy. In other chapters I have engaged the impossible in terms of mimesis and a textuality without end. Here I discuss the impossible as desire and its place in contemporary feminist pedagogy. I focus on feminism and desire because woman has been marked in some contemporary cultural critiques as the barred other: "There is no such thing as *The* woman" (Lacan, "God and the *Jouissance* of ~~The~~ Woman" 144). To become other than a fantasy of man, an excluded "not all" (144), woman, according to these discourses, must find her desire in a feminine *jouissance* "*beyond the phallus*" (145) and beyond masculine fantasies (Copjec, *Read My Desire* 224–27; K. Campbell, *Jacques Lacan* 86–87). Desire in feminist pedagogy, therefore, is teaching the unrepresentable "*jouissance* proper to her" (Lacan, "God and the *Jouissance* of ~~The~~ Woman" 145).

Becoming woman, as I discussed in chapter 3, is for Deleuze and Guattari the general condition (for men and women) of moving away from what they consider to be molar and totalizing identities, such as class, and becoming a body without organs, a field of flow that is absolute desire beyond all codes. In contemporary critique, to teach desire in the classroom is an act of resistance against normative representations; it is to begin to become the body without organs—a transgressive subject whose desires break through pleasure and supersede class relations.

The Imperative of Desire

Feminism in the classroom of contemporary capitalism, when it actually recognizes itself as feminist, is largely a ludic feminism. By *ludic feminism*, in general, I mean a feminism that has rearticulated politics almost exclusively as a cultural politics of desire and signs, as links of affect and language effects—a mode of rhetoric aimed at changing cultural representations and concerned with voicing the silenced desires and experiences of women and other marginalized people (Ebert, *Ludic Feminism*). Ludic pedagogy is a libidinal pedagogy of desire: the bliss of the body, ecstatic textuality, and the sensual surfaces of the everyday. The notion of desire and its pleasures take many forms in feminist pedagogy (Heng). They range from the familiar experiential feminist ideas of desire as "feelings," "affect," "empathy," and the breaking of norms (Sedgwick) to views of desire as an "excess" of rational and ideological limits (Garber, Kipnis, Probyn). When ludic pedagogy declares that "the order of desire is the order of production" (Deleuze and Guattari, *Anti-Oedipus* 296), it understands production not as the relations of production (labor) but as a production of flows, as in the body without organs.

In abandoning materialism, ludic feminism has largely abandoned politics as emancipation (Laclau, "Beyond Emancipation")—politics as a collective practice directed at transforming existing social institutions and the exploitative divisions of labor so that economic resources and cultural power can be equally distributed "to each according to his needs!" (Marx, *Gotha Programme* 10). But ludic feminism ignores the relations of property and, following (mostly) Foucault, understands power as diffuse, asystematic, contingent, and marked by chance and arbitrariness rather than historically determined by production practices. It deploys conventional theories of psychoanalysis (Lacanian rereadings and rereadings of these rereadings), putting the desiring subject at the center of its politics and its way of making sense of reality under capitalism. For ludic feminism, "the social field is immediately invested by desire[;] . . . it is the historically determined product of desire" (Deleuze and Guattari, *Anti-Oedipus* 29), and desire is considered the revolutionary force that can break the hegemony of class bipolarity (240–62). Ludic feminism sees capitalism as a regime of decoding (innovation, freedom from restriction) and recoding (through a monetary equivalence for decoded flows) and essentially as a repression of desire, of territorialization of the body without organs.

I take the other side: capitalism is not a cultural regime of coding, "axiomatization" or (de)territorialization of desire (Deleuze and Guattari, *Thousand Plateaus* 454–73) but a system of wage labor. Capital is a social relation and not money ("axiomatization"); it is accumulated alienated labor based on the unequal exchange of wages for labor power.

The contest about pedagogy is ultimately a class matter being fought out mostly under the signs of libidinal economy and political economy: the signs, in short, of desire and labor. Feminist pedagogy, like other pedagogies, does not escape the fundamental binary of capitalism: the struggle between two classes—the class of owners and the class of workers. But this class antagonism is mediated, and its class character is dispersed through concepts, tropes, and knowledge practices in the pedagogy of desire.

Pedagogies of desire, at their most radical moment, are pedagogies of liberation—specifically individual libidinal liberation, not collective freedom from necessity. In order to map the affective logic behind the rule of desire in feminist pedagogies and examine some of their underlying assumptions, I would like to begin with the question of desire and the ways in which it is theorized in two contesting views that are now canonical in feminist pedagogies. Although they are formally and methodologically at odds with each other, they are both extensions of the same class ideology.

In his theory of the subject, Jacques Lacan makes a distinction between desire, demand, and need. Need is a relation to a specific object; it is physical and is satisfied by that object. Demand is a demand for love from the other; it is still addressed to an object but is a satisfaction that does not really satisfy: "Demand in itself bears on something other than the satisfaction it calls for" (*Ecrits* 286). Desire is radically different from both need and demand because it is deep-seated in the unconscious; it is not aimed at an empirical object but is a relation to an ideal, a phantasy. Desire is "neither the appetite for satisfaction, nor the demand for love, but the difference resulting from the subtraction of the first from the second, the very phenomenon of their splitting *[Spaltung]*" (287). Desire, in other words, is the unrepresentable remainder (263, 265) that is beyond need and demand, an unfulfillable "lack." This lack is ontological and constitutive of the subject, which means that the subject is fashioned by an endless striving to fill the lack but always fails. The substitute for the lost object of desire is always what Lacan calls *objet petit a* (*Ecrits*, 292–325; *Four Fundamental Concepts* 112–18, 184–86, 272–76), a substitute that in turn sets off a chain of imaginary substitutions that keep desire active and in process. The subject, in other words, obtains a continuing series of "material" objects even though (or rather because) these material objects never correspond with the lost object of jouissance—an imaginary gap always separates them.

The writings of Gilles Deleuze and Felix Guattari (*Anti-Oedipus, Thousand Plateaus*) contest the notion of desire as lack. Some of the contested issues surface in Slavoj Žižek's *Organs without Bodies*. For Deleuze and Guattari the "traditional logic of desire" is "all wrong" (*Anti-Oedipus* 25) because it posits "desire as a lack" and so is idealist. In all classical theories, according to Deleuze and Guattari, "[T]he reality of the object . . . produced by desire, is . . . a psychic reality" (25). In these theories, the real object that desire lacks is related to an extrinsic natural or social production, whereas desire is seen as intrinsically producing an imaginary object that functions as a double reality, "as though there were a 'dreamed-of object behind every real object'" (25–26). This, they maintain, denies the materiality of desire and consequently leads to an idealist theory: the world as constituted by phantoms conjured up by desire. In contrast, they propose desire as a field of energy, a material flow: "If desire produces, its product is real" (26). Desire is seen as both autonomous and productive in its own right. For Deleuze and Guattari, in other words, desire is an autonomous positive force. It defies any social determination, and because it is not simply a dormant power within the subject but a productive energy, it shapes the social in many ways.

Desire is the materiality of the body without organs, which is "that which one desires and by which one desires" (*Thousand Plateaus*, 165). It is important to emphasize that for these authors—as for all other ludic theorists—materiality is a form of embodied spirituality, or, to use Derrida's annotation again, a "materiality without materialism and even perhaps without matter" ("Typewriter Ribbon" 281). Deleuze's notion of "machine" (as in desiring machines) is therefore essentially postmechanical; it is more a mystical vitalism that he inherits from Bergson than a physical construct. Materiality as a sublime spirituality is, for Deleuze, a means of resistance to conceptuality and therefore to all regulated social meanings.

Lacan's and Deleuze and Guattari's theories of desire offer radically different views of the subject and social relations. Both, however, perform the ideological work of capital: to invert the relation of the material ("needs") and the cultural ("desire") and represent the cultural as an agency that not only is autonomous from the material but actually produces the material. Desire, in other words, turns the subject into an entity that is constituted immanently and is thus free from any outside social and historical conditions. Deleuze and Guattari, of course, do write a great deal about the relation between society and desire, but the relation they posit is a state of in-betweenness without determination. Existing relations, in other words, are constructed in a state of equilibrium that is an affirmation of the way things are: "There are no desiring-machines that exist outside the social machines . . . and no social machines without desiring machines" (*Anti-Oedipus* 340).

Desire, however, is not unrepresentable; it is the effect of social relations under the regime of wage labor. Its complexities are the twists of subjectivity caused by the alienation of labor under capitalism and not the mysterious outcome of the unconscious, an élan vital, or the body without organs (which is itself the alienated body of labor). In *Wage-Labour* and in *Capital,* Marx addresses this issue and writes, "Our wants and pleasures have their origin in society; we therefore measure them in relation to society" (33). Lacan, Deleuze, and Guattari all argue against Marx's materialist theory and state that desire is not the effect of social relations of production and is thus independent of material needs.

Lacan does this by theorizing needs as completely different from desire, so that desire is self-making. Deleuze and Guattari argue that "desire has nothing to do with a natural or spontaneous determination; there is no desire but assembling, assembled, desire" (*Thousand Plateaus* 399). They maintain that desire should not be understood "as something supported by needs" (26). But this is a class theory masquerading as neutral knowledge. In class societies economic resources are not distributed equally (to each according to his needs), so there are unfulfilled needs, and these produce desire. Through their idealist moves, Lacanian and post-Lacanian psychoanalysis have posited desire as the base of all needs and legitimated the voracious appetites for consumption of the dominant class: if desire (which is assumed to constitute the subject) produces needs and needs are simply illusions of the local fulfillment of desire, then the quest for pursuing desire (consumption) is a never-ending one. This is the logic of capital instituted as the law of the subject. The more the subject consumes, the less fulfilled it becomes; there is a fissure in its excess (desire). Alienated desire is deployed as the very mark of subjectivity and thus is constitutive of being (The Real) itself. However, an actual material gap exists between needs and desires for the other class— the proletariat. For this class there is a profound lack of material objects available to meet its needs (material desires).

Lacan as well as Deleuze and Guattari spiritualize the social everyday through their notions of desire and remove it from the reach of social reason and critique. They are located in the Western tradition of idealism in which the material is obscured by the spiritual, and consequently, the social contradictions of class societies have been mystified as the unrepresentable and unexplainable, the complex higher realities of the "cogito" (Descartes), "things in themselves" (Kant), "spirit" (Hegel), "duration" (Bergson), "hospitality" (Derrida), or the "performative" (Butler). Similarly, desire in contemporary critique is the trope-concept by which the materialist world is translated into cultural spiritualism through such terms as *flows, lines of flights, body without organs,* and *gaze.*

This spiritualizing of the everyday by desire follows a class logic: inversion of the relation of use-value (labor) and exchange value (market), that is, production and consumption. The effect is to represent the market rather than labor as the source of value and depict consumption (lifestyle), not class, as constitutive of subjectivity. Deleuze and Guattari take this displacement even further; they rewrite needs (the material) as the dematerialized effects—the "counterproducts"—of a now-materialized desire that is their cause and producer. They claim that "desire is not bolstered by needs, but rather the contrary; needs are derived from desire" (*Anti-Oedipus* 27). This double move—cutting off desire from need and then reappropriating need as the product of autonomous desire— isolates desire from actual historical needs (use value) and posits desire (exchange value) itself as a self-propelling and compelling social force. This move, which has become common in contemporary cultural theory (for example, Baudrillard, *Mirror of Production*), produces an affective environment for cultural critique in which it is taken for granted that "the general theory of society is a generalized theory of flows" (*Anti-Oedipus* 262). This is the social theory that underlies pedagogy of desire today.

Entrepreneurs of Affect

"Desire," Elaine Marks writes, "is the central force of teaching" ("Memory" 3). Her statement is significant in part because it is included in one of the columns she wrote as the president of the MLA, which makes it symptomatic of the way desire and pedagogies of desire are affirmed by the existing social institutions. It is telling that what she finds "tedious and boring are readings of literary texts that focus uniquely on promoting social change." Instead she defends "what gives pleasure and what gives pain without rewards and without remedies ("In Defense" 2). The criterion, for her, of the kinds of pedagogies that should be practiced in the humanities is whether they focus on desire, a pedagogy that marginalizes social change in favor of "relationships" ("Memory" 3). Marks articulates the pedagogy of desire in readings of three French writers (Desbordes-Valmore, Colette, and Barthes) who "propose different modes of writing desire" in and about schools from "the teacher as molder and model," as Marks sums these up, "to the school as an erotic space of pleasure to the seminar as a space where desire circulates among participants" ("Memory" 3).

One version of this pedagogy of desire, that of bell hooks, is a performative of its erotics and demonstrates some of the reactionary implications of such a pedagogy and the feminism to which it appeals. In her "Eros, Eroticism, and the Pedagogical Process," she writes that eros is a "motivating force" in the classroom (194) and "provide[s] an epistemological grounding informing how we know what we know" (195). In other words, for hooks "the erotic in the classroom" is a force for pedagogy "to transform consciousness" (194). In her passion for passion, however, hooks largely elides the problems with erotic pedagogy. Not the least of these is its anticollective character, which make class consciousness disappear. Hers is little more than a romanticized bourgeois notion of love as excitation for the liberation of individual consciousness. But a revolutionary, materialist praxis of love is not simply a matter of liberating the consciousness of individuals or giving them an "erotic" high. It is based on a shared collective struggle to eliminate exploitation. As Samora Machel writes, "Love can only exist between free and equal people who have the same ideals and commitment in serving the masses and the revolution. This is the basis upon which the moral and emotional affinity which constitutes love is built" ("Women's Liberation" 164).

Whereas a materialist praxis of love is linked to an emancipatory politics, bourgeois erotic pedagogy is based on love as sensual bliss and risks being exploitative. These difficulties are quite evident in the way Jane Gallop has elaborated an erotic pedagogy. In her "Knot a Love Story" (*Anecdotal* 100–111), Gallop tells "a story of desire arising within the scene of pedagogy, where it is unclear whether this is really teaching or really sex" (105). She would, of course, argue that this is exactly the place of desiring pedagogy: the undecidable boundaries of pedagogy and affects where uncertainty itself becomes a teaching of the impossible and points to the impossibility of teaching. Uncertainty, however, is not a mark of the complexity of pedagogy but a feature of capitalism, part of its framing economics. Capitalism "cannot exist without constantly revolutionizing the instruments of production, and thereby the relations of production, and with them the whole relations of society" (Marx and Engels, *Manifesto* 487). Uncertainty is the effect of this need to relentlessly expand the market and therefore change the conditions of production and seek new ways to access cheap labor, which causes "uninterrupted disturbance of all social conditions" (487). The pedagogy of desire turns the conditions of production under capitalism into an epistemology of cutting-edge teaching and makes undecidability (the contradictory nature of the market and its ontological oscillations) into an ethical imperative (Derrida, *Limited Inc.* 116). The overriding problem here, as in all sites of the everyday under capitalism, is that the scene of pedagogy is an institutional power relation—it is not a free space of equals, nor is it situated in an egalitarian society.

For Gallop, desire is "part and parcel of a scene of pedagogy" (*Anecdotal* 106). Thus the teacher-student relation becomes what she calls a "drama of resistance and subsequent capitulation" in which she "invests erotically in students," both female and male (107). She articulates the specifics of this erotic investment in the dedication to *Around 1981:*

> To My Students:
> The bright, hot, hip (young) women who fire my thoughts, my loins, my prose. I write this to move, to please, to shake you.

For a desiring pedagogy, therefore, the purpose of knowledge and teaching—especially feminist teaching—is no longer understanding but seduction, no longer explanation and transformation of social institutions but ecstasy about what *is* and the social relations that keep *is* the way it is. In this seemingly free space of ludic pedagogy, the teacher foregrounds her erotic investment in the student, turning the pedagogical encounter into a drama of seduction in which the student is required to give pleasure, to arouse the teacher, to "fire her loins" and to, in turn, be "shaken" and pleasured. The scene of pedagogy is the alienated scene of everyday consumer capitalism, in which the bliss of the corporeal and the thrill of objects are the only signs of being alive. Everything else, the student is taught, is considered to be an abstract totality and a grand narrative that is really a symptom of the fact that "desire is stalemated in a fixation on the demand of the capitalist Other—for labor and for an antagonistic political complement, the 'working class'" (Gibson-Graham, *Postcapi-*

talist 13). Pedagogy becomes a way of teaching adjustment to existing social relations—an extension of capitalist crisis management—using the rhetoric of Left resistance to capital by breaking its codes of sexuality and desire. Capitalism does not need sexual repression to survive; it needs a compliant ("uncertain") labor force that is savvy in the ways of pleasure (consumption) and inexpensive to employ.

Gallop's rapturous account reproduces other aspects of power relations under capital. By interpreting the pedagogical situation in terms of a transference of her own desires, the ludic pedagogue risks coercing and even harassing students since she is in a position of considerable institutional power over them. In fact, such an erotic pedagogy, I argue, more often than not involves serious sexual harassment of students.

It is significant that Jane Gallop was, in fact, involved in a sexual harassment case brought against her by several of her female graduate students. The university found that although Gallop had "not harassed either student . . . she had violated the campus policy discouraging amorous consensual relations between professors and students" and "as a result, a letter of reprimand *will* go into her file" (Talbot, "Most Dangerous Method" 25). For Gallop the incident was a "joke"—a joke that "her sexual preference was graduate students" and a "florid public kiss" (25). But the pedagogy of the joke for Gallop, as she makes clear in the introduction to her collection *Pedagogy: The Question of Impersonation*—based on a pedagogical conference that she coordinated—is part of a pedagogy of desire: pleasuring and pleasing between teacher and student. Her jokes are not so much intended to promote knowledge as they are "motivated," Gallop says, "by my desire to please the students," in particular, that special student whom she calls "my best partner in repartee" (3). Gallop's erotic pedagogy was very disturbing to many students, some of whom protested at the conference and attempted to articulate how oppressive they found they found the relation between a pedagogy of desire and specific teaching practices to be.

Gallop's response to such protests and critiques has been to try to deconstruct not only the notion of sexual harassment but also antiharassment policy. In "The Lecherous Professor: A Reading" (*Anecdotal* 36–50), she argues that sexual harassment is fundamentally a problem of "heterosexism" and that "to combat sexual harassment, we must disrupt rather than subscribe to this ambient heterosexism" (47). Gallop seeks to "distinguish sexuality from sexism" (47)—desire from discrimination. She does so by undertaking a "deconstruction of the theorizing that underwrites the policies" against harassment and contends that "'we' do not even know what the word 'sex' refers to in sexual harassment"

(44). It involves, according to Gallop, a heterosexism that conflates, "on the one hand, sex, and on the other hand, sex": that is, sex as the "division of human beings into sexes" and sex "meaning sexuality, sexual behavior, sexual attraction" (44). She goes on to claim that "contrary to popular belief, the word 'sexual' in the phrase 'sexual harassment' does not mean that the harassment is sexual (i.e. lascivious), but rather that it is harassment *on the basis of sex*" (44, emphasis in original)—which in Gallop's pedagogy would be sex "as the division of human beings into sexes" (44), that is, on the basis of gender. She thus equates sexual harassment with sex discrimination and sexism (significantly, both these terms remain unexamined and unspecified in her "deconstruction"). In other words, Gallop's deconstructive double move reproduces sexual harassment as both heterosexist—conflating "sexuality and relations between the sexes as synonymous" (46)—and not about sexuality but sexism. But such a move, like other such quasi-deconstructive readings, puts forth an opportunistic interpretation that goes against the very anti-binarism of deconstruction she claims to be deploying. A rigorous—and not self-advancing—"deconstruction of the theorizing that underwrites the policies" (39) of antiharassment would instead demonstrate that there is no such thing as sex outside sex, no pure sexuality (in any sense) outside gender, and no gender outside sexuality. The two, for deconstructionists, are constituted by the same economies of différance and thus are not binaries but are imbricated in each other. By the same logic, heterosexuality and homosexuality, like sex and gender, are in a relation of supplementarity and not opposition.

If sexuality is removed from sexual harassment, then the latter, as (heterosexist) sex discrimination, can only be *gender* discrimination, that is, discrimination against the opposite sex, primarily by men against women. This is the crux of the issue for Gallop; she contends that "if we cut sexual harassment free from gender, we will deform it beyond recognition" (48). What is at stake in Gallop's self-serving rewriting of sexual harassment as heterosexism and gender discrimination is the erasure of power and the excision of sexuality—as a free space of desire—separate from and in excess of power and the political economy of sexual harassment. This move is marked by her opposition to sexual harassment as "a professional rather than a gender issue," to quote, as she does, Billie Wright Dziech (Gallop, *Anecdotal* 47–48). Sexual harassment as a professional issue is fundamentally a question of institutional power and its uses and abuses: it is about the professional relations—that is, institutional power relations—in which faculty and student are situated more than it is about gender. Gallop's deconstructive reading of harassment is a formalist move that entirely elides the basic issue of material power and sutures over the relation of sexuality to subject positions in a power relation. She is concerned that separating sexual harassment from gender will also separate it from feminism (48–49), and then "the fight against harassment" will no longer be "a struggle against sexism but a moral crusade against sexuality" (50). But to limit sexual harassment, as Gallop does, to a narrow notion of (gender) discrimination from which the dimensions of sexuality and power have been removed is to put forth a highly restrictive notion of harassment that is blind to its most common and widespread aspect: the producing of a hostile environment. Similarly, to neglect the relations of power in erotic pedagogy is to posit the free circulation of the teacher's desire and desiring as if the institutional structures of power had evaporated into a "free market" of consummative pleasures. Even if the teacher's seductive practices and drama of desiring (to stay within Gallop's own scenario) "disrupt . . . heterosexism" and exceed gender—focusing not on the other sex but on the same—the teacher is still the one with more institutional power, and thus the seductive relation is an unequal relation not free of sexual harassment. Erotic pedagogy, as a historical and material practice, generates sexual behavior and discourses that for students in an institutional setting are unwelcome and demeaning and create an intimidating, hostile, and offensive work environment that interferes with their ability to do their intellectual and professional work.

Gallop's anecdotal theory about sexuality, gender, and sexual harassment is neither an argument nor an analysis. It is, in the guise of a rule-breaking act of freedom, an affective reproduction of the workings of the market through the pedagogy of desire, a demand for the deregulation of pedagogy for the benefit of the entrepreneur of desire. Her pedagogy of desire is the theoretical performative of the way in which love and sex, in both theoretical and popular culture discourses (for example, Kipnis), are deployed as tropes through which cultural nonconformities of desire and norm-smashing acts of pleasures are used to secure conformities with economic practices that are essential for the working of capitalism.

The rebellion against norms of desire as an act of liberation is more passionately pursued by bell hooks in books that are situated in the middle discourses of culture between popular culture and critical writing. In "Good Sex: Passionate Pedagogy" (in *Teaching Community*), hooks moves beyond the statements she made in "Eros, Eroticism, and the Pedagogical Process" (from *Teaching to Transgress*) and more aggressively asks for the deregulation of pedagogy and an end to efforts to "police desire" (*Teaching Community* 147). She defends "faculty members who become involved in romantic relationships with a student" and "nurture" the student's sexual "maturation process" (154) and goes to great lengths to try to separate "positive uses of desire" and "student/faculty erotic bonding" that "enhance self-actualization" (151) from "relations where professors use sexuality to coerce and dominate students" (142). Hooks's analysis is very problematic: it posits desire as excessive and power as individually "negotiable" rather than institutional and structural, and it claims that the exploitation of students is "falsely constructed as gender neutral" when "the real political issues . . . have more to do with the construction of masculinity within patriarchy and the eroticization of domination . . . male professors abusing students" (145). She obscures the material and institutional aspects of power and instead accounts for the "abuse of power" as effects of cultural "constructions of masculinity" and as individual acts by "primarily males" (144). She trivializes and stereotypes this as a problem of "smart nerdy guys who didn't get sex in high school" and need a "power imbalance to be able to get it up and keep it up" (148). Moreover, hooks, following the current cultural orthodoxies (Foucault, *History of Sexuality* 1: 92–102), separates power from domination, condemning the "eroticization of domination" (mostly male) while affirming "eroticization of power" as an aspect of "female sexual agency" or, more specifically, the eroticization of the powerful (male) as an object of desire: "We fantasized," she says "about the pleasure and danger of having sex with a powerful man" (148). In a contradictory move, hooks acknowledges that "relationships where there are serious power imbalances can be a breeding ground for victimization" (152) then, in effect, dismisses this situation by universalizing the way things are: "This is true in all relationships in life. Power must be negotiated. Part of maturing is learning how to cope" (152). Her answer to the problem of abuse of power seems to be little more than learning how to cope with inequality; "maturing" means learning how to accept one's own subjugation! What is astonishing, of course, is that she makes this argument in the name of a Left pedagogy.

It is a symptomatic "coincidence" that as some feminists increasingly gain positions of institutional power they attempt, like hooks, Gallop, and Kipnis, to obscure the role of structural power in their own practices. Following the ludic logic popularized by Derrida, Lacan, Deleuze and Guattari, Butler, and Irigaray, hooks makes desire itself an excess, a transgressive remainder that she claims is a "democratic equalizing force—the fierce reminder of the limitations of hierarchy and status" (155). The erotic is thus "a space of transgression that can undermine politics of domination" (151). How? The erotic relation is seen as an isolated, ahistorical, noninstitutional "free" space of "free" individual desire that undoes hierarchies through the reversible, negotiable relation of seducer and seduced. But the professor-student relation is not a free space outside institutions and domination. The negotiation of power in an unequal relationship is always one in which the person with (institutional) power sets the terms. This is the logic of the free market, in which individuals are "free" to negotiate in an unequal space that always privileges the owners (the powerful). As I have already suggested, the erotic pedagogy of hooks and Gallop involves a normalization of the logic of capitalism and its class politics. In declaring desire to be autonomous and beyond the bounds of regulation (harassment policies, policing of desire), they are rearticulating the demands for deregulating all transactions in a "free" market.

The "debate over . . . erotic relationships between professors and students" is, for hooks, "one of the newest arenas where assertions of female sexual agency are under attack" (142). For hooks, to deny the "erotic feelings . . . between teachers and students . . . precludes the recognition of accountability and responsibility" (155). In making this argument, hooks recycles the old entrepreneurial logic rearticulated in Leftist rhetoric as agency. What she calls agency is the validation of individual consumer choice and free pursuit of one's aims in a commodity culture where desire is the trope of consumption.

It is a sign of the desire politics of this new feminism of (and for) institutionally powerful women that Teresa de Lauretis in *The Practice of Love* champions psychoanalysis for "the power it grants women—the power of seducing and being seduced as sexed and desiring subjects" (xvii). To reduce the agency of women to that of sexed, desiring subjects is part of a class politics in which material economic agency is marginalized in favor of the agency of desire and the power of seduction. This is an agency that is necessary for the bourgeoisie—the consuming class pursuing the circuit of desire (consumption) in commodity capitalism. It is a notion of agency that entirely displaces the question of need. I leave aside the point that these views are so at home in conservative thought that they form its grounding arguments (Wright) and are disseminated throughout popular culture in such classic postfeminist books as Camille Paglia's *Sexual Personae*, Naomi Wolf's *Fire with Fire*, and Katie Roiphe's *Morning After*, all of which advance a poetics of consumption and free-market ("material girl") individuality in the name of empowering women, promoting self-actualization, and warning against "victim feminism."

The way desire is understood in ludic feminism in terms of a circuit of discourse and desire between two individuals—two bourgeois monads—who are completely isolated from the social contradictions and historical conditions that determine their relation shows how ludic feminism has become an accomplice of capitalism. This is a notion of desire that obscures the economic conditions of its own possibility. To define oneself, to define significant social relations such as the pedagogical scene, almost entirely in terms of personal erotics and desire requires a very privileged social position—one in which fundamental needs are already met. Such an eroticized understanding of human relations is not available, nor in any way useful, for women struggling to meet basic social needs for themselves and their families. It presupposes an ahistorical and quite misleading notion of desire and sexuality as the effects of the free negotiation of equal individuals. In so doing, it not only denies the institutional power relations inherent in the pedagogical situation but also erases the economic reality of sexuality and desire as commodities in capitalism at a time when hundreds of thousands of women, young girls, and boys are not only not equal but are being sold, kidnapped, and coerced into prostitution in the international sex trade (Campbell and O'Neill, Kempadoo and Doezema). Ludic feminists continue to isolate their theories and pedagogical practices of desire from social relations and to exclude the material realities of sexual violence and exploitation that are the conditions of daily life for innumerable women and children.

Another popular version of affective pedagogy that sees teaching as a scene for the acting out of desires is one in which desire is not so much erotic as maternal. This is a nurturing pedagogy that seeks to create a safe space, a compassionate place for the pursuit of feelings and pleasures. Jane Tompkins's essay the "Pedagogy of the Distressed" is an exemplar of the logic of affect in this pedagogy. In it Tompkins develops what she calls "teaching as a maternal or coaching activity" (660). Like other forms of the ludic pedagogy of desire, it is a mode of teaching that tries "never to lose sight of the fleshly, desiring selves who were engaged in discussing hegemony or ideology or whatever" (658). She brings to the classroom Grosz's lessons in corporeality, discussed above. Argument, mode of inquiry, logic of interpretation, and concepts are irrelevant in such a classroom. What matters is the corporeal: how the teacher and students feel. This model of teaching attempts to "democratize the classroom," according to Tompkins, by "break[ing] down the barrier between public discourse and private feeling, between knowledge and experience" (658).

Tompkins's essay, which begins by invoking Paulo Freire's *Pedagogy of the Oppressed*, is symptomatic of the metropolitan appropriations of the periphery's revolutionary struggles for the pleasure and desires of first-world bourgeois academics. Tompkins erases the relationship in the international division of labor between Freire's oppressed—the impoverished peasants and workers in South America—and First-World university professors and students. This is not an uncommon move among academic uses of Freire, but Tompkins goes considerably further: she turns a pedagogy aimed at emancipating students from economic oppression into a pedagogy designed primarily to free teachers from emotional distress. Thus not only is the aim of this pedagogy no longer revolutionary, but it is not even aimed at students. Instead it gives priority to the emotional wants of the teacher as the basis for "democratizing the classroom." According to Tompkins, "the politics of the classroom begins with the teacher's treatment of and regard for him or her self. A kinder more sensitive attitude toward one's own needs as a human being . . . can bring greater sensitivity to the needs of students and a more sympathetic understanding of their positions, both as workers in the academy and as people in the wider world" ("Pedagogy of the Distressed" 660). But as Michael Carroll, points out, "her advice has almost no relevance to those of us who teach heavy course-loads" because "what goes on in the average college English classroom and its attendant conditions-of-labor has been excluded" ("Comment" 600).

The problem—one that informs all pedagogies of desire, not only Tompkins's—is that the basic concepts in the pedagogy of desire—the personal, feelings, pleasure, the erotic, liberation, support, congeniality—are all highly restrictive, ahistorical notions. Desire, feelings, and pleasure are all understood as the fundamental, immanent, essential, and defining attributes of an identity as a person, and the person is understood as a singularity. Although singularity is meant to stand for autonomous individuality, it is actually a symptom of an isolated, alienated bourgeois subject, a monad who is assumed to be free from economic necessity and historical determinacy but, in her everyday life, is trapped in the economic.

Grounding pedagogy on the free expression of desiring selves, however, does not result in a very productive classroom, even in its own terms. As Tompkins admits, "The course was in some respects a nightmare. There were days when people went at each other so destructively that students cried after class or got migraine headaches" (658). She passes over this quickly without any critical analysis, seeming to accept it as a natural part of the expression of feelings. But, in fact, nurturing pedagogy raises a number of problems for an effective feminism. It so reifies an anti-intellectual and transsocial individualism that it supplants any conceptual social and collective knowledge with an acting-out, a performing of emotions. The reason the students' emotional outpourings are so destructive in ludic classrooms is that they have not been provided with the concepts and historical frames for understanding and explaining their seemingly private, unique, individual feelings and desires.

This is what the socialist thinker Dorothy Healey calls asking "substantive questions about the meaning of our own experience" *(Dorothy Healy Remembers* 58). Instead each student's feelings are considered both unique and equal to those of everyone else, regardless of their class conditions. To critique anyone's experience, to unpack it and point to its material conditions, is seen as an unleashing of violence or as a direct attack on the student's identity. The nurturing pedagogical situation provides no means for a critical understanding of the student's emotions and desires or an analysis of the ways in which seemingly unique feelings participate in and reproduce unequal and unjust social relations. At best such a method can describe how the student feels, but it is unable to explain the way the student's feelings are not spontaneous but are constructed from existing socioeconomic power relations. As Sue Clegg has argued, "Oppression is experienced in terms of being black, or being a woman, or being Irish, or being gay, but it cannot be explained by virtue of this experience. For that we need an analysis that goes beyond experience. These oppressions . . . are connected to the central dynamics of capitalist exploitation" ("Theories of Racism" 112).

Such knowledge, however, requires critique, which is largely dismissed as attack in pedagogies of nurturing and as repressive in erotic pedagogy. Critique, in short, is considered antithetical to pleasure and even to feminism itself, in whose discourses it is often represented as "trashing" (Gallop, Hirsch, and Miller, "Criticizing Feminist Criticism," 349–69).

I want to return to my discussion of Elizabeth Grosz's corporeal feminism and examine some of its pedagogical implications. Corporeal pedagogy evolves around the flows and fluids and differences of the (female) body, which for Grosz is the basis on which women can "develop autonomous modes of self-understanding and positions from which to challenge male knowledges and paradigms" *(Volatile Bodies* 19). Her corporeal feminism and its pedagogy are grounded, as I have indicated, in "a nondichtomous understanding of the body" (21) as "pure difference" (21). The subject of pedagogy is "no longer seen as an entity—whether psychical or corporeal—but fundamentally as an effect of the pure difference that constitutes all modes of materiality" (208). Grosz develops this notion in direct analogy to de Saussure's idea of language as "difference" (de Saussure, *Course in General Linguistics* 111–22), and Derrida's radicalization of de Saussure as "différance" *(Margins* 1–27), which she rereads in terms of a Deleuzian notion of desire.

Difference, for Grosz and other pedagogues of desire, is the critique of essentialism. Grosz, however, turns difference into a new corporeal foundationalism in which sexual difference is " originary and constitutive" (*Volatile Bodies* 209) and "occupies a preontological—certainly a preepistemological—terrain insofar as it makes possible what things or entities, what beings, exist . . . and insofar as it must preexist and condition what we can know" (209). Her "pure difference," in other words, is the ground for a new corporeal identity. It is a new ludic essentialism founded on the *arche* essence of an absolute, ahistorical, and ontologically irreducible sexual difference. She writes this difference as the effect of "a material specificity and determinateness" of "bodies" that "exert . . . resistance . . . to the processes of cultural inscription" (190). The materiality of the body and its specificity is, I have suggested, a spiritual "materiality without materialism"; its main function is to unravel conceptuality (abstract, fixed meanings) and thus assert the pure difference that is unrepresentable.

This is, of course, a neo-Platonism, the Platonism of the body concrete. In Grosz's pedagogy, materiality is the generic name of corporeality and anticonceptuality, a theme that dominates post-theory. For all her claims for a theory of the historical specificity of "bodies—male or female, black, brown, white, large or small" (*Volatile Bodies* 19), Grosz erases the real historical, material specificity of bodies, the materiality constituted not by pure difference but by the historical differences produced in struggles over the divisions of labor, surplus labor, and property. Sexual difference supersedes class (18) and is an autonomous flow, a bodily vitalism.

The core of Grosz's pedagogy is her marginalization of the conceptual. She demonstrates this in her "experiment" with a "Deleuzian feminism" (*Volatile Bodies* 180), in which she deploys Deleuze and Guattari's binary "rhizomatic"/"arboreal" (in spite of her own injunctions against dichotomous pedagogies). The arboreal (the systematic understanding of society) in pedagogy is put aside (because it is totalizing) in the interest of a "rhizomatics"—a concrete, specific, discontinuous, heterogeneous description of bodies in terms of their "intensities and flows" (160–83). Bodies in a rhizomatics of desire are "assemblages" of differences, "fragments of a desiring machine" (167–68), "heterogeneous, disparate, discontinuous alignments or linkages" (167). They have (and here she quotes Deleuze and Guattari directly) "neither base nor superstructure" but follow the "imperative of endless experimentation, metamorphosis, or transmutation" (167–68). The function of pedagogy is to teach the rhizomatics of the corporeal, the specific. This is, of course, the curriculum of capital: it aims at saturating everyday consciousness with endless details, teaching that each detail should be honored for its difference, and ensuring that the material logic connecting them remains invisible. To tease out the logic that underlies the seeming autonomy of details is, for Grosz, an act of violence. In the name of the rhizome, her pedagogy represses the knowledge of social totality by which students can grasp the material forces that actually determine everyday life under capitalism.

In support of her pedagogy of the body, she cites the lesson of what she calls the "definitive phenomenological study of the experience of being/having breasts" (204) by Iris Young ("Breasted"). Young deploys an "Irigarayan metaphorics of fluids . . . [that] befuddles and complicates [the] Cartesian ontology" (Grosz, *Volatile Bodies* 204) and deconstructs the common coding and alienating objectification of the female body. Young argues that if we "imagine the woman's point of view, the breasted body become blurry, mushy, indefinite, multiple and without clear identity. . . . A metaphysics generated from feminine desire, Luce Irigaray suggests, might conceptualize being as fluid . . . [and] would tend to privilege the living, moving, pulsing over the inert dead matter of the Cartesian World view" ("Breasted" 192–93).

In other words, a corporeal knowledge that "traces the libidinal pathway," "corporeal flows," and trajectories of fluids "across women's bodies" is seen as a liberatory deconstruction of the binaries of Western metaphysics and its alienating codings of women's bodies. But what is omitted is the determined materiality of the body as the effect of social struggles brought about by the forces and relations of production—the divisions of labor and exploitation. Such valorized, libidinal meanings of corporeal flows, fluids, and intensities are, to a large degree, the privilege of prosperity: they are class-specific. They erase the laboring body, the body of need.

The faith-based practices of the pedagogy of desire and the neo-Platonism that underlies its arguments find full articulation in Eve Kosofsky Sedgwick's lessons about "affect, pedagogy, [and] performativity." In her "Pedagogy of Buddhism" (*Touching Feeling* 153–81), she rewrites pedagogy as lessons in the corporeal holy. It assumes that the student is the bearer of a "template of truth," and all pedagogy has to do is make her "realize" it. This is, of course, a recycling of the theosophical commonplace that one can only learn what one already knows. Pedagogy, accordingly, is an arrival at oneness—where "seeing" and "realizing" merge (167) and go beyond conceptual knowledge, which is binary. This lesson also makes clear that such reading practices as deconstruction, which operate as the logic of arguments in books such as Gallop's *Anecdotal Theory*, are part of this religiomystical tradition (165–66).

Gallop, hooks, Tompkins, Grosz, and Sedgwick all write from a Leftist perspective, and they do so amid struggles against the repressive norms and practices of established ideas and institutions. But they make up the new institution, and their thoughts are institutional. Their writings have established a cognitive environment in which feminism and its knowledge have been reduced to affect, the ineffable, and the body. Feminist pedagogy has become a meditation on desire and its unrepresentable difference. This is not a curriculum aimed at freedom from necessity; it is a curriculum of repression that is not a struggle against but an extension of the economic priorities of capitalism. This feminism has now become hegemonic.

The Pedagogy of Critique

In an essay titled "Critical Thought as Solvent to Doxa," Loïc Wacquant writes that there are two senses to the notion of critique:

> a sense one could call Kantian . . . which refers to the evaluative exami-
> nation of categories and forms of knowledge in order to determine their
> cognitive validity and value; and a Marxian sense, which trains the weap-
> ons of reason at socio-historical reality and sets itself the task of bringing
> to light the hidden forms of domination and exploitation which shape it
> so as to reveal by contrast the alternatives they thwart and exclude (recall
> Horkheimer's definition of "critical theory" as theory that is at the same
> time explanatory, normative, practical, and reflexive). (n.p.)

Wacquant, like most contemporary thinkers, takes a middle ground and writes that "the most fruitful critical thought is that which situates itself at the confluence of these two traditions" (n.p.).

Pedagogy of critique is grounded in what Wacquant calls a "Marxian sense" of critique. It is a materialist critique whose purpose is not simply to perform an immanent examination of the cognitive validity of categories and forms of knowledge but to relate these categories to the "outside" conditions of their possibility. Categories of knowledge are effects—not of language or the thought of individual thinkers—but, as Marx explains in *Capital*, they "are forms of thought which are socially valid, and therefore objective, for the relations of production belonging to this historically determined mode of social production" (1: 169). History, in other words, determines the "inside" and shapes the language by which it is articulated. In *Poverty of Philosophy*, Marx is even more direct. Discussing economics, he writes that its "categories are only the theoretical expression, the abstractions of social relations of produc-tion" (165). The role of (materialist) critique, therefore, is to begin with an immanent investigation of a system or a practice in its own terms but then to relate these "inside" terms to their "outside" historical and social conditions. Interpretive logic, like categories of knowledge, is historical and is shaped by social relations. It is only through analysis of these conditions that one may understand, for example, that the reason the dominant regime of representation focuses on the micropractices of difference is to conceal the material logic of capital, which actually produces these seemingly autonomous practices and their details.

Materialism—in "materialist critique"—means, as I wrote in chapter 1, the worldliness of human practices that constantly revolutionize the relations of production, making human history, in particular, progress toward freedom from necessity. Materialism consists of the objective productive activities of humans that involve them in social relations under definite historical conditions that are independent of their will and are shaped by struggles between contesting classes over the surplus produced by social labor. Materiality, which is deployed in the pedagogy of desire, on the other hand, is the contemplative corporeality of the body, language, textuality, the medium of representation, and the flow of affects. Materiality, in this speculative tradition which has its modern roots in Feuerbach, is a cultural effect of resistance to determinate meanings, conceptuality, and totality. It is a performativity, a meaning that is spectral and an effect of archives and memories. It is a materiality that understands "matter as a sign" in oscillations (Butler, *Bodies* 49) and not an effect of labor.

The project of critique, in the sense that I outline here, has come under increasing attack, as might be expected, from ludic feminists (Butler, "What Is Critique?") and theorists (Foucault, "What Is Critique?"), who generally argue that critique, especially in its materialist sense, is a modernist project and an outcome of the will to truth. It is, therefore, considered a normative act and, as such, a repressive totalization. Instead these critics propose an immanent critique with difference and of difference—a critique of the inside from the inside. Some, like Butler, argue that critique itself as a mode of understanding should always be critique of the specific so as to avoid essentializing it ("What Is Critique?"). The goal is to turn critique into an immanent reading of the social in its own terms without examining their relations to their outside. This confines critique to a local description without connecting what is described to its outside, which can "explain it."

Derrida, who, in spite of his formal statements, continues the tradition of Kantian critique, offers what is perhaps the most concise epistemological criticism of critique. He argues that critique has no ground because there is no "outside" (separate from the economy of signification of the inside) from which to critique (*Grammatology* 30–73). To put it differently, the conditions of the outside are the same as those of the inside: they are both language effects, outcomes of representation. There is nothing outside representation. Everything, therefore, is representation, which cannot critique representation but can only bear witness as "It deconstructs it-self" ("Letter to a Japanese Friend" 274 -75). The knowledge of social totality ("outside") that critique promises, according to Derrida, is impossible because totalization is representation and is thus deconstructed by the very language within which it is articulated. To be clear, the impossibility of totalization is caused, not by the proliferation of practices in the outside that cannot be mastered by concepts, not because there is "too much" in the outside, but because language, in which inevitably knowledge of the outside is formed, "excludes totalization" (Derrida, *Writing and Difference* 289). Language is a "field" of "play, that is to say, a field of infinite substitutions . . . there is something missing from it: a center which arrests and grounds the play of substitutions. . . . [T]his movement of play, permitted by the lack or absence of a center or origin, is the movement of supplementarity. One cannot determine the center and exhaust totalization because the sign which replaces the center, which supplements it, taking the center's place in its absence— this sign is added, occurs as a surplus, as a supplement" (289). "Supplementarity" is an addition that adds because there is a lack in what is supposed to be a plenitude: "if it fills, it is as if one fills a void" (Derrida, *Grammatology* 145). It renders totalization impossible.

Instead of materialist critique—which explains the inside by its relation to the outside of production in order to change it—contemporary feminism deploys such reading strategies as "resignification," a mode of close description that Luce Irigaray calls "mimesis" and "immanent critique." These discursive strategies and their variants are modes of intervention from the inside and dwell on the microsigns of difference in representation.

Resignification is perhaps best theorized by Michel Foucault as "the appropriation of a vocabulary turned against those who had once used it" ("Nietzsche" 154). Butler regards the strategy to be an effective political intervention: "The public assertion of 'queerness' enacts performativity as citationality for the purpose of resignifying the abjection of homosexuality into defiance and legitimacy" (*Bodies* 21). Resignification, in other words, changes representation and in doing so produces a new cultural imaginary that is less repressive.

Irigaray considers mimesis to be a resistance to the closure of meanings and, thus, an integral part of gender politics. Description ("mimesis"), for Irigaray, is a practice in freedom for women from masculine totalization. In mimesis as she uses the term,

> One must assume the feminine role deliberately. Which means already to convert a form of subordination into an affirmation, and thus to begin to thwart it. . . . To play with mimesis is thus, for a woman, to try to recover the place of her exploitation by discourse, without allowing herself to be simply reduced to it. It means to submit herself—inasmuch as she is on the side of the "perceptible," of "matter"—to "ideas," in particular to ideas about herself that are elaborated in/by a masculine logic, but so as to make "visible," by an effect of playful repetition, what was supposed to remain invisible. (*Sex Which Is Not One* 76)

By the practice of mimesis, Irigaray means the need for women to take up cultural traits attributed to them and by their "playful repetitions" exhaust their current meaning and performatively create new positive ones. She proposes mimesis as an activist resignification: to describe in order to transform.

Linguistic and epistemological questions are not the only criticisms of critique. In addition, critique is said to have lost its transformative ability on historical grounds. For instance, what are seen as radical changes in capitalism are viewed as shifting the center of social life from production to consumption. As a result, the gap between the cultural and the material is said to have closed, and the two are no longer considered distinguishable (Hall, "The Centrality of Culture"). "Everything in our social life," as Jameson puts it, "can be said to have become 'cultural'" (*Postmodernism* 48). For ludic theorists, in other words, the critical distance that distinguished the critical practices of Horkheimer, Adorno, and other Marxists of the Frankfurt School is no longer obtainable in a fully commodified postmodern culture. There is no longer any place from which one can mount a critique of culture. In the contemporary, ludic theorists claim, we all think in a middle space without any critical distance to enable transformative explanations.

We are all post-critique-al now.

These views are offered as philosophical and historical criticisms of the ground of materialist critique and to point to its crisis, if not its death. Yet they are more philosophical and historical expressions of a certain class interest than they are critical inquiries into the grounds of critique. Their aim, in the end, is to represent the knowledge of social totality that materialist critique produces as a reductionism (Butler, *Undoing Gender* 138; Grosz, *Volatile Bodies* 165, 180; Derrida, *Specters of Marx* 55, 85, 90). Instead of offering contrary views such as Steven Weinberg's "Two Cheers for Reductionism," which would undoubtedly be marked by ludic feminists as reading from the outside and thus subjected to the same kind of criticism used to marginalize materialist critique, I focus on the structure of the arguments, logic, and grounds of these criticisms. I read them, in other words, not from their outside but in their own terms.

Like all class theories, criticisms of critique are fraught with contradictions that are not simply cognitive or the results of the intellectual shortcomings of their authors but are reflections of the contradictions in the social conditions that produce them: "The ruling ideas are nothing more than the ideal expression of the dominant material relations; the dominant material relations grasped as ideas" (Marx and Engels, *German Ideology* 59) If these critiques are read reflexively, that is, if they are analyzed by the very terms that they use to analyze materialist critique, they will lose their critical authority and collapse from their own contradictions.

Their notion that critique is normative and thus represses the freedom of the other, for example, is based on the assumption that a nonnormative discourse is (a) possible and (b) closer to Truth than is critique. The critique of the normative, in other words, is itself normative (it is based on the norm that the normative is repressive and the nonnormative, liberating). It rejects critique as normative by norms of its own. The criticism that critique is a logocentric attempt to reclaim presence (truth) from the abyss of absence is itself grounded in truth: the truth that there is no truth outside representation. In other words, the truth that there is no truth outside language—and that what is in language is simply representation—is considered truer than the truth of critique that grounds its truth in "the centrality of relations of production" (Grosz, *Volatile* Bodies 165). The norms and truth on which the criticism of critique is based are as totalizing as the totalization that they find repressive in materialist critique. Derrida's "There is nothing outside of the text" (*Grammatology* 158) is an absolutist statement no matter how one interprets it.

The question, in other words, is not one of norm, truth, or totalization—which are parts of all discourses and practices—but the particular kind and how they further or resist the interests of a particular class. The mode of interpretation (critique, resignification, deconstruction, mimesis, immanent critique, and so on) that one offers depends on which class one sides with and on which side of history one struggles. "The question whether objective truth can be attributed to human thinking is not a question of theory but is a practical question. Man must prove the truth, i.e. the reality and power, the this-worldliness of his thinking in practice" (Marx, "Theses on Feuerbach" 3).

Resignification, mimesis, and immanent critique do not transform the system that produces women as lesser subjects in order to normalize the exploitation of their labor at the point of production. All they do is to rewrite woman and rearrange the attributes that subjugate her within the system. The system, not woman, is the sole beneficiary of resignification, mimesis, and immanent critique. These interpretive acts are not struggle strategies for women but, rather, styles of renewal and reinvigoration of the system.

Unlike these rewritings, which reaffirm in a somewhat new language the system of wage labor with only minor internal reforms, materialist critique aims at ending class rule. It goes beyond description and explains the working of wage labor and the abstract structures that cannot be experienced directly but underwrite it. Materialist critique unpacks the philosophical and theoretical arguments that provide concepts for legitimizing wage labor and marks the textual representations that make it seem a normal part of life. In short, instead of focusing on micropractices (prison, gender, education, war, literature, and so on) in local and regional terms, materialist critique relates these practices to the macrostructures of capitalism and provides the knowledges necessary to put an end to exploitation. At the center of these knowledges is class critique. Pedagogy of critique is a class critique of social relations and the knowledges they produce. Its subject is wage labor, not the body without organs. An exemplary lesson in pedagogy of critique is provided by Marx, who concludes chapter 6 of *Capital*, "The Buying and Selling of Labour-Power," by addressing the sphere within which wages are exchanged for labor power and the way this exchange is represented in the legal, philosophical, and representational apparatuses of capitalism as equal. He provides knowledge of the structures of wage labor and the theoretical discourses that sustain it. I have quoted this passage before and will refer to it again and again. Here is the full version:

> We now know how the value paid by the purchaser to the possessor of this peculiar commodity, labour-power, is determined. The use-value which the former gets in exchange, manifests itself only in the actual usufruct, in the consumption of the labour-power. The money-owner buys everything necessary for this purpose, such as raw material, in the market, and pays for it at its full value. The consumption of labour-power is at one and the same time the production of commodities and of surplus-value. The consumption of labour-power is completed, as is the case of every other commodity, outside the limits of the market or the sphere of circulation. Accompanied by Mr. Moneybags and by the possessor of labour-power, we therefore take leave for a time of this noisy sphere, where everything takes place on the surface and in view of all men, and follow them both into the hidden abode of production, on whose threshold there stares us in the face "No admittance except

on business." Here we shall see, not only how capital produces, but how capital is produced. We shall at last force the secret of profit making.

This sphere that we are deserting, within whose boundaries the sale and purchase of labour-power goes on, is in fact a very Eden of the innate rights of man. There alone rule Freedom, Equality, Property and Bentham. Freedom, because both buyer and seller of a commodity, say of labour-power, are constrained only by their own free will. They contract as free agents, and the agreement they come to, is but the form in which they give legal expression to their common will. Equality, because each enters into relation with the other, as with a simple owner of commodities, and they exchange equivalent for equivalent. Property, because each disposes only of what is his own. And Bentham, because each looks only to himself. The only force that brings them together and puts them in relation with each other, is the selfishness, the gain and the private interests of each. Each looks to himself only, and no one troubles himself about the rest, and just because they do so, do they all, in accordance with the pre-established harmony of things, or under the auspices of an all-shrewd providence, work together to their mutual advantage, for the common weal and in the interest of all.

On leaving this sphere of simple circulation or of exchange of commodities, which furnishes the "Free-trader vulgaris" with his views and ideas, and with the standard by which he judges a society based on capital and wages, we think we can perceive a change in the physiognomy of our dramatis personae. He, who before was the money-owner, now strides in front as capitalist; the possessor of labour-power follows as his labourer. The one with an air of importance, smirking, intent on business; the other, timid and holding back, like one who is bringing his own hide to market and has nothing to expect but—a hiding.

Materialist critique is fundamental to a transformative feminist politics. Through critique the subject develops historical knowledges of the social totality: she acquires, in other words, an understanding of how the existing social institutions (motherhood, child care, love, paternity, taxation, family, . . . and so on) are part of the social relations of production, how they are located in exploitative relations of difference, and how they can be changed. Materialist critique, in other words, is that knowledge practice that historically situates the conditions of possibility of what empirically exists under capitalist relations of class difference—particularly the division of labor—and, more important, points to what is suppressed by the empirically existing: what could be, instead of what actually is. Critique indicates, in other words, that what exists is not necessarily real or true but only the actuality under wage labor. The role of critique in pedagogy is exactly this: the production of historical knowledges and class consciousness of the social relations, knowledges that mark the transformability of existing social arrangements and the possibility of a different social organization—one that is free from necessity.

Quite simply then, the pedagogy of critique is a mode of social knowing that inquires into what is not said, into the silences and the suppressed or the missing, in order to unconceal operations of economic and political power underlying the myriad concrete details and seemingly disparate events and representations of our lives. It shows how apparently disconnected zones of culture are in fact linked by the highly differentiated and dispersed operation of the systematic, abstract logic of the exploitation of the division of labor that informs all the practices of culture and society. It reveals how seemingly unique concrete experiences are in fact the common effect of social relations of production in wage labor capitalism. In sum, materialist critique both disrupts that which represents itself as natural and thus as inevitable and explains how it is materially produced. Critique, in other words, enables us to explain how social differences, specifically gender, race, sexuality, and class, have been systematically produced and continue to operate within regimes of exploitation—namely, the international division of labor in global capitalism—so we can change them. It is the means for producing politically effective and transformative knowledges.

The claim of affective pedagogy is that it sets the subject free by making available to her or him the unruly force of pleasure and the unrestrained flows of desire, thereby turning her or him into an oppositional subject who cuts through established representations and codings to find access to a deterritorialized subjectivity. But the radicality of this self, at its most volatile moment, is the radicality of the class politics of the ruling class, a class for whom the question of poverty no longer exists. The only question left for it, as I have already indicated, is the question of liberty as the freedom of desire. Yet this is a liberty acquired at the expense of the poverty of others. The pedagogy of critique engages these issues by situating itself not in the space of the self, not in the space of desire, not in the space of liberation, but in the revolutionary site of collectivity, need, and emancipation.

The core of the pedagogy of critique is that education is not simply for enlightening the individual to see through the arbitrariness of signification and the violence of established representations. It recognizes that it is a historical practice and, as such, it is always part of the larger forces of production and relations of production. It understands that all pedagogies are, in one way or the other, aimed at producing an efficient labor force. Unlike the pedagogy of desire, the pedagogy of critique does not simply teach that knowledge is another name for power, nor does it marginalize knowledge as a detour of desire. It acknowledges the fissures in social practices—including its own—but it demonstrates that they are historical and not textual or epistemological. It, therefore, does not retreat into mysticism by declaring the task of teaching to be the teaching of the impossible and, in doing so, legitimate the way things are. Instead, the pedagogy of critique is a worldly teaching of the worldly.

Material Breasts, Breasts of Desire

To show the actual consequences of the pedagogy of desire and the pedagogy of critique, I return to the body once again, specifically to breasts. Instead of reading breasts in terms of a libidinal economy as the site of the corporeal flows of fluids and intensities of desire (Gallop, "The Teacher's Breasts" 23–35), I want to offer a materialist critique of the class and labor relations conditioning the way breasts are "lived," "experienced," and "made intelligible"—a political economy of breasts (Ebert, *Ludic Feminism*, 239–41). Currently, lactation and breastfeeding are being revalorized in advanced capitalist countries, especially among the upper-middle classes. In recent years, there have been increasing claims about the nutritional and health benefits of mother's milk and breastfeeding. It is significant that the studies that validate breastfeeding and the corporeality of the subjectivity of the mother are appearing at a time of considerable unemployment and corporate attempts to "downsize" the labor force, including managerial and professional positions, in the United States.

In the neocolonies of global capitalism, however, the ideological construction of such corporeal practices as lactation is often quite "other." The political economy of breastfeeding is very different, for example, in the Alto do Cruzerio of northeastern Brazil, a poverty-stricken, highly exploited region of "cloying sugarcane fields amid hunger and disease" described by Nancy Scheper-Hughes in *Death without Weeping* (31). Here, the changing relation of production—the transition from semi-subsistence peasantry to wage labor and the commodification of food, especially infant formula—has led to extreme hunger and poverty. It has produced radical changes not only in the ideological representation of lactation but in the materiality of baby's milk and practices of maternity. In short, the changing relations of production under global capitalism have substantially altered women's lived relation to their own bodies and to their infant children. The effects have been devastating: this area of Brazil accounts for "a quarter [of] all childhood deaths in Latin America," deaths that are largely attributable to the "precipitous" decline in breastfeeding in Brazil (316–17). Scheper-Hughes argues that "a fairly direct and positive correlation exists between infant survival and breast feed-ing," yet "each generation of mothers in the Third World is less likely than the previous one to breast-feed offspring. This is especially true of rural migrants to urban areas, where wage labor and the work available to women are incompatible with breast-feeding" (316–17).

Nearly all Alto women suffer from acute hunger and overwork, from the very material needs whose validity and materiality are erased by such theorists as Deleuze and Guattari. These women do not celebrate the liberatory feminine flow of corporeal fluids and desires. Instead they perceive their breast milk, according to Scheper-Hughes, as "bad," as "infected, dirty, and diseased . . . as 'unfit' for the infant" (326). For Alto women, "human milk appeared blue, thin, watery" in contrast, to the "rich" and "strong" formulas they offer to their "often small, puny in-fants" (325). Moreover, the provision of infant formula plays a crucial role in demonstrating paternity and establishing the child's legitimacy. With the transition to wage labor, marriages, according to Scheper-Hughes, have become "less formal, more consensual, and more transitory in the shantytown . . . the definition of a 'husband' . . . is a functional one. A husband is the man who provides food for his woman and her children," especially the expensive infant formula (323). The father, rather than the mother, has become the provider of baby's milk. As the father ar-rives "bearing the prestigious purple-labeled can of Nestle . . . a woman will say to her newborn . . . 'Clap your hands, little one; your milk has arrived'!" (323–24). For the exploited women living at the "foot of the cane," at the foot of global capitalism, the medium of the body is not the liberatory zone of libidinal paths of desire—these are indulgences of the privileged. Instead the bodies of these women are sites where the class contradictions and exploitative relations of capitalism are acted out in the daily pain of desperate need.

The pedagogy of critique provides students with explanatory con-cepts that enable them to make these connections and to see how the pleasures of privilege and the trajectory of desires of the affluent are dependent on the poverty of need of the Alto women working in the sugar cane fields and processing factories of northeastern Brazil. It en-ables students to engage the class politics of libidinal theories, develop class consciousness, and consequently see the material conditions that libidinal theories conceal. The pedagogy of critique, in sum, provides the conceptual means by which students can develop historical knowledges of the social totality and acquire an understanding of how the existing social institutions have all come about, how they have been located in exploitative relations of labor, and how they can be changed.

5. Chick Lit: "Not Your Mother's Romance Novels"

A Condition That Requires Illusion

Romance novels (such as Harlequin romances) are fantasies, or to be more precise, as Marx says, they are *"the fantastic realization of the human essence since the human essence has not acquired any true reality"* ("Critique of Hegel's Philosophy of Right" 244, emphasis in original). At the same time, these fantasies, to continue using Marx's argument, express a real yearning for "true reality"—a reality in which one is not alienated from oneself and others. Fantasies are illusions that promise to cure alienation. By providing an *illusory* happiness, however, romances obscure the struggles for *real* happiness. To critique these illusions is, at the same time, to call for the building of a true reality that does not need illusions to make it livable.

To say that romances are texts of fantasies, however, is to appeal to a cultural obviousness that is not all that obvious. It covers over the considerable textual, social, and ideological complexity by means of which romance novels shape the popular imaginary in order to reconcile readers with the structural contradictions of capitalism. These contradictions, which arise from the promise of equality and the negation of that promise in actual labor relations, are at the heart of romance novels. I argue that although romance novels represent themselves as narratives of a natural intimacy between men and women (romance novels are almost exclusively heterosexual), they construct that intimacy in such a way that the reader not only accepts the contradictions of capitalism but concedes that these contradictions are natural and normal, and thus there is no need for any substantial change in the order of things. The central tension in the romance novel is, of course, a sexual tension that is resolved in the promise of genuine love. This seemingly natural tension and its apparently natural resolution make up an ideological narrative strategy to provide a general cultural pattern for resolving (or promising to resolve) all social tensions, especially the material tensions produced by the contradictions of labor and capital. The resolution of tensions in romances, in other words, is a cultural lesson for solving problems in such a way that the existing social division of labor and property relations are left intact and are seen as normal and the result of a natural evolution of history.

As a matter of cultural politics it is important to note that although, in cultural terms, romance novels are among the least validated forms of writing and have almost no "cultural capital," to use Pierre Bourdieu's term, they are the most widely read of all forms of books—fiction and nonfiction. What makes reading romances (which are assumed to be perhaps the most simple if not simplistic form of writing) so difficult is what might be called their double narration. They are experienced as intensely private pleasures, yet they are profoundly social. Their writerly identity, therefore, is a spectral in-betweenness. To foreground either the intimate or the social in one's reading is to read reductively. Although moving back and forth between the two modes might seem more balanced and offer a more sophisticated and nuanced reading, it is actually an act of ideological fence-sitting. In reading romances—more than other modes of writings—one has to take sides in order to tease out their layered social, cultural, and personal implications and imbrications. Although commonly regarded to be escape literature disconnected from reality (and thus mere "fantasy"), the romance novel is in fact one of the main cultural practices through which contemporary reality is constructed, understood, and experienced. In part this is because, under capitalism, daily reality is constructed mostly through commodity relations—consumptions that provide or promise to provide pleasure. Pleasure—the exchange of all exchanges, the commodifier of all commodities—is itself turned into a commodity in romance. It is pleasure that makes the commodity desirable (that is, exchangeable). In a sense, then, romance is a cultural place in which the reader is taught how to experience seemingly natural pleasures naturally and where the natural itself and natural pleasures are carefully constructed and used to interpellate the subject into class divisions and the property relations that underlie them. Romances, in other words, deploy sexual pleasure and the promise of love to produce subjects as workers who are avid consumers and through whom capitalism normalizes its relations.

Desiring Production

To put it differently, romances are what Gilles Deleuze and Felix Guattari in *Anti-Oedipus* call "desiring production" (1–9). By means of this trope, they attempt to bring Freud (desire) and Marx (labor) together and reunderstand desire (which is seen as a "lack" in Freud and, later, Lacan) as an active producing force: "Desire causes the current to flow, itself flows in turn, and breaks the flows" (5). Deleuze and Guattari regard capitalism as a regime that has separated the two (273–382). I argue that it is capitalism that has brought them together and normalized their merging by such theories as Deleuze and Guattari's "production desire" and its outcome, namely, the body without organs (9–16; *Thousand Plateaus* 149–66). Capitalism renders surplus labor part of the economies of desire through desiring consumption: "Production is immediately consumption" (*Anti-Oedipus* 4). Romances are the cultural spheres in which surplus labor and desire are fused, and the two become part of the identity of the lovers. Labor, which produces reality, is thus obscured (in both Deleuze and Guattari and in Harlequin romances) by desire and its flows and counterflows in the body without organs (28–29). Deleuze and Guattari use desiring production to critique Freud's idea of repression, but their critique is not so much an affirmation of desire (against Freud and Lacan) as a discursive obscuring of the material alienation of labor. Their idea of desire, in other words, conceals alienation and converts the alienation of labor into a desiring production, an activity. Romances are texts of desiring production, machines of desires/desiring machines, which turn the alienation of labor into the erotics of flows and lines of flights.

They are active and activating texts that secure the relations of pleasure and consumption that capitalism deploys to represent the existing world not as the only way things are but as the only way things can be. In short, romance novels are the cultural capillaries through which ideology circulates and in its circulation normalizes the subject of desiring production. In Elizabeth Lowell's romances, for example—with such telling titles as *Pearl Cove, Jade Island,* and *Midnight in Ruby Bayou*— the natural orgasmic pleasures of sex are transformed into an erotics of the production of consumption. The two become so commingled that the organic sensuousness of the body is inseparable from the sublime opulence of the commodity. The novel, in other words, first makes sex the transcendental moment of union—the "endless, wrenching ecstasy" (*Pearl Cove* 161)—that surpasses all representations and explanation. It then extends this postanalytical orgasmic experience to the obtaining and owning of commodities. *Pearl Cove,* for example, concludes with the ecstatic pleasure of possessing the lost treasure of the "Black Trinity"— a multimillion-dollar black-rainbow pearl necklace—whose "gleaming unearthly beauty" arouses the bliss of "[e]xcitement and serenity . . . [s]ecret dreams and impossible miracles" (405).

Romances are texts that, through a social fantasy (experienced as active desire), fill in the "lack" in women's lives and, in doing so, put women in their place in existing class relations. The immense diversity in romances is the effect of this social placing of women. Romances, in other words, are plotted and written in the specific styles and with types of characters that have the cultural power to attract the reader, convincing her to take up a particular class position. The traditional romance is mostly directed, for example, to women whose position in labor relations is what stratification theorists call the "middle class," while the emerging contemporary variation of romance, which is often called chick lit, is more clearly addressed to women who are actually or potentially part of the upper-middle class.

To write what I have just written—that romance is an effect of class relations and a cultural means for interpellating women into certain class positions—is to go against the current views of both class and romance. In the dominant form of contemporary cultural theory, sexuality, love, and the affective in general are assumed to be independent of class and the social relations of production, or, as I have implied in my reading of Deleuze and Guattari, are inseparable from each other. They are seen not as effects of the material base of culture (namely, its labor relations) but as materialities in themselves.

Contemporary cultural theory regards "popular culture" in all its forms to be an active resistance against class relations, racism, and confining sexual and gender relations. I think such readings of popular culture as those by Stuart Hall, Michel de Certeau, John Fiske, and Angela McRobbie, which find moments of resistance to capital and consumption in almost all texts of popular culture, obscure the economies of popular culture. These critics have a tendency to dismiss Adorno and other critics of popular culture for their elitism, but they themselves practice a new, more accommodating form of elitism: that of popular culture and its hyperresistant consumers. Popular culture now, as Adorno has argued, "transfers the profit motive naked onto cultural forms," making cultural texts into "commodities through and through" (*Culture Industry* 99–100). This results in what Adorno calls the "two-faced irony" that "the consciousness of the consumers themselves is split between the prescribed fun which is supplied to them by the culture industry and a not particularly well-hidden doubt about its blessings." The "gratification" that popular culture provides, according to Adorno, is also "a deception which is nonetheless transparent to them" (103). Popular culture offers, then, a contradictory and conflicted protest that is itself part of capitalism.

Class, the Classy, and Consumption

Several times I have referred to class and property. Because both play important roles in my interpretation of romance, I would like to briefly annotate them. By *class* I do not mean what most social stratification theories mean. I believe they conceal class antagonisms by mapping the social as a scene of different levels of lifestyles, income, and jobs. As I have argued in my other texts, however, class is not a cultural lifestyle, a person's taste, accent, income, occupation, status, power, or prestige. These are all important features of social life, but they are not class— they are effects of class.

Class is an explanation of the social structures of exploitation. The cause of class divisions is the process of production through which the labor of the many is appropriated by the few. Because production is the material basis of the social world, class is a material social relation, or to be more specific, it is a relation of owning. Obviously, it is not owning just anything but owning that which produces more owning. Owning your home does not make you an owner, but owning labor (living and past) does because labor is "a commodity" that "possesses the peculiar property of being a source of value" (Marx, *Capital* 1: 270). In all class societies people are reduced to what they own and, therefore, are divided into only two classes: those who own the labor of others and make profits from it, and the others, whose labor is appropriated from them. In capitalism, more specifically, the others own only their labor and sell it for wages, which they then pay back to the owners of labor to buy (depending on when and where in the world they live) food, medicine, housing, cars, books, DVDs, Xboxes, and so on, which they need to live and to educate and entertain themselves so they are ready—and in a fairly good emotional state—to go back to work for the owners of labor. Owning the labor of others makes you an owner, but owning a home or a car, a refrigerator or an Xbox, items that are often mentioned as a sign that nowadays everyone is an owner and there are no classes, does not.

Using the labor of others brings you profit; owning an Xbox returns your wages to the owners. There is no middle ground between the two: the middle class is an ideological illusion used to cloud class binaries and conceal the fact that under capitalism society is breaking up more rigidly into two classes whose opposition cannot be dissolved in the hybrid of a playful in-betweenness of the middle-class (Ebert and Zavarzadeh, *Class in Culture* 3–4).

The romance novel is one of the ideological discourses through which the illusion of middle class is normalized and made to seem a reflection of society itself. This fantasy is made more realistic by the way capitalism and its cultural products, such as romances, focus on the individual and individuality, which is a convenient cover-up for class differences. Even though every single day Americans come face to face with the brutal realities of the huge economic disparities that contradict their cultural belief in equality, they feel quite nervous thinking of themselves in terms of class. There is something vaguely sinister and even anti-American about class.

People fear class because it makes them confront the actuality that social disparities are not individualistic and therefore exceptional, or casual and accidental, but are built into the system of wage labor. Social differences are systemic, not eccentric. Class makes people acknowledge that the affluence of the few is the direct result of the wage labor of the many, who live in dull and depressing houses and apartments, have unhealthy diets, send their children to mediocre and dilapidated schools lacking basic educational facilities, and survive on "hope."

Because the objective economics of class differences cannot be denied, this reality is mystified and converted into cultural values. Texts of popular culture such as romances and chick lit play a crucial role in the translation of the economic into the cultural and in neutralizing the contradictions of capitalism. They do this by turning class—which is the effect of economic inequalities—into a cultural difference: a matter of style, of prestige, of having a sense of elegance, a refined taste in wine, an educated accent, and so on. As Paul Fussell notes, "Regardless of the money you've inherited your social class is still most clearly visible when you say things" (*Class* 18). Through popular culture, for the most part, *class* is distorted into being *classy*. This translation is ideologically very useful because if class is simply a matter of elegance, taste, and good manners, then anyone—rich or poor—can acquire it. Class in popular culture is mostly a question of cultural sophistication. In chick lit people are differentiated not by their economic access but by their taste, manners, and style. In Clare Naylor's *Dog Handling*, for example, the heroine's best friend is a poor but fashionably elegant woman who refuses at first to marry the man she loves because she mistakes him for a stable-hand, since he dresses more "like a groom" with his jeans and "scuffed brown boots" than a race-horse owner (76). In short, the economics of social differences are represented as personal. As an expression of taste and lifestyle, this "neutered" class is actually seen as adding to the diversity and richness of social life instead of being a social problem that should be eliminated. Not only is class not eliminated, but anyone who talks about eliminating it is laughed at or thought to be unrealistic, if not totally "outmoded" in her thinking (Gibson-Graham, *End of Capitalism* 52–56, 263).

In romance novels and chick lit, freedom and equality are linked to a person's consuming powers, which makes the source of class differences unclear. One's class, as I have already indicated, is determined not by how much one makes but where one stands in the social division of labor. In romance novels this distinction is blurred by the focus on consumption and income. For example in Jane Green's *Mr. Maybe* the heroine dissolves class boundaries at will simply by changing her wardrobe. By dressing right, "preferably in designer clothes" (purchased with an overdraft), she feels she can "hold [her] head up high and walk in anywhere feeling good" and date one of the "most eligible bachelors in Britain," who is "hugely rich" (152–53, 149).

"Not Your Mother's Romance Novels"

In thematic and cultural terms, contemporary romance narratives range all the way from chaste love to the highly erotic and from medieval fantasies to romantic suspense and thrillers. In formal terms, they include both the traditional romance (such as Harlequin and historical romances) and chick lit. The latter has become a major popular culture phenomenon and, in spite of its short history, has attracted a great deal of media attention. An *ABC Evening News* report devoted a fairly long segment to it and, in a rather dramatic way, informed the viewers that although their major theme is love, chick lit books are "not your mother's romance novels" (ABC News, 23 August 2003). The ABC segment went on to state that "chick lit" features "everyday women in their 20's and 30's," and in it "nobody's got a great job, nobody has a perfect body and God knows, none of them has a perfect boyfriend." The novels, as one chick lit Web site claims, are highly realistic narratives "with real, true-to-life characters & loads of boyfriend angst" and without fantasies about "the dashing, but brooding, tycoon that whisks the ever-so-genteel heroine

into the sunset" ("What Is Chick Lit?" n.p.). Although it may be full of
"messy detail" and represent its characters as "so-real-you-can-pinch-
'em people liv[ing] their lives in a funny, thrilling, sad world" ("What Is
Chick Lit?" n.p.), the narratives are, in many ways, as rooted in fantasy
as any mainstream romance.

Chick lit is not so much a new genre as it is another of the diverse
forms of the romance narratives that dominate so much of the popular
imaginary. It shares many of the textual, cultural, and structural traits
of romance narratives, but there are telling differences that are effects
of the changing relations of women to labor and that show class differences in the popular imaginary. Indeed, chick lit is "not your mother's
romance." It is the romance of postcontemporary *cynical reason.*

The most striking feature of chick lit is its representation of love.
In more traditional romances—such as novels by Nora Roberts, Johanna
Lindsey, Elizabeth Lowell, Linda Howard, and Karen Robards—love and
lust, sex and sensuousness, passion and tenderness are all unified and
focused on the figure of a primary male hero. In other words, traditional
romances are highly gendered, and the differences between the two genders form the main narrative energy of the novel. In these romances, man
is the main signifier. In chick lit, however, all of these elements—love,
lust, passion, and male figures—are ironically rewritten, disrupted, and
dispersed. As one of Clare Naylor's heroines comments in response to a
declaration of love—"getting back with an ex is such a cliché. It's like
. . . being turned on by a man driving a Ferrari. Sure, it happens, but not
to people with any taste" (*Dog Handling* 289). Love becomes an uncertain performance—as Lucy says at the end of Keyes's *Lucy Sullivan Is
Getting Married,* "Daniel swears he loves me. He certainly *acts* as if he
does. And, you know, I'm halfway to believing him" (61). It is ideologically significant, however, that in spite of the playful displacement of
love in chick lit, it is still affirmed in the end in a more or less serious
(conventional) tone. In both mainstream romance and chick lit, love is
the master signifier that generates equivalences between the sensual and
the conceptual, sensualizes property, and establishes a relation of similar-
ity between having and being. Even in Jennifer Weiner's cynical tale of
love gone bad, *Good in Bed,* in which the heroine proclaims, "Love is for
suckers," she declares "I *do* . . . I *will*" to love at the end. In short, by the
end of every romance, as Clare Naylor's heroine in *Love: A User's Guide,*
puts it, "I get to have my cake and eat it . . . interchangeable romance and
reality in the same bed" (278). Just as important, as Catherine Alliott's
single mom discovers at the end of *A Married Man,* not only does love
fill "a huge gaping hole," it also comes with a fantastic house (407).

Romance narratives are fantasies of fulfillment—sexual, emotional and economic. Conventional romances are narratives of *wanting* that immerse the reader in this fantasy by saturating the text with erotic signifiers and tropes of sensual arousal. The plot is a repeating dynamic of sexual tension, anticipation, climax, and release, culminating in an imaginary completeness and unity in love. This fantasy of unity is essentially a fantasy of security, which is most often lacking in the life of the middle-class reader. The idea of unifying love, in other words, is part of the class politics of mainstream romances. Chick lit, with its upper-middle-class readers, has enough (economic) security to afford to be not only analytically skeptical about love as a unifier but to become cynical about the whole idea of love as fulfillment. Its reader knows somewhere in the back of her mind that security is not simply emotional but, in the system of wage labor, is always and ultimately a matter of hard economics. What makes chick lit the romance of cynical reason is that it knows that love is not the answer to the alienation and frustrations of daily life but, nonetheless, it desires love and, in doing so ideologically, affirms it (Žižek, *Sublime Object* 11–53; Sloterdijk, *Critique of Cynical Reason* 5). The rebellion of cynical reason, in other words, is more of a safety valve for the system than a critique for change.

Cynical Reason and Love with a Wink

Since I have used and will use the concepts of cynical romance and cynical reason, I should say that by *cynical* I mean the following: the heroine maintains an ironic distance from love and regards herself to be too sophisticated for the all-too-familiar plot of sexual and emotional fulfillment, but nonetheless she loves to be loved—that desire, as Weiner's Cannie puts it, for "the feeling of falling in love, of being loved, of being worthy. *Treasured*" (*Good in Bed* 316, emphasis in original). The cynical consciousness in chick lit, as in other texts of culture, is a double consciousness, one divided between knowledge and desire. It knows that love is a bourgeois ideology used to normalize mostly heterosexual relations and through them the institution of the "modern family" with, as Engels argues in *The Origin of the Family, Private Property, and the State*, "its particular character of man's domination over woman" and its role as one of the central "economic units" of class societies (181). The heterosexual family is not a natural unit in chick lit, which substitutes what Jane Green calls, a new "urban family" of friends and neighbors. The cynical consciousness, however, suppresses this knowledge in the pragmatic interest of her desire. Although "love—*or something like it*" (emphasis added), as the back-cover blurb of Valerie Frankel's *Accidental Virgin* describes it, prevails in chick lit, it is ironically displaced in these novels. "You won't find the usual corny love scenes here," declares Chicklit.us.com. In a sense chick lit cleanses romance of "corny love" with an almost clinical description of passion—so dispassionate that it becomes ironic. Naylor describes one sexual encounter thus: "Luke took her glass out of her hand and kissed her. Just like that. No messing. It was nice. . . . But it was nothing to how it would feel later, when she played the little details back to herself, rewound the conversation" (12). What adds to this irony is the realism of style in chick lit and its minimalist rhetoric, which often turns these narratives into continuous cultural understatements about women and love in the new labor force. This ironic distance, achieved by a bare realism and sparse description of sex, is perhaps the most important difference between chick lit and "your mother's romances," in which irony is seen as a destroyer of passion and love can never be corny—it is, rather, what Elizabeth Lowell calls a "pleasure whose piercing sweetness was like silver lightning stitching through his soul" (*Pearl Cove* 363). What is, of course, critiqued in the dry ironies of chick lit is the sentimentalism that is the cultural marker of the middle class. Sentimentalism is represented as an inability to think clearly: thinking clearly means having a self-reflexive, even double consciousness and a sharp sense of ironic distance, which, in the end, is essentially a return to bourgeois pragmatism—pragmatism with a wink.

Corniness, which is said to be absent in chick lit, is the representation in traditional romances of the sensual and the emotional, passion and affect, as inseparable and as attached to the figure of the male hero. He is perceived to be the signifier of desire but in actuality is a signifier of the phallus, which, as Lacan explains, is the sign of power that is ultimately derived not from physical strength (although that is what is emphasized in romance) but from his access to power—that is, to property (*Ecrits*, 285). In Lowell's Donovan series, for example, the Donovan brothers, who appear in *Jade Island* and in *Pearl Cove*, are multimillion-aire dealers in precious gems and metals. Of course, the signifier does not settle on a single meaning but overflows with meanings that open up the possibility of interminable interpretations. This excess of meaning marks the signifier of the erotic, which in the traditional romance is the male hero, who inaugurates and completes the heroine's sexual arousal and emotional awakening. The signifier, in other words, sutures love, lust, tenderness, and care with power and property in order to provide an imaginary unity through the heterosexual union that is the condition of possibility of the family—the custodian of property.

The surfeit of signifiers of the erotic is one of the main textual devices by which mainstream romances recruit women, or "interpellate" them, as Louis Althusser puts it (*Lenin and Philosophy* 170–83), into the social relations of production. The erotic in these romances is so closely tied to property that it is difficult to separate the two—passion between a woman and a man is also and at the same time passion for the property signified by such tropes as gold, diamonds, pearls, estates, and castles. In Lowell's *Running Scared*, for instance, the intense, ecstatic sensation the heroine feels when touching her lover is the same sensation she feels when touching his priceless Celtic gold collection. In chick lit the main narrative device of irony delays and postpones such interpellation. This is why chick lit is at times read as resistance to ideology and a critique of bourgeois love and its association of money with marriage.

Yet chick lit is as much a product of class relations and ideology as what it parodies and ironically plays with. The ironic interpellation of heroine and reader in chick lit tends to be represented as urban and sophisticated, so sophisticated that they develop what Sloterdijk (*Critique of Cynical Reason* 5) and, following him, Žižek(*Sublime Object* 29) call "enlightened false consciousness." By this they mean the state of consciousness in which one knows that one is acting falsely "but still one does not renounce it" (*Sublime Object* 29). The heroine of chick lit knows love is a cultural fantasy but still seeks it because in doing so she is also seeking some kind of meaning to shield her from the dissatisfaction and drudgery of her work and the emptiness of her life. Love is the (cynical) cure for the alienation of labor.

The ideological interest of chick lit is not in the fulfillment of the individual, although that is, of course, the surface theme of these novels. Rather, such fulfillment is used in order to normalize the larger class structures. Making love an intimate emotion, without which a woman's life is incomplete, is more a legitimization of class relations and a valorization of private property as the core of social identity than it is an indication of emotional fulfillment. In chick lit, as in romances as a whole, the social relations of property are secured and naturalized through personal relations of intimacy. Without property, love is represented as incomplete: as sheer sentimentality, which is not an adult emotion. To be in love (for bourgeois ideology) is simultaneously to concede the necessity of a social system in which private property provides the framework of a secure life. Both forms are texts of desire through which ideology normalizes class. In traditional romances this is done in a mimetic narrative and without irony, but chick lit does it with an ironic attitude and in a much more subtle mode of realism, in which the mimetic is interspersed with a metafictional self-reflexivity and mixed with mock introspection like that made famous in *Bridget Jones's Diary*. Note that some of the most well known chick-lit narratives use first-person narration, which allows a great deal of space for self-talking and brooding by the narrator. Feminist critics such as A. Rochelle Mabry claim that the "move to first-person narration is an especially significant change from the third-person narration employed in most traditional romance novels. . . . [It] not only strengthens the heroine's voice and increases the reader's opportunities to identify with her but also offers at least a temporary escape from the feeling of constantly being watched or controlled by a male-dominated society" ("About a Girl" 195–96). However, the popularity of the first-person point of view in chick lit, I argue, owes more to the ideological desire to occlude the daily contradictions of class. First-person narration is a device by which the writer attempts to screen out the deep alienation of labor that engulfs the lives of the characters by representing the social contradictions that cause alienation as personal anxieties, inadequacies, and brooding. More often than not, the technique fails to obscure the alienation completely, and what is supposed to be self-reflection becomes self-indulgence. First-person narrative cannot fully suture the fissures between reality and representation, and it is in recognition of this failing, that, for example, Jane Green says she is "sick" of first-person narration in chick lit (Whelehan 69).

Romancing Capital

As capitalism becomes more sophisticated and complex in its labor relations, its ability to absorb critiques of its practices increases and, with it, its tolerance for ideological resistance. The emergence of irony in women's romances, in other words, is not so much a sign of an emerging resistance to the bourgeois ideology of love as it is simply a more self-reflexive accommodation of it. After playfully displacing love, the ironic eventually accepts it and the property with which it is associated, but it does so with a wink. Chick lit is not all that different from recent television commercials that playfully point to themselves and self-reflexively mark themselves as nuanced commercials in order to enhance their effect on more educated, well-to-do viewers. Property-with-a-wink is still property; the objective class interests that it embodies are not negated by subjective attitudes.

To see the working of class politics and the ideology of private property as the doubles of love—in both romance and chick lit—all one has to do is to read the "signature" moment in any mainstream romance, that is, the first description of the hero as seen by the heroine. In Lowell's *Pearl Cove*, for instance, the heroine, Hannah, opens the door to the hero: "And then she could only stare. She had forgotten Archer's dark male beauty, the intelligence in his light, changeable eyes, his height and physical power, the sensual promise of his mouth. Her husband had been a wild blond Viking. Archer was a dark angel who made a woman want . . . everything" (43–44).

This scene contains the kernel of the primary narrative code of the conventional romances—the binary opposition between legitimate and illegitimate masculinity—Mr. Right (Archer) and Mr. Wrong (her destructive and now-dead husband). The scene demonstrates how the hero inaugurates the social fantasy that the romance will fill the desires—the lack—in the woman who wants everything," how it will provide an imaginary completeness, a wholeness to oppose the everyday realities of the alienation of labor: fragmentation, disaffection, separation, emptiness, loneliness, and loss.

This first narrative encounter of hero and heroine launches the hero as the "dark" figure of desire, the signifier of the heroine's and—through a readerly identification—the reader's wanting. As both the instigator of desire and the agent of its fulfillment, the hero sets in motion the proliferation of signifiers of sensuousness and excitement. Not only is the heroine's desire literally activated and stimulated by the "sensual promise" that the hero represents, but more important, the ordinary and the mundane are infused with sensuousness as a way of completely immersing the reader in the social fantasy of heterosexual love. Every unconscious move and bodily aspect of the other in the romance narrative is an erotic provocation, arousing desire. Even the simple act of eating pineapple, in which Archer is feeding an exhausted, dazed Hannah "as though he were feeding his niece" (48), turns sexually exciting. Watching Hannah "nibbling" on her sandwich, Archer thinks that "a lap full of ice water was exactly what he needed to get his mind off her nipples and quick tongue" (49) because "wanting like that made a man lose control" (49). Such erotic intensity is intended to signify instantaneous, immanent connection to the other as one's true and everlasting soul mate. In conventional romances, however, it takes the entire narrative for the heroine to trust that the hero—to whom she is intensely attracted from the start—is the right man and to realize the inevitability of their togetherness and thus find fulfillment. The trust is achieved after the heroine assures herself of the hero's access to wealth. It is this access that finally makes the hero desirable even though the desire is expressed in the vocabularies of body and soul.

In other words, it is part of the ideological process of the romance that the right man is always a man of property, either possessing or protecting it. The right man is always a signifier not only of love but also of capitalism and the regime of private property. Desire in romance is always a desire not only for love but also for property or love as property. If the object of desire does not *own* property, he is the *protector* of the property, as is the case with the detectives, soldiers, and others serving capital in romance narratives. (Increasingly, with the recent preponderance of private security agencies and fighting forces—in fact and fiction—these "protectors" are becoming richly compensated and newly propertied.) No matter how self-sufficient a woman may seem to be in mainstream romance, she is always dependent on the male hero, in one way or another, for economic protection, whether it is to save her business (Jayne Ann Krentz, *Flash*), to find missing treasure (Lowell, *Running Scared*), or simply for financial well-being. To marry in a romance narrative is, more often than not, to marry property. In Lowell's *Pearl Cove,* the heroine is very well aware that to be a woman alone is to risk being propertyless, even destitute—her greatest fear is to be alone, to be like the street walkers and sex workers, "*standing on a street corner in Rio. No money. No hope*" (392, emphasis in original). The novel ends with the heroine proclaiming her love for the hero and declaring, "I want it all, Archer. The Black Trinity. The baby. You. You most of all" (406). Of course, Archer is a man of property, a tycoon, and the treasure he finds for her is worth millions—so indeed love fulfills the desires of the woman who "wants . . . everything." The fulfillment fantasy at the core of romance is really economic although it is represented as nonmaterial, as erotic and emotional.

There is a strong correlation between this dream of property and erotic pleasure in mainstream romance and the actual economic situation of many of its readers. According to a Romance Writers Association reader survey, only 39 percent of romance readers are employed full-time. Of the remaining 61 percent, a full 41 percent are not in the labor force at all, another 16 percent work part-time, and the rest are unemployed. These numbers suggest that at least 61 percent of romance readers are economically dependent on the income of others. (This information is from the 1998 reader survey posted on their Web site; it is interesting that all employment statistics have been dropped from the more recent reader survey posted on their Web site in 2007: http://www.rwanational.org/cs/ the_romance_genre/romance_literature_statistics/readership_statistics.) The economic situation of romance readers closely parallels their marital status as recorded in both studies: the 1998 survey reported that 49.5

percent were married, with another 11 percent either widowed or separated; the most recent statistics (2005) show a similar pattern 50 percent married and 13 percent widowed, divorced or separated. Even among romance readers who are working, whether part-time or full-time, there is a tendency to see their earnings as supplementing the family income and as secondary to the husband's. To a very large degree these are indeed "your mother's romances" in that 65 percent of romance readers are over the age of thirty-five (in both surveys). The fantasy of a propertied male who can take care of the heroine and her children is thus an imaginary pleasure that speaks to many a reader's real economic situation.

Although the same statistical information is not available for chick lit readers, there is a strong assumption by the publishing industry of a demographic identity among its authors, characters, and readers. The female heroines in chick lit—like the authors and, it is assumed, their audience—are predominately well-educated, mostly single career women in their twenties and thirties. Keep in mind that these assumptions carry enough weight to justify considerable spending on the part of publishers and booksellers to target this audience. Also, I think it is safe to say that the economic expectations of the majority of these women are quite different from those of their mother's generation—and the typical romance reader—in that they assume, perhaps reluctantly, that they are financially responsible for themselves and expect to work not simply at jobs but in careers that provide both meaning and economic security. But these assumptions are not easily realized in this economy, and chick lit is also marked by considerable disappointment and dissatisfaction. The heroines frequently have careers in privileged fields such as the media, fashion, and public relations. Although these jobs, as one of Jane Green's heroines notes (*Mr. Maybe* 4), may have "sounded glamorous, exciting" at first, they are often accompanied by considerable drudgery and relatively low pay.

Love as Decentered Capitalism

Part of the fulfillment fantasy of chick lit moves beyond the male to a career-revival romance: giving the heroine a Cinderella makeover, not so much for herself, but for her job—as when Bridget Jones chucks her tedious job to become a celebrity TV reporter or when Clare Naylor's accountant turns a flea-market craft into an internationally famous bikini business (*Dog Handling*). One of the more notable job fantasies is in Sue Margolis's *Apocalipstick*, in which the heroine turns a lowly assignment to write a mundane cosmetic column into an award-winning exposé of corruption in the international cosmetics industry that earns her a personal call from the prime minister of Britain "to thank [her] for saving the African peace deal" (309).

Greater participation in the labor force not only provides chick lit heroines and readers with economic self-sufficiency but also considerable sexual freedom. By not being economically dependent on a man, as in traditional romance narratives, chick lit heroines do not have the immediate economic need to tie themselves to a male provider. Of course, not every romance heroine is as financially dependent on the hero as Hannah is in *Pearl Cove,* but in nearly every conventional romance, money is the nexus of relations between hero and heroine, with the heroine in some way dependent on the male's greater proximity to property.

In traditional romances, as in early industrial capitalism, property is solidified in the ownership of one person. In chick lit, however, as in more advanced forms of capitalism in which capital is dispersed among many stockholders, property is no longer so closely associated with one person (the man). Rather, like the signifiers of love and sexuality, it is decentered and diffused. This follows the shifts in the relations of exchange in capitalism as a whole and the increasing inclusion of women in the workplace. The historical changes that have given women greater earning power have also rearticulated property relationships, with economic power and earnings more widely distributed among women and men—at least in the upper-middle-class fractions. Money as the nexus of relationships does not disappear in chick lit; if anything, it acquires more prominence. But it is no longer centralized in the figure of the male; it is much more dispersed and multipolar, located in a more complex negotiation and sharing between women and men.

The economics of love and love as economics are comically displayed in Jane Green's *Mr. Maybe,* which opens with the heroine declaring that the novel's sexy hero, Nick, "was never supposed to be The One, for God's sake. . . . There was the money thing, for a start. My job as a PR might not be the highest-paying job in the universe, but it pays the bills, pays the mortgage, and leaves me just enough for the odd bit of retail therapy. Nick, on the other hand, didn't earn a penny. . . . [W]hat I always say is I don't mind if he can't pay for me, but I do bloody well mind if he can't pay for himself" (1).

As an unemployed writer, Nick is thus relegated to the category of a "fling" (2), and the heroine spends much of the novel trying to convince herself to forget Nick and marry a very boring, unappealing multimillionaire so that she can fulfill her "dreams of being a rich man's wife and a lady who lunches" (36). Her case is the case of the double interpellation of women into the ideology of love and labor. Toward the end of the novel, she realizes (in response to one set of discourses of ideology) that "money isn't everything." But, at the same time, she is also called on by ideology to concede that "all that means," she says, "is that I'll have to make it myself" (329). In other words, property is not negated but, rather, is negotiated in terms of its ownership. It is significant, however, that Nick, who needed "some money, some stability" in his life and needed to get his "novel published" (119), has, by the end of the novel, signed a contract and, in his words, obtained "a publishing deal." The contract allows him to join the ranks of Mr. Right—he is now a man of property. Unlike traditional romance, in chick lit, property shifts, and its shifts, like those of the stock market, produce instability in the relation between the hero and the heroine. Money is still "the thing," but it is no longer securely attached to the male. It is more mobile, fluid, and dispersed. But no man is the "right one" without it, and no love is a real love without a man with property.

The Tender and Finicky Signifiers of Class

With relative economic self-sufficiency and the decentering of property comes a more ironic and self-reflexive attitude toward romance among readers and writers alike. Thus chick lit both desires and ironically disrupts the fantasy of love, property, and fulfillment that romance promises; its narratives oscillate between ironically displacing and reinstating love with the right man—whose own property status is now more uncertain. Love itself is no longer the stable, secure signified that it is in conventional romance. As the back cover of the chick lit novel *Doghandling* explains, "love is more *finicky* than a Chihuahua in a Prada handbag" (emphasis added). Love as a "finicky" signifier—as elusive, slipping, and uncertain—is the textual dynamic of chick lit in which cynical heroines ironically chase the possibilities of love through serial affairs and sexual experimentations with all the wrong men in hopes of finally finding Mr. Right and grasping love as a real, permanent commitment—*maybe.* In fact, *Mr. Maybe* ends with the heroine, who is not yet aware of Nick's publishing deal, declaring, "I don't know how I feel about you yet, I think it's still a little early for me to talk about love, but I know that I do love being with you" (357).

Love may be the elusive goal of chick lit, but it is also highly suspect and uncertain. The heroines seek, if not love, then *"something like it"* (Frankel, *Accidental Virgin*). All the conventional signifiers of love in romance—sensuousness, arousal, and erotic intensity, on one hand, and affection and gentleness, on the other—dissolve, slip way, and have no

fixity. Desire becomes a floating signifier transferred from one male figure to another, as the "late twenty- and thirty-something singles (a.k.a.
singletons)" indulge in "just sex" and lustful flings in their "search for
the perfect partner" ("What Is Chick Lit?"). The seeming unity of lust and
love (which is the main narrative theme of traditional romance) breaks
up in chick lit, in large part because the male figure has become such a
precarious anchor, unable to reliably secure the unity of property, passion, and tenderness on which the fulfillment fantasy depends. In a sense
chick lit is the narrative of capitalism in crisis, in which the volatility
of the ownership of property intensifies but property remains the only
thing that matters. In chick lit, the lovers become a chain of signification
whose main signified is love itself.

The heroine of Alisa Kwitney's *Dominant Blonde*, for example, says,
"I think I've slept with way too many guys, but if I've behaved like a slut,
it's because I'm a romantic. I may like the guy, I may be attracted, but
once we get into bed it all seems to fall apart, and then I know there's
really no rescuing it, so I move on" (181). Men are still the heroine's
predominate preoccupation in chick lit, but there is rarely a single male
figure that is represented, from the beginning, as a reliable and consistent focus for her desire. This is in large part because the property relations between the sexes is in such a state of flux. As a result there is a
comic and almost chaotic proliferation of male sexual figures, disrupted
relationships, and sexual experimentation—what the Web site Chicklit
.us.com describes as "lust, bed-hopping, unresolved sexual tension & bad
behavior." This sexual disarray gives chick lit its sense of fun and hipness. It is, however, a rather melancholic hipness. It is more an attempt
to overcome alienation than an attempt to achieve happiness, since happiness has become such a remote and unobtainable state. This desiring
and, at the same time, knowing that the desire will not be fulfilled adds
to the cynicism of chick lit's narrators.

In spite of all the obstacles, there is still a compelling desire in chick
lit to revive the fulfillment fantasy and contain the play of sexual signifiers by reasserting the primacy of love at the end of the novel and yok-
ing lust and love together again in a single dominant man with property,
albeit in an often hesitant and tentative way, as in *Mr. Maybe*. The unity
of lust and love is resecured by the figure of the tender male lover. In
a reversal of the erotics of traditional romance, *tenderness* in chick lit
signifies love and a commitment (of sorts). This is made quite explicit by
Jane Green in her best-selling novel *Jemima J*, when Jemima explains that
sex at last with the right man (Ben) "was so completely different from
being with Brad"—the man who cynically uses the heroine—"I mean,

the sex was amazing with Brad, but . . . that's all it was, just great sex. There was no tenderness, no love, just passion" (361). By finally joining lust and love together in an imaginary fantasy of fulfillment, chick lit participates in the same structure as every other romance. At the same time it insists on an ironic jarring of any certitudes: love may prevail in the end, but it is still halting and uncertain. This hesitation is a response to the more unstable relations of property and general volatility of capital in its global movements.

Valerie Frankel's heroine in *Accidental Virgin* chooses one lover from a series of candidates, with the qualification "that maybe she could. Love him. Someday, in the not-too-distant (or dismal) future" (277). For Clare Naylor, "big commitment and stuff" is given a parodic turn, as the heroine of *Dog Handling* proclaims, "They were going to be a dog-owning bona fide couple with responsibilities and a life together, all three of them" (341).

Unlike traditional romances, which are saturated with tropes of sensual hunger and satiation, chick lit keeps a more mocking and self-reflexive distance from its desires. Sexual scenes are given a more minimalist, almost Zola-esque, naturalistic treatment, avoiding all the tropic excesses of traditional romances. Chick lit often spends more time examining the angst that follows sex than the pleasures it provoked. Bridget Jones's description of her first sexual encounter with the object of her desire, Daniel, is not only an after-the-fact summary, it skips entirely any discussion of the erotics of the act and only notes that "[i]t was so lovely." She focuses, instead, on enumerating the "down points" of the mundane conversation that followed (52). The euphoria of the day after gives way to anxiety as she notes that she feels "as if I have just sat an exam and must wait for my results" (52). Self-conscious and critical, she is well aware that unlike her mother's generation, she is spending her time "mooch[ing] about being all paranoid and diffident" and buried in "self-help books" (52–53) and taking more pleasure in a self-reflexive agonizing over sex than in the relations themselves.

Chick lit texts are narratives of dissatisfaction that relish the emotional intensity of sexual melancholia rather than eroticism. Much of the comic effect of these books results from the melodramatic excesses of this melancholia carried to the point of parody. In addition to the British novel *Bridget Jones's Diary*, one of the more famous American chick lit texts, Jennifer Weiner's *Good in Bed*, which indulges in an ironic orgy of melancholy, is also exemplary. This is the ultimate breakup tale: it disparages romantic love at the same time as it reinstates it. Wallowing in an excess of dejection, despondency, and despair, Weiner's jilted heroine discovers not only that her ex-boyfriend is writing a sex column about their relationship but that she's pregnant with his child. She suffers a traumatic accident at the hands of his lover, causing her to nearly lose her child, and becomes anorexic after suffering from months of postpartum depression. This leads her to declare, "I felt like a spectacle of a woman, a sob story, a freak. How must I look, really? I imagined myself on the street that night, my shoe falling apart, sweaty, filthy, my breasts leaking. They should take a picture, put my poster up in every junior high school, staple it in bookstores next to the Harlequin novels and the self-help books about finding your soulmate, your life partner, your one true love. I could be a warning; I could turn girls away from my fate" (352).

This parodic warning against romance is followed by her melodramatic proclamation: "Love is for suckers, and I'm not going to be a sucker ever again" (353). Of course, for the reader this is saturated with the cynical pleasures of enlightened false consciousness since she is making these declarations to the very man who on the next page will turn out to be the tender lover who gives her "that feeling of being safe, of being tucked in and taken care of" (354). Although he may not be able to give her "everything"—as with the hyper-propertied hero of traditional romances—he is sufficiently propertied to declare, "I will give you whatever I can," and that includes her desire for "a house with hardwood floors" (354).

Chick lit is the narrative of an unhappy consciousness—the cynical, enlightened false consciousness that Peter Sloterdijk describes as "well-off and miserable at the same time" (5). Recognizing that love, in the existing social situation, is an ideological fraud, they seek it anyway—because its fantasy of fulfillment is the only form of meaning that the popular imaginary makes available to them. As Slavoj Žižek writes, "[T]hey know very well what they are doing, yet they are doing it" ("Spectre" 8). Cynical consciousness is not simply a personal matter. It is the performance of a bourgeois class consciousness, what Hegel called the "unhappy, inwardly disrupted consciousness" divided against itself (*Phenomenology*, 126), torn by the contradictions between what it knows and what it desires.

What the women of chick lit—its authors, readers and heroines—"know" but cannot afford to recognize is that it is not only romance that is an ideological fraud; it is the whole thing—the emptiness of consumption, the claims of equality, and the loneliness, the unending loneliness of their lives. To cure the alienation caused by property relations, they resort to consumption. They shop, as amply demonstrated in Sophie Kinsella's popular series of chick lit consumption fantasies (for example, *Confessions of a Shopaholic, Shopaholic Takes Manhattan, Shopaholic*

Ties the Knot). They shop for just the right pumps, the trendiest brand names, and, as the cover of Kwitney's *Dominant Blonde* declares, "for the perfect boyfriend *and* the perfect hair color." They also shop for just the right romance novel or chick lit narrative to resolve these contradictions for them ideologically. This is the crux of chick lit and all romances: they are articulations of commodity relations through which women consume a fantasy in order to try to assuage the alienation caused by the commodity relations of capitalism. This alienation is not simply psychological, existential, or theological. It is economic: the alienation of labor within the system of wage labor. Love is represented as an affective space, free from the alienation of labor, but it is the very sphere of alienated labor.

Deterritorializing Love and Money

Like its binary class structure, capitalism has a binary commonsense. On one level it puts love and money in opposition to each other at the two ends of cultural representation. On this level, love is regarded as a person's most intimate emotion and is constitutive of his or her emotional and affective identity, whereas money is seen as an "extra," something social and therefore not essential to one's true self. Such segregation is ineffective in advanced capitalism. As I discussed above, Deleuze and Guattari's notion of desiring production and related theoretical concepts deterritorialize love and money and then reterritorialize them, linking them through the flows and lines of flights of desire. Capitalism needs a labor force that is highly motivated, ambitious, competitive, and worldly. If love and money were separated, it would be hard to find such a labor force because all the people would withdraw into an affective space and become hermits for love rather than hard workers who seek wealth through property and who validate capitalism and work for its advancement.

The joining of love and money, therefore, is another task of ideology; thus the necessity of Deleuze and Guattari's concept of desire as an active force in constructing the consciousness of the middle classes and the central role that popular culture plays in integrating, or reterritorializing, the two. Women's romances in all their variety are part of this ideological apparatus by which women are called recruited into desiring production and the workforce or are trained to be mothers of those who will become part of the workforce. In romance novels, the intensity of passion, sensuousness, and individual intimacy that are associated with love are extended to commodities as tropes of property. Romance narratives, which on a first reading seem to be all about intimacy and love, are allegories of property.

6. Red Love

The ruinous impact that capitalism and the free market have had on Russia give new urgency to the question of the relations of gender, sexuality, and capitalism in cultural critique. It also opens up a space in transformative critique for a serious reconsideration of the early Soviet and Bolshevik experiments in order to revaluate some of the revolutionary possibilities that socialism has raised for the emancipation of women. Of special importance in this regard is the work of Alexandra Kollontai, who was a strong critic of capitalism as well as an unrelenting revolutionary theorist and critic on behalf of the development of a true worker's society and the full emancipation of working women. More important, she had a profound revolutionary understanding of the radical changes that the nascent socialist society would need to make from the beginning if it were not to reproduce the gender inequalities and sexual norms of capitalism in a new form.

Alexandra Kollontai is, I believe, a touchstone in cultural critique for understanding the relation of women to both capitalism and socialism and for thinking beyond the historical limits of the existing society to envision the fundamentals of an egalitarian, nonexploitative and post-gender future. But to reread Kollontai today is to raise questions not only about the revolutionary value of her work but also about the historicity of our own reading. In order to avoid subsuming her revolutionary insights, we need to read dialectically the current historical situation and the one from which Kollontai was writing—turning our critique-al attention not only to the limits in which she worked but also to the limits of our own situation, including the realities of the post-Soviet state as well as the resurgence of antisocialist ideologies in the neoliberal marketplace.

One of the first problems is the way knowledge about Kollontai has been erased from cultural memory. Aside from a brief revival of interest in the 1970s and early 1980s, she is largely forgotten among feminists and socialists alike. As a Marxist revolutionary and Bolshevik, Kollontai struggled for the economic, social, and sexual emancipation of women in Europe and Russia during the first decades of the twentieth century. She played a leading role in the revolutionary struggles of the time and was considered, along with Trotsky and Lunacharsky, to be among the most dynamic speakers on behalf of the Russian Revolution (Kollontai, *Selected Writings* 108). She was also a key participant in the formation of the early Soviet state, becoming the first to head the Department of Social Welfare in the new Soviet Union and later was head of the Women's Department. Kollontai summed up her life by saying that "women and their fate occupied me all my life and concern for their lot brought me to socialism" (*Selected Writings* 30). She was deeply committed to the class struggle and convinced that the emancipation of women required not only the end of capitalism but also a concerted effort to transform personal relations along with the struggle for social change. As part of this effort, she worked especially hard to make socialism responsive to the needs of women and children and to create new communist sexual principles for a worker's state. She pioneered the development of social welfare and collective child care, the reform of marriage and property laws, the freeing of women from the isolated drudgery of the home and collectivization of domestic work, and the articulation of a new theory of sexuality for a collective society. But she was also a prominent critic of the bureaucratization and dominant economic policies of the early Soviet state. This led to her being marginalized, especially during Stalin's rule, and her ideas were suppressed as she was, in effect, exiled to a series of diplomatic posts from which she was not allowed to return until the last years of her life.

But this is all largely forgotten. If Kollontai is remembered at all, it is likely that she is misrecognized as a proponent of the "glass of water theory" of sexuality, which was commonly seen as a defense of promiscuity and "free love"—the idea that sex should be as easily satisfied as quenching one's thirst by drinking a glass of water. Not only did she not originate this theory, but her antibourgeois theories developed a much more complex view that understood sexuality as both a social and a historical relation (see Kollontai, *Selected Writings* 13; Clements, *Bol-*

shevik Feminist 231). Nonetheless, charges of sexual extremism were widely attributed to Kollontai in the West and in the Soviet Union (for example, Gray, *Soviet Women* 94) as a way of ideologically distorting and undermining her transformative understanding of human interpersonal relations and social change.

Approaching Kollontai and the issue of a red theory of sexuality today, one has to contend with even more ideological distortions, not the least of which is the attempt to suppress the history of revolutionary workers' movements and class struggle and the efforts to try to reduce Marxism to an accommodationist post-Marxism. We read Kollontai at a time when the socialist emancipation of women has been marginalized in East and West alike and when many (former) socialist feminists, particularly those in the West, such as Iris Young and J. K. Gibson-Graham, have embraced ludic politics and an accommodationist economics. It is also a time when theories of sexuality are dominated by discourses of desire, and the separation of sexuality from class has become a commonplace slogan, making the autonomy of desire the marker of human freedom.

Such positions are completely antithetical to the revolutionary class consciousness and profoundly materialist understanding that Kollontai brought to her work concerning sexuality. Throughout her political writings, public speeches, and fiction as well as in her political work, Kollontai consistently held to historical materialist principles and a revolutionary commitment to the emancipation of women, to the workers' struggle, and to a radical reunderstanding of bourgeois notions of sexuality and love.

There are three core principles around which her work developed: First, a rigorous materialist analysis of the historically varied forms of love and sexuality and their class basis; second, an unwavering commitment to the role and importance of the workers' collective in building the new society and in shaping interpersonal relations; and third, the firm conviction that effective social change involves the dialectical interrelation of ideological struggle and economic change.

In "Sexual Relations and Class Struggle," Kollontai criticizes the

> idea that proletarian sexual morality is no more than "superstructure," and that there is no place for any change in this sphere until the economic base of society has been changed. As if the ideology of a certain class is formed only when the breakdown in the socio-economic relationships, guaranteeing the dominance of that class, has been completed! All the experience of history teaches us that a social group works out its ideology, and consequently its sexual morality, in the process of its struggle with hostile social forces. (*Selected Writings* 249)

Kollontai argued, in other words, for the necessity of carrying out ideological struggle over the structure of gender and sexual relations *simultaneously* with the social and economic struggles. This is, I think, one of her most important lessons for cultural critique today. What is at stake is the dialectical relation between base and superstructure in the most specific ways. In working out its "ideology, and consequently its sexual morality, in the process of its struggle with hostile social forces," the social group is not only struggling to change consciousness but also is working out its priorities for social change. In this dialectical relation, the ideological struggle helps shape the priorities for developing the socioeconomic structures necessary to support new social relations and the new revolutionary consciousness.

Kollontai was quite aware of this dynamic, as she made clear in her last public speech in 1926, "On Marriage and Everyday Life" (*Selected Writings* 300–311). The ideological struggle taking place at the time between a resurgence of petit bourgeois notions of an entrenched, patriarchal family and the "new lifestyles" of the proletariat was a result, Kollontai argued, of the "class contradictions" still existing in the new society. The emancipation of women, she contended, required a political commitment of economic resources to provide for the welfare of women (many of whom were unemployed and still involved in domestic labor) in order to free them from financial dependency on individual men and property relations and to enable them to become full and productive members of the labor force. Thus she argued repeatedly for a "worker's state" that "aim[ed] to support every mother, married or unmarried, while she is suckling her child, and to establish maternity homes, day nurseries and other such facilities in every city and village, in order to give women the opportunity to combine work in society with maternity" (*Selected Writings* 257). In short, for her the "socialist approach" meant a profound social and material commitment to women so that "every woman has the right to desire and strive to be free from anxieties when bringing up her child, and to be free from the fear that some day she and the child will find themselves in need and without any means of sustenance" (*Selected Writings* 308–9).

There was important political and ideological support among the more radical Bolsheviks for this understanding of the socialist approach to the situation of women. The Communist Party program of 1919 declared that the party was "not confining itself to formal equality of women, the party strives to liberate them from the material burdens of obsolete household work by replacing it by communal houses, public eating places, central laundries, nurseries, etc." (quoted in Munoz and Woods,

"Marxism" 5). But these goals were nearly overwhelmed by the social and economic circumstances of the time—including the devastation of a world war with its massive destruction of the economy, the social infrastructure, and the population, followed by revolution and civil war— as well as by the resurgence of reactionary ideologies and economic and political practices that increasingly came to the fore with the New Economic Program (NEP) and the rise of bureaucratic centralism. The high rates of unemployment in these years, as well as the political conflicts about how to allocate scarce resources, meant that women's economic needs were considerably shortchanged. As Trotsky explained in 1923,

> [t]he workers' state must become wealthier in order that it may be possible seriously to tackle the public education of children and the releasing of the family from the burden of the kitchen and laundry. Socialisation of family housekeeping and public education of children are unthinkable without a marked improvement in our economics as a whole. We need more socialist economic forms. Only under such conditions can we free the family from the functions and cares that now oppress and disintegrate it. ("Old Family to the New" 26)

Lacking the economic means for substantial material reforms in women's condition, the early Soviet state focused its progressive efforts on legislative and political changes and made significant advances on this front. As Lenin pointed out on the second anniversary of the Bolshevik revolution, "In the course of two years of Soviet power in one of the most backward countries of Europe more has been done to emancipate woman, to make her the equal of the 'strong' sex, than has been done during the past 130 years by all the advanced, enlightened, 'democratic' republics of the world taken together" ("Status of Women" 122). This revolutionary progressiveness extended to all issues of sexuality as well, including homosexuality. "Soviet legislation," according to the director of the Moscow Institute of Social Hygiene, Dr. Grigorii Batkis, writing in 1923, "bases itself on the following principle: *It declares the absolute non-interference of the state and society into sexual matters, so long as no one's interests are encroached upon.* Concerning homosexuality, sodomy, and various other forms of sexual gratification, which are set down in European legislation as offenses against public morality—Soviet legislation treats these exactly the same as so-called 'natural' intercourse (quoted in 1917 Collective 375, emphasis in original).

This "government by proclamation," as Gail Lapidus notes, "was the least costly of mechanisms for social change, but it symbolized the commitment of the new regime to new values" (*Women in Soviet Soci-*

ety 58). And it did indeed lead to considerable changes in the situation of women, gays, lesbians, and transgendered persons. Many of these legislative changes, Lapidus argues, provided "the juridical foundation for women's economic independence" (59). Some of the more noteworthy legal and political advances included granting full citizenship to women; legislating an end to gender and sexual discrimination and restrictions on women's freedom of movement; establishing the basic principle of equal pay for equal work; substantially changing property relationships and inheritance laws and thereby weakening male authority; giving women "equal rights to hold land, to act as heads of households"; mandating revolutionary changes in the family code such as lifting restrictions on divorce, recognizing "unregistered marriages" and legalizing abortion, and in the "Moslem communities of Central Asia," outlawing such common practices as "abduction, forced marriage, the payment of *kalym* (bride price), and polygamy" (59–61).

But Lenin made clear that this was not enough:

> Notwithstanding all the laws emancipating woman, she continues to be a *domestic slave*, because *petty housework* crushes, strangles, stultifies and degrades her, chains her to the kitchen and the nursery, and she wastes her labour on barbarously unproductive, petty, nerve-racking, stultifying and crushing drudgery. The real *emancipation of women*, real *communism*, will begin only where and when an all-out struggle begins (led by the proletariat wielding the state power) against this petty housekeeping, or rather when its *wholesale transformation* into a large-scale socialist economy begins. ("A Great Beginning" 429, emphasis in original)

Only after Lenin's death, however, with the rapid economic progress of the Five Year Plans under Stalin, were women incorporated into the labor force in significant numbers; by 1939 women made up 41.6 percent of the industrial labor force and "an even higher proportion of manual laborers" (Lapidus, *Women in Soviet Society* 99). It is this economic growth that made "the desirable objective"—to create "a network of public child-care institutions and communal services"—a "pressing economic need" (98). But while the economic conditions for the emancipation of women were finally developing, the political and ideological situation had changed substantially by the 1930s. The "all-out struggle" that Lenin called for was largely derailed by the defeat of the workers in their efforts to "wield the state power." The Soviet Union became a "deformed worker's state" in which, Trotsky argued, "the bureaucracy . . . shattered the revolutionary vanguard of the proletariat" (*Revolution Betrayed* 92) and "defeated the program of Lenin" (94). For "by freeing the bureaucracy from the control of the proletarian vanguard . . . democratic centralism gave place to bureaucratic centralism" (98). In this climate, according to Trotsky, "the growth of the productive forces has been accompanied by an extreme development of all forms of inequality, privilege and advantage, and therewith of bureaucratism" (112). One of the mainstays of both this productive growth and the inequality was a reinscription of forms of the gender division of labor in the Soviet Union, such as the feminization of some industries (for example, textiles and health care) and gendered wage inequities, which continued until the period of perestroika and contributed to the violent discrimination against women and exclusion from the labor force that occurred under market reforms.

Thus, instead of fulfilling the Bolshevik goals of emancipating women from economic inequality, the tyranny of domestic labor, and patriarchal family relations, the rise of bureaucratic centralism in the Soviet Union "strengthened not the socialist, but the bourgeois features of the state" (Trotsky, *Revolution Betrayed* 113) and supported a reactionary revival of the family, an inadequacy of social services for workers (day care, public canteens, and so on), and the criminalization of homosexuality and promoted a gendered division of labor, including women's double burden of full-time work both outside the home and within it. This "retreat," Trotsky argued, meant that

> marriage and family laws established by the October revolution, once the object of its legitimate pride, are being made over and mutilated by vast borrowings from the law treasuries of bourgeois countries. . . . [It] not only assumes forms of disgusting hypocrisy, but also is going infinitely farther than the iron economic necessity demands. To the objective causes producing this return to such bourgeois forms as the payment of alimony, there is added the social interest of the ruling stratum in the deepening of bourgeois law. The most compelling motive of the present cult of the family is undoubtedly the need of the bureaucracy for a stable hierarchy of relations, and for the disciplining of youth by means of 40,000,000 points of support for authority and power. (*Revolution Betrayed* 153)

In other words, the contradictory practices that affected women and sexuality in the Soviet Union can be explained in part by the centrality of women's labor for economic growth, which accounts for their unprecedented access to high levels of education and professional work—unavailable to women in the West until recently—and to social services such as child care (however inadequate) to enable their participation. At the same time, the domination of an authoritarian bureaucratic centralism as "the planter and protector of inequality" (Trotsky, *Revolution*

Betrayed 113) depended in large part on the gendered divisions of labor and the reinstatement of the patriarchal, heterosexual family to maintain its power and privileges.

Kollontai would be quite critical not only of the deteriorating material and social conditions of women since the revival of capitalism in the Russian Federation but especially of the sexual exploitation of women. She would be, I think, relentless in cutting through the ideological masquerade of exploitation as a form of freedom and equally critical of the way Left cultural politics and "post" theories of sexuality in the West have contributed to this masquerade, mainly by their profound neglect of the economic basis of the "emotional and psychological" and the unavoidable class determinations of love and sexuality. "Sexual relations, family and marriage," Kollontai argues, "are historical categories, phenomena which develop in accordance with the economic relations that exist at the given level of production" (*Selected Writings* 225) and that change under pressure from the economic. "Social and economic changes," she continues, create conditions "that demand and give rise to a new basis for psychological experience" and "change all our ideas about the role of women in social life and undermine the sexual morality of the bourgeoisie" (*Selected Writings* 246). The current reifications of desire in the works of such authors as Deleuze and Guattari, Kristeva, Gallop, Butler, Grosz, Sedgwick, de Lauretis, and Gibson-Graham generate a concept of desire not only as independent of the economic but also as primarily an individual circuit of pleasure and posit liberation as mainly the free play of desire.

In contrast, Kollontai puts forth a complex materialist and collective vision of desire and sexuality. "Love," she argues, "is a profoundly social emotion. Love is not in the least a 'private' matter concerning only the two loving persons: love possess a uniting element which is valuable to the collective" (*Selected Writings* 278–79). At the core of all of her thinking about sexuality is her analysis of the way "each historical (and therefore economic) epoch in the development of society has its own ideal of marriage and its own sexual morality. . . . Different economic systems have different moral codes. Not only each stage in the development of society, but each class has its corresponding sexual morality . . . the more firmly established the principles of private property, the stricter the moral code." Kollontai thus finds that "the ideal of love in marriage only begins to appear when, with the emergence of the bourgeoisie, the family loses its productive functions and remains a consumer unit also serving as a vehicle for the preservation of accumulated capital" (284).

Kollontai makes the important argument that the very development in capitalist society of a sexualized love "that embraced both the flesh and soul" (*Selected Writings* 283)—as opposed to feudal notions of chaste, chivalrous love—becomes the primary ideological mechanism for securing marital cooperation and stability in the project of accumulating and preserving capital. This is, I think, one of the ideological factors behind the "back to home" movement as Russian society tries to adapt to the ruthless logic of private property. In capitalism, Kollontai argues, nearly all sexual relations are, of necessity, economic and property relations. The legal ones, that is, those relating to marriage, are all "grounded in (a) material and financial considerations, [and] (b) economic dependence of the female sex on the family breadwinner—the husband—rather than the social collective" (225). The other side of bourgeois marriage in capitalism is prostitution.

Prostitution and pornography have divided contemporary feminists, particularly as concerns the issues of sex workers' rights, identity, and self-determination (for example, Kempadoo and Doezema; Nagle). All too often these debates are isolated from basic economic questions of exploitation of labor and become empty claims for the freedom of "choice" and the "free expression" of sexuality, as in Drucilla Cornell's argument that what is needed is to protect women's "imaginary domain" so they have the right to the self-representation of their "sexuate beings" as sex workers and to organize (*Heart of Freedom* 45–58). At most, such arguments may help alleviate the worst conditions (for example, by enabling sex workers to organize) but they in no way engage the structure of exploitative relations. In contrast, Kollontai cuts straight through these empty debates to go right to the core of exploitative relations, showing the connections between the economic exploitation of sex workers and the commodification of everyday labor relations under capitalism. As she argues in "Prostitution and Ways of Fighting It,"

> the sale of women's labour . . . is closely and inseparably connected with the sale of the female body. . . . This is the horror and hopelessness that results from the exploitation of labour by capital. When a woman's wages are insufficient to keep her alive, the sale of favours seems a possible subsidiary occupation. The hypocritical morality of bourgeois society encourages prostitution by the structure of its exploitative economy, while at the same time mercilessly covering with contempt any girl or woman who is forced to take this path. (*Selected Writings* 263)

The root condition of capitalism is the buying and selling of people's labor power as a commodity to produce profit, and the commodification and sale of women's labor is inseparable from the sale of the female body.

In fact, Kollontai would find the current massive expansion of prostitution within Russia and the international sex trafficking in women and children quite predictable under global capitalism. "The trade in women's flesh," she wrote, "is not surprising when you consider that the whole bourgeois way of life is based on buying and selling" (*Selected Writings* 264). This is the most significant factor in the exploitation of women in Russia today: the return of people buying and selling other people's labor for profit, long outlawed under socialism, revives the direct exploitation of people, the outright buying and selling of women's flesh, their bodies and sexual labor. In a *Nightline* special report titled "Russian Revolutions: Sex in Russia," Ted Koppel noted that "the ranks of prostitutes in Moscow have swollen from around 15,000 to more than 70,000. That estimate from Moscow's police. Other observers suggest the numbers are actually much higher." A Russian man comments that "Russian prostitution . . . is pure economy. It's . . . just a case of survival," and Robin Montgomery, a researcher working with "Russian prostitutes," says that it "comes down to one word: necessity. . . . If you want to put food on the table, if you want to pay for your studies, if you want to buy nice clothes, it comes down to [the fact that] sex work is the most lucrative, it has a future and most romanticized job there is available for women in Russia today. The market is sex" ("Russian Revolutions").

But it is not only organized prostitution that involves the buying and selling of women as a sexual commodity. The sale of sexual favors as a "subsidiary occupation" to supplement inadequate wages or as a strategy of subsistence survival is increasingly seen as a "smart" choice and has led to "undercover prostitution," which Bridger, Kay, and Pinnick describe as "a deliberate decision [by women] to use their beauty and sexuality to 'buy' for themselves the comforts and lifestyle to which their training and professional work simply does not give them ready access. The deal involves finding a rich lover, or better still, a husband from the business world, who will amply provide for them" (*No More Heroines?* 174–75). But these are rarely the good deals they seem. Instead, women find that they are "treated just like any other asset. This means they can be dumped when they become 'obsolete' or sold off in the event of financial difficulties, ending up in a more overt form of prostitution"—as in the case of one woman whose businessman lover went bankrupt and "sold her to his friends together with his dacha. For 5,000 dollars" (176).

The only way to end prostitution, Kollontai argued, was to struggle against the conditions that compelled women to find prostitution a necessary means of subsistence. In 1921 she argued that the "workers' revolution in Russia has shattered the basis of capitalism and has struck a blow at the former dependence of women upon men" as well as eliminating the "main sources of prostitution—private property and the policy of strengthening of the family." But she also recognized that "communism was still a long way off." In the "transitional period," she insisted, "other factors are still in force. Homelessness, neglect, bad housing conditions, loneliness and low wages for women are still with us. . . . These and other economic and social conditions lead women to prostitute their bodies" (*Selected Writings* 265). Thus, as Kollontai made very clear, "to struggle against prostitution chiefly means to struggle against these conditions" (266). For as "the first All-Russian Congress of Peasant and Working Woman" stated, "A woman of the Soviet labour republic is a free citizen with equal rights, and cannot and must not be the object of buying and selling" (266).

This is the fundamental difference between capitalism and socialism. Capitalism continues to define freedom as the right of individuals to sell themselves and the right of those with money to buy others. This usually means buying and selling labor, but it also entails the buying and selling of people's sexuality and even their bodies. Over the years, democracy has tried to put some constraints on the buying and selling of people under capitalism, applying legal sanctions against some forms—notably slavery. The injunction against slavery is necessary to legitimate the market. As Marx argues in chapter 6 of *Capital* (vol. 1), slavery is made illegal under bourgeois democracy because otherwise it would unmask the (fraudulent) notion of the free exchange of "wages" for "labor power" that is the founding myth of capitalism and its political regime—bourgeois democracy—as a ruling class ideology. The legitimacy of capitalism, the free market, and democracy all depend on the narrative that in the free market, the worker and

> the owner of money meet in the market, and enter into relations with each other on a footing of equality as owners of commodities, with the sole difference that one is a buyer, the other a seller; both are therefore equal in the eyes of the law. For this relation to continue, the proprietor of labour-power must always sell it for a limited period only, for if he were to sell it in a lump, once and all, he would be selling himself, converting himself from a free man into a slave, from an owner of a commodity into a commodity. He must constantly treat his labour-power as his own property, his own commodity, and he can do this only by placing it at the disposal of the buyer, i.e. handing it over to the buyer for him to consume, for a definite period of time, temporarily. In this way he manages both to alienate [*veraussern*] his labour-power and to avoid renouncing his rights of ownership over it. (1: 271)

Marx further clarifies the seemingly free relation between labor and capital in chapter 28 of *Capital* by stating that this relation is ruled by "the silent compulsion of economic relations[, which] sets the seal on the domination of the capitalist over the worker" (899). The formal ("legal") injunctions against slavery, however, have not put an end to it—wage labor is a hidden form of slavery (through the exploitation of "surplus labor"), and prostitution and other forms of sexual slavery are structural features of bourgeois democracy and the free market.

The struggle against prostitution, as Kollontai and the early history of the revolutionary workers' state make clear, needs to be the struggle, first, against wage labor—against the rule of private property and the buying and selling of people—and, second, against the array of social and economic conditions that compel women to take up prostitution.

The principle of socialism is that, as Kollontai says, "All citizens are equal before the work collective. . . . A woman provides for herself not by marriage but by the part she plays in production and the contribution she makes to the people's wealth" (*Selected Writings* 265). An effective socialist society struggles to fully realize this principle and provide the material basis for the emancipation of women. The distortions of socialism in the Soviet Union had a very uneven and troubled history and brought an inadequate realization of women's economic and social emancipation. But abandoning this principle and reinstating the capitalist system has been catastrophic for the majority of women in the new market economies of the Russian Federation.

Kollontai's unwavering materialist analysis of love and sexuality makes her a revolutionary for our own time. Her work poses a serious challenge to the uncritical erasure in theoretical and critical work in East and West of the economic exchange, commodification, and capital accumulation involved in sexual relations under capitalism. Women's economic dependence on husbands is intensifying in the Russian Federation as women are being forced out of the workplace. Today's dual-income family, whether in the West or the East, just as much as the "male breadwinner" family, is a unit of consumption—and, in the case of the owning class, a unit of capital accumulation. What has changed is the enormous expansion of the commodification and exploitation of sexuality and bodies for profit, whether in prostitution, pornography, or the mass media. This commodification is an inescapable aspect of our lives and our sexuality in capitalism, but it is largely absent from our understandings of sexuality. Instead we find the valorization of transgressive or guilty pleasures and sensuous excesses represented as a liberating force from the writings of such feminist theorists as Luce Irigaray, Hélène Cixous,

Elspeth Probyn, and Laura Kipnis, to the pornographic broadsheets and sex manuals saturating Moscow streets. What we lose sight of is how this fetishization of pleasure and sensuality is itself an effect of capitalist commodification of pleasures. It is necessary therefore to ask how subversive are theories of sexuality that obscure the economic relations of desire and the class interests embedded in its current forms.

Kollontai takes her materialist analysis further and critiques the form of sexual subjectivity that emerges from the class interests and economic relations of capitalism. Briefly, she analyses the "contemporary psyche" as characterized by an "extreme individuality, egoism that has become a cult," by property relations ("the idea of 'possessing' the married partner"), and by "the belief that the two sexes are unequal, that they are of unequal worth in every way, in every sphere, including the sexual sphere" (*Selected Writings* 242). It only takes a moment's observation to show how strongly these features have continued in global capitalism and, especially, how intensely they are being revived in the new market economies, particularly in the Russian Federation.

What is most fundamental in capitalism is the extraordinary way in which relations of sexuality, love, and desiring are grounded in property relations. The "bourgeoisie," Kollontai argues, "have carefully tended and fostered the ideal of absolute possession of the 'contracted partner's' emotional as well as physical 'I,' thus extending the concept of property rights to include the right to the other person's whole spiritual and emotional world" (*Selected Writings* 242). The constant perpetuation of this subjectivity is one of the primary projects of bourgeois ideology from operas such as *Carmen* to popular romance novels and chick lit. In all these forms the measure of love and sexual desiring is the fantasy of possessing the object of desire. This logic of property relations is making strong inroads into changing personal relations under capitalism in Russia. As one Russian woman told Bridger and her colleagues: "Attitudes to women are changing from the traditions of the past. Women today are looked upon as some kind of personal possession. Attitudes are certainly getting worse and worse, men seem to think that anything goes. They think they have the right to take what they want, by force if need be" (180–81).

"Healthy sexual instinct," Kollontai argues, "has been turned by monstrous social and economic relations . . . into unhealthy carnality. The sexual act has become an aim in itself—just another way of obtaining pleasure, through lust sharpened with excesses and through distorted, harmful titillation's of the flesh. . . . Prostitution is the organized expression of this distortion of the sex drive" (*Selected Writings* 286). This may sound rather puritanical to some, for under capitalism there is an increasing acceptance of anything that will intensify the pleasures of sensuousness—even pain and violence. But Kollontai demonstrates that the pursuit of pleasure as a performance of freedom is a very specific historical practice of the owning classes and is *not* the basis for egalitarian, sharing relations of mutual sexual pleasure and personal regard among people. The valorization of excessive stimulation, excitation, and sensation as ends in themselves distorts human relations and capabilities and is a direct reflection of the alienating commodification and exploitation of human relations that arises with capitalism. Claudia Broyelle extends this analysis in her book *Women's Liberation in China*, in which she writes about sexuality under capitalism: "In a society where the division of labor becomes more accentuated, where the vast majority of people are deliberately deprived of creativity, where work has no other value than its explicit *monetary one*, sexuality becomes *a means of escaping from society through self-centered sexual consumption, rather than the full expression of interpersonal relationships*" (pt. 5, p. 2).

In the West, Left sexual theories commonly represent sexual excess and transgressive pleasures as subversive of bourgeois morality (for example, in Kipnis) and thus as emancipatory practices. This is a frequent defense of pornography in contemporary cultural critique (for example, see Penley, "Crackers and Whackers"). But to use it is to fundamentally misrecognize the relations involved and instead to further promote the bourgeois ideology of individual consumption and personal gratification against the interests and well-being of others. The Left has embraced an "anti-repressive hypothesis" of sexuality that is no different in its effects and no more antibourgeois than the "repressive hypothesis" that Foucault describes. The "'putting into discourse of sex,'" he explains, "has been subjected to a mechanism of increasing incitement; . . . the techniques of power exercised over sex have obeyed a principle . . . of dissemination and implantation of polymorphous sexualities" (*History of Sexuality* 12).

In fact, the "increasing incitement" and excitation of sex is exactly what capitalism requires for the continuing proliferation of sexual commodification and control of subjectivities. As Reimut Reiche states in *Sexuality and Class Struggle*, "desublimation" becomes yet another form of repression and control: when "individual sublimation is collectively broken down," the individual is subjected to "the same powers which engineered his desublimation, and they henceforth decide for him how he is to behave . . . when and how he reacts in an openly sexual way, and when and how he curbs or gives free rein to aggressive urges" (135).

Against bourgeois property relations and individual gratification in sexual relations, Kollontai argues that socialist relations of production, which are no longer organized around profit and the exploitation of labor of others, create the conditions for profoundly different interpersonal relations. These conditions make possible what she calls a new "communist morality," that is, new principles of living for a workers' collective. Thus, "As regards sexual relations, communist morality demands first of all *an end to all relations based on financial or other economic considerations.* The buying and selling of caresses destroys the sense of equality between the sexes, and thus undermines the basis of solidarity without which communist society cannot exist. . . . The stronger the ties between the members of the collective as a whole, the less the need to reinforce marital relations" (*Selected Writings* 230, emphasis added).

The basic principles that Kollontai articulates for a "communist morality" still hold, as does the daily need to struggle for such no exploitative relations. Kollontai opens up a complex, integrated, and materialist understanding of the revolutionary possibility of relationships that are no longer based in any way on commodification, economic exchange, or financial considerations. Instead, she envisions truly free—that is, equal—relations of love and comradeship necessary both for human fulfillment and for sustaining the connections among members in a collective. This is the basis, for Kollontai, of a new class practice, a "proletarian morality" that "replace[s] the all-embracing and exclusive marital love of bourgeois culture" with "three basic principles: 1. Equality in relationships. . . . 2. Mutual recognition of the rights of the other, of the fact that one does not own the heart and soul of the other (the sense of property, encouraged by bourgeois culture). 3. Comradely sensitivity, the ability to listen and understand the inner workings of the loved person (bourgeois culture demanded this only from the woman)" (*Selected Writings* 291).

Kollontai firmly believed in the emancipator potential of noncommodified and thus nonpossessive relations among free individuals not bound by economic dependency. She believed in the social value of what she called "love-solidarity" based on comradeship and equality and contended these would "become the lever" in communist society that "competition and self-love were in the bourgeois society" (*Selected Writings* 290).

Although Kollontai's articulation of human relations is heterosexual (she speaks only about relations between the sexes), her views of postpatriarchal, nonexclusive relationships open up the possibility for a radical postheterosexual society. At the core of her "communist morality" is the belief in the development of various degrees and kinds of intimacy—of sexuality, love, comradeship—among individuals, connecting them in a collective. These intimate relations in no way preclude intimacy between members of the same sex and, in fact, a multiple, complex intimacy across differences of sex and race follows from such an open, nonexclusive, nonsingular "morality." Kollontai, in short, shows the way to develop a revolutionary sexual theory in which sexual difference is no longer the basis for the social division of desire because it is no longer the basis for the social division of labor. An egalitarian workers' collective based on communist relations of production—in which, as Marx states in his *Critique of the Gotha Programme,* the needs of all are met—would abolish the exploitation of differences. Thus differences of sexuality and race would no longer be the basis of inequality, privilege, and the exploitation of others and no longer the basis of divisions of desire and labor. Such radical changes will not occur automatically—they require, as Kollontai makes very clear, unrelenting, all-embracing social and ideological struggle as an integral part of the class struggle to build a new social formation.

Does Kollontai's vision of communist sexuality seem utopian? Only if we accept as inevitable capitalism and its tyranny of individualism. But for Kollontai and other Bolsheviks in the early years of the workers' state, such revolutionary relationships were a very real historical possibility. Their failure is a historical, political, and economic problem that needs to be carefully analyzed, not merely erased as obsolete, in order to learn why they failed and how to actualize the full possibilities of the free and equal relations of love, sexuality, and social collectivity that Kollontai articulated. What such an examination would enable us to understand is how profoundly dialectical is the problem, how inseparable are the economic and the ideological, how fully integrated are sex and class, and how sexual freedom depends on the material economic means to meet people's needs.

Kollontai's theory of sexuality shows the way to develop an emancipatory theory, a red theory of love as an understanding of the inseparable dialectical relation of sex and the material relations of production. A red theory of love is a commitment to ending the economic exploitation and commodification of relations and the social divisions of labor and desire. It is the struggle to build free and equal relations in which desire is neither simply sexual nor exclusive but involves a solidarity of multiple connections and interrelations to others as well as to the work and welfare of the collective. Such relations cannot be developed in a social formation dominated by property relations as the signifiers of individual freedom. What needs to be done is to struggle toward red love—toward sexual and comradely solidarity.

7. Globalization, the "Multitude," and Cynical Critique

Globalization without Referents

By now a common code for the free market, globalization has become more a state of desire in contemporary cultural critique than an objective condition. After all the mandatory qualifications of "for better and for worse" are made (for example, Derrida et al., *Philosophy in a Time of Terror* 123) and all the requisite doubts and discontents are expressed (Stiglitz, *Globalization and its Discontents*), globalization is represented in this interpretive imaginary as an actual or yet-to-come condition of cultural heterogeneity, self-sovereignty, and inclusiveness beyond the regulatory authority of the (nation-) state. Globalization, in these critiques, "can yield immense benefits. . . . [G]lobalization of knowledge has brought improved health, with life spans increasing at a rapid pace. How can one put a price on these benefits of globalization?" (Stiglitz, "Globalism's Discontents" 3). In contemporary cultural critique, globalization is depicted as the space of a new cosmopolitanism with engagement, and a plurality without pluralism, where "democratization has more of a chance" (Derrida et al., *Philosophy in a Time of Terror* 123).

"Normal" cultural critique (to recall Thomas Kuhn's term for hegemonic knowledge paradigms) has, generally, been a cheerleader for globalization—both within institutional structures of cultural knowledge, as exemplified in the special issue of *PMLA* titled "Globalizing Literary Studies"—and outside them, as in Thomas Friedman's *The World Is*

Flat. While expressing some routine dissent, normal cultural critique has largely rejoiced in capitalist globalization, describing it as a process by which the local and resistance have been energized. As a result, new, hybrid cultures are believed to develop and are seen as marked by diversity, heterogeneity, and fusion, what Roland Robertson, adopting the Japanese term *dochakuka,* calls "glocal" (*Globalization* 173) and Ronald Stade and Gurdun Dahl, in their tribute to Ulf Hannerz, who seems to have first used the term, elaborate as "creolization" ("Globalization, Creolization"). The social and economic implications of globalization as desire acquire even greater ideological clarity in Arjun Appadurai's *Modernity at Large,* in which he argues that globalization has related the world in new ways through nonbinary mediascapes, ethnoscapes, technofinancescapes and, consequently, produced a new complex of connections that make the social and the cultural less determinate, less closure-seeking. Globalization, for Appadurai, is a Deleuzian cosmopolitan body without organs—a site of links of hybrid lines of flights and flows of desire, a translocal locality.

Friedman and Appadurai seem to be in a strange (political) cohabitation in recent cultural critique. But actually the political differences between progressives (Appadurai) and conservatives (Friedman) melt into air when they join the carnival of globalization. They both follow corporate scripts of globalization. Their only difference is that the Left script finds a cultural resistance to corporate norms in the local and context-specific adaptations of globalization. In India, for example, as a result of a local culture of vegetarianism, a McDonald's "burger" is creolized into a burger look-alike made of peas, potatoes, and carrots mixed with Indian spices. This "glocalization" is what the progressive media celebrate in order to conceal the actual economic brutalities that capital commits against workers. Nicholas Kristof, for example, in his review of *Golden Arches East,* writes that "in many countries McDonald's has been absorbed by local communities and become assimilated, so that it is no longer thought of as a foreign restaurant and in some ways no longer functions as one" (n.p.).

The proliferation of heterogeneity is one of the management strategies that global capitalism deploys to increase sales and profit, but it is depicted in Left cultural critique as the assertion of local culture and as an instance of resistance against corporate power. This is because most progressive critics of globalization—although they think of themselves as forward-looking, even cutting-edge thinkers—nonetheless still regard capitalism in rather outdated terms as a normative regime that imposes homogeneity everywhere. Therefore, they consider these trivial heterogeneities as marks of local cultural transgressions. Douglas Kellner writes that from a postmodern perspective McDonald's is "the paradigm of mass homogeneity, sameness and standardization, which erases individuality, specificity, and difference" (*Media Spectacle* 50). In actuality, however, capitalism, today is the main producer of heterogeneity, singularity, locality, and norm-breaking in consumption. When it comes to desire for consumption, capitalism is the sponsor of the heterogeneous and the singular consumer whose affects it represents as uncanny—as unexplainable as the enigma of subjectivity itself.

Even in its most radical moments of opposition to globalization, progressive cultural critique has not been against capitalism (which is its root) but has stood, in the words of the World Social Forum Charter of Principles, "in opposition to a process of globalization commanded by the large multinational corporations" (World Social Forum, n.p.). Cultural critique, in other words, has opposed *corporations*, not *capitalism:* it has sought to reform corporate capitalism, not to end capitalism. In fact, capitalism is not seen as a very active factor in the globalization of culture, which is the means by which English (the "first language" of capitalism) is installed as the universal medium for banking, managing global sweatshops, and the conduct of imperialist wars. Stephen Greenblatt, for example, writes that the "globalization of literary studies is not principally a phenomenon of . . . the spread of English on the wings of international capitalism" (59).

Given the unbearable consequences of globalization (Petras and Veltmeyer, *Globalization Unmasked;* Olivera, *Water War in Bolivia*), few critics give it direct support. Yet the ideology of capitalism works its way through their various arguments and qualifications. In the end, most conclude that although globalization may not be the best way to reorganize the world, in reality, other ways of organizing it are worse. Globalization, in other words, is legitimated with a wise tone of discontent and in an understated language that is more effective because it carries with it the mark of thoughtfulness.

In reality, globalization *is* the worst. It has made wage labor (which is missing from, for example, Derrida's discourse on globalization/*mondialisation*) the universal regime of work. It has suspended all strong labor laws and finance regulations so that capital can travel freely across national borders to invest, trade, and own property all over the world, as well as set wages and receive huge tax benefits at the expense of workers. It has limited the rights of workers to unionize in order to improve their conditions and, through national and local governments, has placed severe restrictions on their movements (immigration) so that there is always a ready army of unemployed people who can be deployed to bring down wages and eliminate the benefits (for instance, pensions and health-care) of other workers throughout the world. It has used democracy as a cover for imposing the free market on people of the world and transferring public wealth to the private sector by commodifying water, healthcare, education, energy, food, and transportation. It has increased the gap be-tween poor and rich countries, ruined the environment, and turned the "working day" into a nightmare of unending exploitation for workers who, unprotected by any laws, have only two options: consent to being exploited at an ever-increasing rate or live a life of extreme poverty and want in everlasting uncertainty.

Normal critique is a web of class contradictions, some of which show in its understanding of culture. These contradictions are not the results of any analytical negligence on the part of critics but are the outcomes of the social conditions that produce them. Cultural critique insists on the autonomy of culture at the same time that it argues for the way technological revolutions (from Fordism to post-Fordism or from labor to knowledge) have changed culture. The technological dynamic is a familiar line of argument that extends, in its modern form and with dif-ferent degrees of emphasis, from McLuhan through Baudrillard to Sherry Turkle, who contend that spectral and fractured identities emerge from new technologies, and Donna Haraway, who theorizes the emergence of new cyborg subjects. Along similar lines, Derrida argues that globalizing democracy "owe[s] a great deal, almost everything perhaps, to television, to the communication of models, norms, images, information products, and so on" (*Philosophy in a Time of Terror* 123) and that e-mail and digital inscription (*Archive Fever*) have introduced new levels of difference into the everyday (*Paper Machine*). The technological changes are assumed to be so radical that they are seen as transforming not only the contents of culture but also its very epistemological status: culture "can no lon-ger be studied as some unimportant, secondary, or dependent variable in what makes the modern world move and shake, but has to be seen as something primary and constitutive, determining its shape and character as well as its inner life" (Hall, "Centrality of Culture" 215).

At the same time that cultural critique argues for the transforma-tion of culture as the result of technological changes, it also maintains the contradictory position that culture is not dependent on any force outside itself but is autonomous. Not only is culture self-determining, it actually shapes other spheres of social life such as politics and the economic (Salaman, "Culturing Production"). This argument, which has its modern roots in such books as Max Weber's *Protestant Ethics and the Spirit of Capitalism*, has gone through numerous variations. More recently, Guido Tabellini, has asked, "Does culture have a causal effect on economic development?" He answers by saying, "The data on European regions suggest that it does" ("Culture and Institutions"). Malcolm Waters argues from a somewhat different perspective: "The economy is becoming dominated by lifestyle choices, both in terms of the displacement of production by consumption as the central economic activity and in terms of the diversification of possible occupational experiences. The economy is becoming symbolically mediated and reflexive, which detaches it from locality" (*Globalization* 24).

This view of culture leads to the observation that in the contemporary world "everything in our social life—from economic value and state power to practices and to the very structure of psychic life itself—can be said to have become 'cultural'" (Jameson, *Postmodernism* 48). Jameson attempts to account for this phenomenon by maneuvering between materialism and cultural materialism, which leads him to argue that the "explosion" of culture is the effect of its disappearance as a semiautonomous sphere (48). This mixing of what is basically a form of technological determinism with an insistence on the autonomy of culture is a reflection of capital's contradictory needs. On one hand, it places technology at the center of contemporary social life and contends that wealth is produced by knowledge, not labor, in order to assert that there is no exploitation of labor by capital. On the other, it deploys culture to obscure class differences, which are the effects of exploitation, by spiritualizing social life so that material differences are translated into cultural differences, lifestyles, and matters of personal choice. These contradictions underlie and enable the grand inversion on which the dominant cultural theory of globalization depends, namely, that in the globalized world "production" has been displaced by "consumption" and labor is no longer the source of value.

In these narratives, the "contemporary global order, or disorder, is . . . a structure of flows, a de-centered set of economies of signs in space" (Lasch and Urry, *Economies* 4), in which labor is technologized and culturalized when it is not silenced outright. In the globalized space that Lasch and Urry describe, the "ordinary manufacturing industry is becoming more and more like the production of culture. It is not that commodity manufacture provides the template, and culture follows, but that the culture industries themselves have provided the template" (123). As a consequence of such a transformation in culture, work itself becomes cultural. "Flexible" production has become "reflexive" in the sense that it is grounded more and more in "discursive knowledge" and "has succeeded a material labor process" (60). "Reflexive" production is also a mark of how deeply "culture has penetrated the economy itself" (61). As I have explained elsewhere (Ebert and Zavarzadeh, *Class in Culture*), reflexive production is a concept by which the cultural, within global economies, is substituted for the material. It is the regime of the singular, in which the individual employee is seen as acquiring the opportunity for self-expression—reminiscent of the old, small, liberal nineteenth-century enterprises with their echo of medieval craft guilds—as the actuality of the worker or laborer is shunted to the cultural periphery. Reflexive production (and consumption) are geared more toward the heterogeneity and singularity of the prosperous consumer; they allow the employee to make decisions and put considerable time into production design while using shorter production runs (for a few rich consumers). Reflexivity means individualization. This is seen as greatly transforming the workplace, replacing both the old Taylorist management style and the more recent "just in time" models with a new "shopfloor epistemology" (122), in which the individual employee is not circumscribed by structural constraints but is part of the unencumbered flows and lines of flights, new links and connections without totality. In the reflexive workplace, freedom is not freedom from labor ("necessity," as Marx calls it) but from the *protocols* of labor: how labor is done, not why, as in why have wage labor. The question why is dismissed in globalization discourses as a symptom of the metanarrative of totality.

Globalization in cultural critique today is a form of cosmopolitan spiritualism with a strong aroma of religion, and it is driven by technology. In his essay "Glocal Knowledges" in the *PMLA* issue concerning globalization, Robert Livingston makes the requisite gestures toward its political and economic features, but then he stresses that "globalization is a structure of feeling—'planetary consciousness,' equal parts Mandela [Good] and Milosevic [Evil]—that springs from the media-saturated soil of our daily life" (145). This spiritualism actually frames the entire special issue. In "Literature for the Planet" Wai Chee Dimock assumes that borders are "cultural" practices and narratives of self-construction and not limits set by the relations of labor and capital. The "objective" borders of Iraq and Jordan, however, and the constantly shifting borders of Palestine (regions with the same general culture) are not cultural; they are imposed by the economic interests of imperialist capitalism. Dimock writes that "every new translation" of a literary work will "punch a hole in those borders" (177). But borders are not lifted by translations. They are erased by the uniformity of banking regulations, insurance laws, and tax codes—laws that free capital to travel wherever cheap labor is available. Borders are lines of demarcation drawn by the historical relations of production, the active basis of power, which legitimates itself through "translation" and other cultural products. The unsaid part of globalization's borderless fantasy, which is haunting the interpretive imaginary of cultural critique today, is that a postborder world will be filled with "prosperity for all," but this is actually a legitimization of free trade (Micklethwait and Wooldridge, *Future Perfect*).

Free trade is the ideological discourse of finance capital for erasing labor as the source of wealth and putting "knowledge" (the spirit of invention) in its place. Wealth, in the culturalist theory of globalization, is seen as the result of "thinking" and not the outcome of surplus labor. Relying on this spiritualism, Livingston defines globalization in such terms as "transforming the sense of place" (147), and when such vacuous culturalisms become too embarrassing, he makes equally empty gestures toward the finance side of globalization and names the World Bank and the IMF, as if globalization is simply an effect of banking, finance, trade, or money. This finance determinism is the confusion that Derrida's reading of Marx has introduced into cultural critique: Derrida, according to even his most sympathetic readers, seems to think that finance capital and not labor is basis of the dynamics of world capitalism (Spivak, *Outside* 97–119). Such Derridean reading has produced a growing literature about the impact of, for example, the World Bank and the IMF on culture. But these institutions are not the causes of globalization. The cause is the capitalist relation of production; globalization and the World Bank are the effects.

Within its grand inversion, the cultural theory of globalization represents culturalism as a progressive intervention. The anticolonialism that Rey Chow advances in support of polyethnicity is exemplary. Her essay "How (the) Inscrutable Chinese Led to Globalized Theory," in the same issue of the *PMLA*, evokes the "radical" language of anti-imperialism and offers a subaltern theory of globalization. But imperialism, for Chow, is not part of the worldwide class struggles over surplus labor. Rather, it is a mode of cultural exclusion, not "exploitation" but "oppression." She writes, "To globalize has meant predominately one thing: to subordinate, derogate, or extinguish one's native language, culture, and history, in order to accommodate those of the West" (69). For Chow the problem with globalization is the continuation of modernity, and it is exemplified in Derrida's "hallucinating China" (70). Her modernity, however, is strangely separated from industrial capitalism and its regime of labor. Globalization is a grammatological move for Chow (73): a purely textual and cultural matter that has very little if anything to do with access to the world's cheap labor, energy resources, markets, or banking and insurance regulations.

Stephen Greenblatt's theory of globalization, "Racial Memory and Literary History," is another instance of theory as anecdote—in this case, of course, a multicultural ("global") anecdote. It begins with his listening to a conversation taking place in the back seat of his car between Nadine Gordimer and Carlos Fuentes, both of whom were accompanying him to a dinner party in Cambridge. The two discussed various writers and events that "encapsulated the globalization of literature" (48). His anecdote leads to a view of globalization as a cultural in-betweenness: a "local knowledge" (49) that moves through language, "the slipperiest of human creations," and thus "does not respect borders, and like the imagination, it cannot ultimately be predicted or controlled" (62); it crashes through all limits. Globalization is not, as "Marxist ideology" (49) contends, concerned with the relations of the international division of labor but is, for Greenblatt, the slippery transgressive trajectory of the sign "Oxford," whose play eludes the rigidity of the nation-state in its errancies of reference between Oxford, Mississippi, and Oxford, England (49).

The globalized world in cultural critique is a postclass community based on lifestyle (consumption practices), taste, ideas, and irony (Rorty, *Contingency* 73–95). The ironic is the means by which the prosperous (using the excuse of mistrusting what Rorty calls "final vocabulary") avoid confronting the reality of others whose misery is the condition of their prosperity. Instead of changing the world, the ironist simply "redescribes" it (73). This is the community whose assumptions ground such treatments of globalization as Bill Readings's *University in Ruins*.

Readings's contribution to capital is not in his theory of globalization, which is an eclectic and pragmatic reconciliation of different and often incompatible views and ideologies, but in the way he hollows out materialist critique, replacing it with what he calls "Thought" without referent (159) and in doing so replaces economic explanations of wage labor with a theosophical and religious description of "ruins" as the site of a new society of singularities without totality (Ebert and Zavarzadeh, *Hypohumanities*). Readings begins with a routine description of globalization as an event in which "the nation-state ceases to be the elemental unit of capitalism" (44) and argues that this change puts an end both to the critique of culture, which was canonized by Humboldt's model of knowledge in the modern university (46, 65–66, 68–69), and the critique of "reason" as it was perceived in the Enlightenment and glorified the Kantian notion of the university (14–15, 54–55). In postrational and postnational capitalism that is, in Kenichi Ohmae's words, run by investment, industry, information, and individual (*End of the Nation State* 2–5), critique ("teaching" in Readings's narrative) becomes a practice without referent. It becomes

Thought, whose signification is the effect of the surprising and aleatory play of the sign because Thought is without any "intrinsic meaning" (159). Thought, in other words, is a postconceptual excess that overflows all representations (166–79). It is modeled after "politics" in Derrida (*Politics of Friendship*) as an empty signifier (Laclau, "Empty Signifiers Matter"). Its main function is to keep the space of thought open and protect it from "slipping back into an idea" (160), from becoming thinking (about anything in particular), because thinking will impose closure ("Truth") on Thought. Thought is not thinking that may lead to the production of coherent knowledge (Truth) and enable people to change their world; it is its opposite. It keeps "open the temporality of questioning so as to resist being characterized as a transaction that can be concluded" (19). Thought, in other words, "does not function as an answer but as a question" (160). In this postnational state, Thought is an ongoing playfulness without end; it is a reproduction of the aesthetic reflexivity of the nineteenth-century (art for art's sake). It legitimates, for the globalized world, the pedagogical equivalent of Lasch and Urry's reconstruction of the Victorian workshop and its "shopfloor epistemology."

Thought without thinking is a space in contemporary cultural critique for thoughtful unthoughtfulness. It converts Thought from a public act into a private reflexivity, and by disallowing thinking (about anything other than itself), it shields existing social relations from change. Thought as thinking about something provides Thought with a referent in the social relations of production and, consequently, puts a stop to the play of the sign and totalizes the "ruins"—society as a collection of singularities— into a critique of capitalism. In order to shield capitalism from such a critique (Thought with content), Readings warns against radicalism (163) and against ending the existing social organizations (167) by mocking "Big Politics" (178). Instead, he recommends "rethinking" (163). He seems to know that any commitment (other than to Thought without content) will recognize how such Thought is a strategy for cleansing critique of the social. The globalized world "in ruins" is the ideal of capital because it is a world in fragments, filled with singular subjects with their own singular desires. It is a world in which the particulars obscure the rules and regulations by which heterogeneous ruins are produced and maintained as signs of freedom from totality when, in fact, the ruins are the new totalities of the reflexive workshop, which Readings names the "university."

The university is a code for the workplace of Thought, where new strategies for dealing with identity, knowledge, work, thinking, desire, language, and labor in the post-nation-state culture are forged: strategies that are said to be based not on the Truth of Thought (160) but on its contingent pragmatics. Because Thought has no intrinsic contents, it acquires its content-effect from its nonreferent, namely, the ever shifting-opportunities that capital offers. In not referring to anything in particular (which will limit its opportunities), it makes all opportunities its grand referent. The logic of the nonreference of Thought is the logic of the new global entrepreneur: she does not limit her opportunities for profit (by any specific referent) but keeps her options (referents) open and in ruins, that is, the plural particulars that cannot be totalized. The empty signifier of Thought produces this "absent totality" (Laclau, "Empty Signifiers Matter" 42), which is the space of the global market as the arena of the singular entrepreneur whose interests can never be totalized; they are always glocal, hybrid, heterogeneous, and shifting with the market. In cultural critique today, globalization represents a body without organs, desires without norms, organs without organisms, signs without reference, competition without regulation. Globalization is the other name of anarcho-capitalism.

Globalization as Transnationalism

Theorists of modern globalization have mapped the world as a transnational space beyond the limits of the nation-state. From Saint Simon's pan-Europeanism to Negri and Hardt's empire-ism, postnational theories of globalization, with their various modifications of the state and differing concepts—such as "rationalism" in Weber; "knowledge" in Daniel Bell; "world-system" in Wallerstein; "media" in Marshall McLuhan; "glocalization" in Roland Robertson; "time and space" in Anthony Gidden; "McWorld" in Barber; "flatness" in Friedman—are all responses to the changing needs of capitalism for increasing the rate of surplus labor.

There have been many globalizations in modernity, and like the current one, all have been caused by the requirements of capital to intensify the exploitation of workers beyond national borders in order to increase profits. This has meant that capital has had to constantly reconfigure the state and its geographical borders by means of imperialism. Depending on the historical conditions, this reformation has included such various arrangements as colonialism, inventing new states by breaking up existing ones, establishing the "League of Nations," and spreading "democracy" in order to increase the supply of producers, regardless of their nationality.

Normal cultural critique accommodates the needs of capital for a globalized market and access to cheap labor by treating globalization as the progressive transformation of the world into a new cultural space and depicting the nation-state as an outdated narrative that is repressive of new cultural identities (for example, Bhabha, *Nation and Narration*). The "state," of course, is the other face of class: "the ruling class establishes its joint domination as public power, as the state" (Marx and Engels, *German Ideology* 355), which means the state is the "organized power of one class for oppressing another" (Marx and Engels, *Manifesto* 505). In *Anti-Dühring*, Engels discusses the relation of the state and capital in broader terms, arguing that "the modern state . . . is only the organisation that bourgeois society takes on in order to support the general external conditions of the capitalist mode of production against the encroachments as well of the workers as of individual capitalists. The modern state, no matter what its form, is essentially a capitalist machine, the state of the capitalists, the ideal personification of the total national capital" (266).

Theories about the end of the nation-state are theories that represent class as an outdated residual concept (Derrida, "Politics and Friendship" 204) and argue that labor is no longer the source of wealth; instead, they announce the emergence of knowledge capitalism. Globalization is a theory of a transclass space in which social difference is an effect of the "possibilities for consumption rather than production relations," and the source of power is "individual talents" and not membership in a class because "world class is displaced by a world status system based on consumption, lifestyle and value—commitment" (Waters, *Globalization*, 56, 92).

Because the state is an invention of the owning class for the protection of its "property and interests" (Marx and Engels, *German Ideology* 90), the form of the state has been modified as the structure of property ownership has changed from local to transnational. In the nineteenth and twentieth centuries, various forms of colonialism were deployed to deal with the imperatives of new forms of transnational property within the framework of the nation-state. Now, the more radical shifts in the structure of transnational property demand that the state itself be transformed. In order to increase property on a global scale, capital needs to have access to a high rate of surplus labor. This means higher rates of exploitation of workers in such large numbers that they can only be found outside the borders of individual nation-states. The nation, which was at one time necessary for the development of capitalism, has now become an obstacle. It thus has to change.

At the moment of its emergence from feudalism, capitalism needed to reorganize existing economic structures and relations. The nation and the nation-state are historical responses to that material necessity. Through legislation, the state centralized power and produced uniform codes for taxation, banking, investing, importing and exporting, and enforcement of tariffs. In other words, it normalized the new form of property relations called capitalism. In the nation-state, "independent or but loosely connected provinces with separate interests, laws, governments and systems of taxation, became lumped together into one nation, with one government, one code of laws, one national class-interest, one frontier and one customs tariff" (Marx and Engels, *Manifesto* 489).

Nationally uniform tax laws and finance regulations became the norms, but capital now needs to transgress these norms and rewrite them as transborder agreements such as the World Trade Organization, the North American Free Trade Agreement, and the European Union. What was once a main condition for capitalism's emergence and development has now become one of its major fetters. Capital still needs the nation-state, but it needs one with different functions. It needs it to carry out transnational agreements and enforce them locally. In place of a local nation-state, it needs a *glocal* one. The new functions of the glocal state include using local power to administer global rules and do the policing work for capital: preventing workers' strikes, reducing national taxes for capital, deregulating economic policies, lowering environmental safeguards, and setting capital free to reduce or eliminate workers' benefits, pensions, and job safety. "The executive of the modern State is but a committee for managing the common affairs of the whole bourgeoisie" and not only the local capitalists, according to Marx and Engels (*Manifesto* 486).

The passing of the present form of the nation-state" s considered by normal cultural critique to be an instance of progress that will set people free from the constraints of national identity and usher in a new cosmopolitanism. These fables of freedom are rooted in the anarcho-capitalist cultural theories derived from Nietzsche's maxim "The state is the coldest of all cold monsters. Coldly, it lies, too; and this lie creeps from its mouth: 'I, the state, am the people'" (*Zarathustra*, 75). Both the progressive (Foucault, "Governmentality"; Deleuze and Guattari, *Anti-Oedipus*) and the conservative (Hayek, *Fatal Conceit*; Yergin and Stanislaw, *Commanding Heights*) converge in this theory of the state. Generally, these views lead to a theory of globalization as a radical agent of liberty that will, once and for all, put an end to the repressive regulatory power of the nation-state. In all such anarcho-capitalist writings, the nation is treated as a narration of totality without difference (Derrida, *Of Hospitality*).

The end of the nation-state in bourgeois narratives is an ideological story that obscures the class basis of the state; what is called its end is really only its modification to fit the new needs of capital. This "ending" is radically different from the withering away of the state that historical materialism has argued for because the ending of the state in bourgeois theories of globalization takes place within the existing class relations. In *Anti-Dühring* Engels argues that in a revolutionary situation the proletariat

> abolishes itself as proletariat, abolishes all class distinctions and class antagonisms, abolishes also the state as state. Society thus far, based upon class antagonisms, had need of the state, that is, of an organisation of the particular class, which was *pro tempore* the exploiting class, for the maintenance of its external conditions of production, and, therefore, especially, for the purpose of forcibly keeping the exploited classes in the condition of oppression corresponding with the given mode of production (slavery, serfdom, wage-labour). The state was the official representative of society as a whole; the gathering of it together into a visible embodiment. But it was this only in so far as it was the state of that class which itself represented, for the time being, society as a whole: in ancient times, the state of slave-owning citizens; in the Middle Ages, the feudal lords; in our own time, the bourgeoisie. When at last it becomes the real representative of the whole of society, it renders itself unnecessary. As soon as there is no longer any social class to be held in subjection; as soon as class rule, and the individual struggle for existence based upon our present anarchy in production, with the collisions and excesses arising from these, are removed, nothing more remains to be repressed, and a special repressive force, a state, is no longer necessary. The first act by virtue of which the state really constitutes itself the representative of the whole of society—the taking possession of the means of production in the name of society—this is, at the same time, its last independent act as a state. State interference in social relations becomes, in one domain after another, superfluous, and then dies out of itself; the government of persons is replaced by the administration of things, and by the conduct of processes of production. The state is not "abolished." *It dies out.* (267–68)

Lenin interprets Engels's distinction between the state's being "abolished" and its withering away by emphasizing Engels's own use of *abolish* at the beginning of this passage: "according to Engels, the bourgeois state does not 'wither away,' but is 'abolished' by the proletariat in the course of revolution. What withers away after this revolution is the proletarian state or semi-state" (*State and Revolution* 397).

The state withers away not because capitalism becomes global and finance capital becomes the source of wealth but because capitalism itself comes to an end. This brings about the end of class rule and a cessation of the inequities of property relations protected by the state. The state withers away in the absence of classes because the state is the effect of class relations and an agent of the ruling class. Without the ruling class there is no need for the state.

However, the end of the nation-state in contemporary cultural critique takes place within class relations. Such theories obscure class relations by declaring the end of what Jameson dismissively calls the "productionist model" of culture, in which culture is seen as the superstructure of a material base (*Postmodernism* 406). They are, in other words, consumptionist theories. By announcing the end of the state (class), they persuade people to free themselves from their national and local identities and seek an ever new, transforming, and variegated ("deconstructed") identity in lifestyles fashioned by consumption. Consumption is therefore portrayed in Left cultural critiques as an activist social intervention: one changes society through one's lifestyle, not by revolution. Consumption, which is the lifeblood of capital, is inverted in normal cultural critique and represented as a resistance against capitalism, thus making it part of the progressive struggles for a different world (Yudice, *Expediency of Culture*; Canclini, *Consumers and Citizens*). As in almost all other aspects of globalization theory, Left and Right merge in their support of capital by depicting consumption as a new form of production. The consumer is constructed in these stories as an active subject whose practices are described (in Left discourses) as "producerly" (Fiske, *Reading the Popular* 107) and who is named a "prosumer" (in Right-wing discourses)—an agent whose activities in the globalized world overcome the divide between consumers and producers created by industrial capitalism and the nation-state (Toffler, *Powershift* 233).

I call this corporate theory of globalization *transnationalism*. It is a globalization that is represented, in Thomas Frank's words, as the "end object of human civilization," a process that "would make us rich, set us free, and generally elevate everything and everyone everywhere" (Frank, *One Market under God* 65). This version of globalization is the effect of the global North's capitalist triumphalism, which compels the "other," in the words of Marx and Engels, "to introduce what it calls civilization into their midst, i.e. to become bourgeois themselves. In a word, it creates a world after its own image" (*Manifesto* 488). It connects people of the world through the uniformity of cultural signs, which are the signs of products; it is a transborder regime of the pleasures of consumption. In transnationalist globalization, culture, not labor, (class) is said to be the dynamic of history as the "economy is becoming dominated by lifestyle choices" (Waters, *Globalization* 24).

In contemporary cultural critique, culture itself is no longer a "way of *struggle*," as E. P. Thompson notes in his critique of Raymond Williams ("Long Revolution" 33), but instead is regarded as an autonomous discourse of oceanic affectivity, "flows of preferences, taste and information" (Waters, *Globalization* 24) and "aesthetic products" (56) because "in a global economic market that has no centre there might be no place in which classes can confront one another" (54).

Internationalism and a New Cultural Critique

Theories of globalization as transnationalism now dominate normal cultural critique, but they occlude the fundamental issues involved in globalization. They claim, for example, that it is "revolutionizing the means of consumption," in the words of George Ritzer, who describes the new world order as the "McDonaldization" of the world (*Enchanting a Disenchanted World*). According to this view the globalized world is a transcultural, eclectic consumption regime that Lyotard parodically describes as one in which "one listens to reggae, watches a western, eats McDonald's food for lunch and local cuisine for dinner, wears Paris perfume in Tokyo and 'retro' clothes in Hong Kong" (*Postmodern Condition* 76). The new world community envisioned in these theories is the community of taste, preferences, and sensibilities.

The transborder territories needed for the free movement of capital are legitimated by these theories' declaration of a post-state world in which human rights are no longer a local issue but a trans-state concern. They argue that the interventions in Bosnia and Kosovo, for example, transcended local nation-state sovereignty to put a stop to genocide or that "regime change" in Iraq was a transnational matter of bringing freedom to people and liberating them from repression by widening the circles of democracy and the rule of law. What is missing from these narratives is that the goal of the intervention—made in the name of human rights—was to free a huge market for global capital, to make energy resources accessible for capital and, most important, to make a sizeable pool of highly skilled but very cheap labor available to it. Where there is no prospect of immediate return for transnational capital, as, for example, in Rwanda, there is no immediate intervention in the name of human rights, either. Human rights are used as a banner for the globalization of exploitation. Transnational theories of globalization are an apologetics for imperialism, a word that is now taboo in cultural critique.

In order to understand what is at stake in globalization and what causes its discontent, it is necessary to go beyond the politico-cultural issues and focus on materialist factors such as labor, class, and exploitation. Some Left theorists, such as Immanuel Wallerstein and Andre Gunder Frank, who are associated with the "world system" and "dependency" perspectives on globalization, have discussed material forces but have interpreted the material to mean trade and markets (as do many neoliberals to their political right). Wallerstein, for instance, regards the capitalist world system to be divided into three zones: the core, the semiperiphery, and the periphery. Each is distinguished from the others by the reach and strength of the state because that is what guarantees the transfer of surplus value and also stands behind capital. He writes that "actors in the market" try to "avoid the normal operation of the market whenever it does not maximize their profit" by deploying state power (*Capitalist World Economy* 95). Imperialism is understood as the logic of the relations among states and the powerful "core" that systematically promotes underdevelopment in the "periphery." In "world system" theory, it is "trade" and not "class" that matters.

I argue that globalization is a struggle over global surplus labor. Contrary to the claims of hegemonic cultural critique, the dynamics of globalization are not new means of communication, such as satellite networks, fax machines, and e-mail. To see the means of communication as the cause of globalization is to make ideology the cause of social change and, in effect, erase labor. This is, of course, what conservative ideologues have done. I have already quoted Derrida concerning the relation between television and democracy. Ronald Reagan made a similar point in his speech to the English Speaking Union: "The communications revolution will be the greatest force for the advancement of human freedom," with the "David of the microchip," photocopiers, and fax machines bringing down the "Goliath of totalitarianism" (Rule, "Reagan Gets Red Carpet" n.p.). Globalization is not a historical mutation, a sudden structural change in capitalism, nor is it an event of discontinuity such as the transformation of Fordism to post-Fordism. It is not the effect of the emergence of a network society, nor is it a shift in the phenomenology of exploitation (from Taylorism to Toyotaism and the reflexive workshop). It is not a matter of changing the status of states, nor the emergence of nongovernmental organizations. Nor is it the expansion of human rights and other legal, political, or cultural matters. These are all effects of the more fundamental processes of the relations of labor and capital.

Globalization is the unfolding of the fundamental contradiction in capitalism, namely, the extraction of surplus labor from the worker—the separation of the worker from the product of her labor—and capital's need to constantly increase the rate of this exploitation in order to raise the rate of profit. Globalization does not begin with this or that geographical discovery that expands the world, as Nayan Chanda argues (*Bound Together*) or with this or that communication technology connecting the unconnected, or with changing the status of the sovereignty of the state.

Rather, it begins with the commodification of labor power itself when human labor becomes a commodity like all others and is exchanged for wages. Capital needs this commodity, whose consumption is the source of value, and conquers the globe to control it. This is why imperialism is a structural feature of capitalism.

In the most simple terms, globalization is the expansion of the commodification of labor on a world scale because it is the only source of capital's profit. In *Capital* Marx gives a detailed analysis of this historical-economic matter and writes that labor power is the only commodity "whose use-value possesses the peculiar property of being a source of value, whose actual consumption, therefore, is itself an embodiment of labor and consequently a creation of value" (1: 164). With the commodification of labor, the ownership of the means of production is thoroughly privatized and the stage is set for competitive capitalism. Capitalism is a social relation based on the accumulation of profit, and profits are obtained by fighting the workers to lower the cost of labor (for example, lowering wages, extending working hours, and the digitalization of labor), allowing the capitalist to compete with other capitalists This requires that the capitalist invest in machinery (that is, constant capital).The more advanced capitalism becomes, the more is invested in machinery. As a result, the organic composition of capital—the ratio between C (constant capital = machinery) and V (variable capital = labor)—changes, and C becomes higher (*Capital* 1: 574ff.). But profit is not produced by machines; it is produced by labor, which means that in order to compete successfully, the capitalist must have access to cheap labor. "Profit and wages," Marx writes, are "in inverse proportion" (*Wage Labour and Capital* 39). Globalization is the process by which capitalists gain access to cheap labor and maintain their competitive rate of profit. Contrary to "world system" theory, which places the market and consumption at the center, Marx writes that profit is "the main factor, not of the distribution of products, but of their production" (*Capital* 3: 1022).

The process of the globalization of exploitation—the ready access to surplus labor—sets in motion a highly complex set of secondary processes. These involve not only transforming the sovereignty of the nation-state, making it into a poststate entity, but also such other changes as developing global postnational banking and investment laws, deregulating markets, altering environmental regulations, and reorganizing the universities. The cultural and political changes that mark globalization are effects of the internationalization of the social relations of production. Normal cultural critique, however, focuses on the effects and suspends all causes because it has already jettisoned the idea of cause. The *Manifesto of the Communist Party*, which puts forth the first materialist theorization of globalization, discusses these cultural and political changes at length:

> The bourgeoisie cannot exist without constantly revolutionizing the instruments of production, and thereby the relations of production, and with them the whole relations of society. Conservation of the old modes of production in unaltered form was, on the contrary, the first condition of existence for all earlier industrial classes. Constant revolutionizing of production, uninterrupted disturbance of all social conditions, everlasting uncertainty and agitation distinguish the bourgeois epoch from all earlier ones. All fixed, fast-frozen relations, with their train of ancient and venerable prejudices and opinions, are swept away, all new-formed ones become antiquated before they can ossify. All that is solid melts into air, all that is holy is profaned, and man is at last compelled to face with sober senses his real conditions of life, and his relations with his kind.
>
> The need of a constantly expanding market for its products chases the bourgeoisie over the whole surface of the globe. It must nestle everywhere, settle everywhere, establish connexions everywhere.
>
> The bourgeoisie has through its exploitation of the world-market given a cosmopolitan character to production and consumption in every country. To the great chagrin of Reactionists, it has drawn from under the feet of industry the national ground on which it stood. All old-established national industries have been destroyed or are daily being destroyed. They are dislodged by new industries, whose introduction becomes a life and death question for all civilized nations, by industries that no longer work up indigenous raw material, but raw material drawn from the remotest zones; industries whose products are consumed, not only at home, but in every quarter of the globe. In place of the old wants, satisfied by the productions of the country, we find new wants, requiring for their satisfaction the products of distant lands and climes. In place of the old local and national seclusion and self-sufficiency, we have intercourse in every direction, universal inter-dependence of nations. And as in material, so also in intellectual production. The intellectual creations of individual nations become common property. National one-sidedness and narrow-mindedness become more and more impossible, and from the numerous national and local literatures, their arises a world literature. (487–88)

Globalization is a dialectical process, and as Marx and Engels argue in the *Manifesto*, the historical forces that move capitalism toward transnational centralization (which is what globalization actually is, contrary to Hardt and Negri's *Empire*) also produce an antagonistic proletarian "internationalism." Against transnational capital rises international labor, which is the other globalization: *globalization as internationalism.* Whereas transnationalism is rooted in trade and markets, internationalism is grounded in production and a rising international class solidarity; it is the effect of collectivity in production, not individualism in consumption.

Contrary to official propaganda (for example, the slogan "A rising tide lifts all boats"), transnational globalization in no way remedies class injustice but, rather, reinforces class relations. That it provides jobs for some of the jobless, as its proponents frequently state, does not mean that it changes the social relations of production. More jobless people may now have jobs, but they are still exploited. Transnational globalization legitimates exploitation and it naturalizes remaking the world as a global sweatshop for capital by depicting capital as the means for lifting the poor of the world out of their abject condition. Consequently, as Thomas Frank notes, global capital, in its populist discourses, portrays all who oppose it as "seeking to deprive the vastly more numerous people of the Third World of the ability to make a decent living" (*One Market under God* 239).

The internationalization of class relations unleashes and unites forces that were previously separate. The artificial boundaries of "nation" and "nationality" that so far have separated the workers of the world are transformed, and people see what capitalist ideology has effectively prevented them from seeing: class, not nation, is the basis of human solidarity; "working people have no country." In spite of itself, globalization gives rise to internationalism, which is the basis of solidarity for constructing a classless society, not because this is the aim of globalization but because this is the force of history.

It is through international class struggles and not the affective Franciscan activism of the "multitude" (Hardt and Negri, *Empire* 60–66, 209–18, 396–407; *Multitude* 97–227) that it is possible to effectively challenge transnational capitalism and support the struggles of an internationalist class subject for emancipation from necessity. Along with these struggles, a new cultural critique is needed: a critique that can demystify everyday consciousness, which is shaped by the immediate empirical actualities of transnational capital, and instead produce a critical and class consciousness about globalization. Such a materialist critique has to indicate, for example, that globalization as internationalism is part of the progress of history toward freedom from necessity and that struggles against transnationalism need to be conducted not by fighting corporations (as advocated by the anarcho-bourgeois, anti-globalization movement) but by overthrowing wage labor.

Globalization, Empire, and Imperialism

Transnationalism obscures the workings of imperialism—how it institutes wage labor and the "free market" throughout the globalized world—and argues instead that imperialism is the "extension of the sovereignty of European nation-states beyond their boundaries" (Hardt and Negri, *Empire* xii). If the globalized world is no longer organized around the sovereignty of the nation-state, then imperialism, for such critics, is displaced by a decentered empire. In other words, imperialism is seen as a political accident of the nation-state and not a structural feature of capitalism. In short, for theories of globalization as transnationalism, capitalism is not identical with imperialism. "Business leaders around the world," according to Michel Hardt, "recognize that imperialism is bad for business because it sets up barriers that hinder global flow" ("Folly of Our Masters" n.p.). This is not an eccentric view but the shared sentiment of the North-Left. In *End of Capitalism (As We Knew It)*, for instance, we read that "some capitalist instances may be quite acceptable" and that if we carefully examine the contexts and conditions of capitalist practices, "we might cease to speak of capitalist imperialism as though empire were an aspect of capitalism's identity" (Gibson-Graham, *End of Capitalism* 247). In *Iraq: The Borrowed Kettle*, Žižek regards imperialism as essentially a political matter, one that he seems to think is best dealt with by means of a cultural decoding that draws on jokes, the unconscious (for instance, Rumsfeld's "forgetting" the "unknown knowns") and, as always, allegorical allusions to "the Real," which always exceeds reality, thus turning it into yet another occasion for the knowing smile of cynical critique. Yet imperialism is more active today than it has been since the rise of capitalism. Capitalism is constitutive of imperialism, through which it violently appropriates the global social surplus labor. Imperialism, in other words, is not a political event in a world of nation-states: it is capitalism's essence. Imperialism is indeed the highest stage of capitalism (Lenin, *Imperialism*).

Although Hardt and Negri, among many others, depict their views as new, their ideas about imperialism simply update a very old Kautskian view that capitalism was to "enter upon a new phase, a phase marked by the transfer of trust methods to international politics, a sort of super-imperialism" or post-imperialist modality (Kautsky, "Imperialism and the War" n.p.). The idea of an ultraimperialism is now the master theory of the Left; it is grounded in the notion that imperialism is not "the highest stage of capitalism" but the effect of intrastate conflicts that, Kautsky maintains, are contrary to the interests of capitalism. The invasions of Afghanistan and Iraq in the early twenty-first century have, of course, turned these Left theories of imperialism into a political joke. The ideological implications of empire as a new centerless world in Hardt and Negri are made clear in Malcolm Waters's argument that in a global world "that has no center there might be no place in which classes can confront one another" (*Globalization* 56). *Empire* is the name of a new business space free from class antagonism.

In the empire without class, the worker, as the agent of history, is replaced by the "multitude," representing the new revolutionary, what Hardt and Negri call the "militant"—"the agent of biopolitical production and resistance" (*Empire* 411). The activism of the new revolutionary is decidedly anti-Leninist: it is based not on "duty or discipline" or deduced from an "ideal plan" but is a cultural intervention that "makes resistance into a counterpower and makes rebellion into a project of love" (413). To put it differently, the militant is the "expresser" of "love" and actor of "rebellion" who rejects Lenin and embraces Saint Francis of Assisi. Saint Francis is exemplary for Hardt and Negri because his practices form a performativity of an affective ethicopolitics ("love," "hospitality") that they call a new "communism."

Saint Francis of Assisi is represented as the empire's cosmopolitan communist of love who adopts poverty in order to feel the condition of the multitude from within and affectively "discovers"—without the mediation of any conceptual analytics—"the ontological power of a new society" (*Empire* 413). Francis denounces "discipline" and becomes an activist of desire ("joyous life") as a means for building a "new" communist community that includes "sister moon, brother sun" (413) and reminds us how we "in our postmodernity" are in his situation. Through this spiritual militancy, with its strong religious aroma, Hardt and Negri produce history as a cultural posthistory, a series of "immaterial" returns (twenty-first-century capitalism and twelfth-century Catholicism are spiritually alike) that eternalize the values of the upper classes of the contemporary North.

Francis is the saint of the new globalization because he normalizes poverty, making it acceptable as a universal mode of living. What is mystified in Hardt and Negri's rewriting of the poverty of Saint Francis and the lessons it can teach the new militant multitude is that his is a *voluntary* poverty—he is the son of a wealthy cloth merchant—that has nothing in common with the poverty of those whose poverty is the direct consequence of imposed class relations. But by turning voluntary poverty into an affective politics (what Hardt and Negri familiarize by the popular term *biopolitics*), Francis makes social change more difficult: if poverty is not only the means of spiritual attainment and inner happiness but also the way to a joyous life, there is no reason at all for social struggle for material equality. In fact, this is the ideology of contemporary transnational globalization. The new global militant is a nomadic Franciscan bourgeois who teaches love, class reconciliation, and holy poverty in place of class struggle for equality: "This is the irrepressible lightness and joy of being [a Fransciscan] communist" (413). The joy of this "true" communism is intensified in the writings of Alain Badiou through the teachings of Saint Paul (*Saint Paul*) and by Žižek's embrace of Christianity in *The Puppet and the Dwarf* and *The Parallax View.* Žižek represents the Pauline community as a collective for making revolution by using a kynicism that reduces revolution to a metaphor of the soul, a spiritual play without referent.

Globalization and Cynical Consciousness

The struggle against transnational globalization and for international class solidarity, however, is not an automatic outcome of history. It requires the development of class consciousness and knowledge of history and theory to learn how to act in a revolutionary historical situation. The advance of class consciousness, however, has been thwarted by one of capital's most effective cultural strategies: the cultivation, both in philosophical and popular culture discourses, of cynical consciousness, which diffuses class consciousness with a wry smile as a mark of its strategic cunning and tactical savviness. Before discussing the working of this cynical consciousness as a normalization of globalization in the writings of Slavoj Žižek, I want to briefly outline the architecture of cynical consciousness and its main strategy of containment, namely, the hybrid interpretations situated in the indeterminate space between cynicism and kynicism. I then argue that a particular mode of cynicism, *hypercynicism*, has become one of the main strategies for the containment and legitimization of capitalism in its global moment, and the writings of Žižek exemplify this move.

Although cynicism is practiced by individuals, it is not an individual matter but a historical condition that Hegel calls the "unhappy, inwardly disrupted consciousness" (*Phenomenology of Spirit* 126). The "unhappy consciousness" is rent within itself because of the conflicts between its knowledge of the "unchangeable"—the principled truth—and its practice, which is derived from the "changeable," the "things of this world." The "unhappy consciousness," Hegel argues, always locates itself in "things of this world" but never forgets its yearning for the unchangeable—the principled truth. In other words, it is the consciousness of the divided subject, torn between the contradictions of what it "knows" and what it "does." This is the schism that Marx and Engels, in *The German Ideology,* understand as constitutive of bourgeois consciousness, which is oscillating in the gap between "theory" and "praxis" and is caused, Marx argues, by what he describes as the alienation of labor (*Manuscripts of 1844* 270–82).

Cynicism is the logic of pragmatism. It opportunistically deploys ideas and beliefs in order to secure its place in the things of this world—to get things done within the existing class structures of access and privilege. Cynical reason is the other of class consciousness. Like Readings's emptying Thought of all referents, Žižek opportunistically redefines politics as a practice without empirical contents ("Class Struggle or Postmodernism?"). As might be expected, he is formally against both what he calls "pure politics" and "post-politics" (*Revolution at the Gates,* 263–76, 297–305), but he practices both according to the situation at hand.

To act politically—for example, to fight transnational globalization because it is plundering the surplus labor of the workers of the world—is to commit oneself to a practice founded on a principle, as Lenin argues in *What Is to Be Done?* But the very idea of a principle brings a smirk to the face of the cynical. This is one reason why Žižek, in *Revolution at the Gates,* rewrites Lenin as a situationist, a post-principle man who only acts strategically. To act in terms of principles is to take risks. The cynic protects herself by depoliticizing the political (reducing it to strategies) and argues that all principles are epistemologically suspect because they are foundationalist, lead to totalization, and erase difference. The cynic reads principle as a performative desire and treats it as a fiction of pleasure to be enjoyed but not taken seriously because seriousness is a pathology. Instead, the cynic advises acting situationally and strategically within the prevailing economies of meanings and the social arrangements they support. She avoids confronting the present social injustice by speculating about a state "to come" (for example, Derrida, *Specters of Marx, Politics of Friendship*). In doing so, she guarantees that things will stay as they are (because she benefits from the existing social relations). In the name of resistance to totalization and honoring the heterogeneous, the cynic obscures the dominant class relations by translating them into cultural difference. In the hybrid spaces of his "Plea for a Return to *Difference,*" for example, Žižek treats the political as a recognition of the singular by diffusing its class constitution into an ethico-ontological effect. Politics, in the writings of the cynical, is always an occasion for speculation and the accumulation of cultural capital. Such speculations are located in the in-betweenness of cynicism and kynicism (Sloterdijk, *Critique of Cynical Reason* 217–18).

Sloterdijk argues that "cynicism is enlightened false consciousness. It is that modernized, unhappy consciousness on which enlightenment has labored. . . . Well-off and miserable at the same time" (*Critique of Cynical Reason* 5). For Sloterdijk, however, cynicism is not simply a divided consciousness but rather a complex one: a savvy double consciousness that lives subtly in the in-betweenness of the cynical and what he calls the "kynical," in other words, the ludic. Hegel, of course, anticipates such a reading and argues that, among other things, "The unhappy consciousness itself is the gazing of one self-consciousness into another, and itself is both" (126). Self-reflexive, enlightened false consciousness supersedes its own falseness by knowing that it is false. In elaborating on this meta-consciousness, Žižek writes that "with a disarming frankness one 'admits everything', yet this full acknowledgement of our power interests does not in any way prevent us from pursuing these interests—the formula of cynicism is no longer the classic Marxian 'they do not know it, but they are doing it'; it is 'they know very well what they are doing, yet they are doing it'" ("Spectre" 8).

An example of a sophisticated de-politicization of politics through the play of the kynical and in the name of antiessentialism is Judith Butler's writing about the political and her parody of classical Marxism. In her widely circulated and popular attack on "Left Conservatism"—her code for classical Marxism—in her essay "Merely Cultural," Butler claims that the Marxist insistence on class in the realm of sexuality is a repression of sexuality, in general, and queer sexuality, in particular. According to Butler, the "charge . . . that a unified and progressive Marxism must return to a materialism based in an objective analysis of class . . . marks" the "resurgence of a certain kind of theoretical anachronism." This leads to the "resurgence of a leftist orthodoxy" that, she says, "work[s] in tandem with a social and sexual conservatism that seeks to make questions of race and sexuality secondary to the 'real' business of politics, producing a new and eerie political formation of neo-conservative Marxisms" ("Merely Cultural" 268).

The cynical consciousness is an excluding consciousness; it designates the noncynic as an outdated epistemological realist who has no place in the order of the "new" reality ("Merely Cultural" 266). Those who oppose Butler's liberal eclecticism and insist on the priority of class over all other social differences—because all social differences, regardless of their cultural identity, are ultimately and always differences of access to material resources and are constructed at the point of production—are marked by her as part of a "theoretical anachronism" that adheres to an equally "anachronistic" materialism (268). Anyone who critiques Butler's position for being "merely cultural" is thus banished in her discourse, delegated to the nonbeing of a nontruth (an "anachronism"). To be clear, in Butler's argument, which is ostensibly a defense of difference, the dissenter (the different) becomes an "error" in time, an instance of the nontruth and thus the "improper."

The cynic, in other words, appoints herself as the norm while smiling at the very idea of the normative. She is the proper-in-time while calling into question the very notion of the proper (Derrida, *Margins of Philosophy*; Butler, *Precarious Life*). Accordingly, only Butler herself is the "proper" truth of time, an "in time" (*khronizein*). The cynic, who smiles at the binary opposition of class as an outdated concept, reproduces with a vengeance the binary of in-time/out-of-time in order to protect her own class interests. The binary, which is ultimately the binary of the material relations of classes, haunts the formal antibinary discourses, which attempt to purge class using the excuse of epistemology. The return of the binary to Butler's "properly" antibinarian declaration (in-time/out-of-time) affirms the historical inevitability of class difference under capital. The cynic, faced with the stubbornness of history and class, takes refuge in kynical savviness. Kynicism, however, does not conceal the fact that Butler acts as the all-knower in-time who is in the fullness of an identitarian plenitude with absolute coherence as the truth of the time, who is the Master of Chronometrics: the rationality (correct measurement) of time. "Merely Cultural" is the postabsolute absolutism that is always at work in the class politics of post-politics.

Butler's kynical alternative to what she calls an anachronistic Left conservatism, with its "objective analysis of class," is a political parody in which she deploys mimicry to empty Marxism of its revolutionary class politics. She performs what she calls a "temporary identification" that involves a "certain ability to identify, approximate, and draw near; it engages an intimacy with the position it appropriates that troubles the voice, the bearing, the performativity of the subject such that the audience or reader does not quite know where it is you stand" ("Merely Cultural" 266). Butler is engaging in a kind of political cross-dressing, a Marxism in drag, in which she temporarily dons Marxist positions and materialist principles, only to shed them even before her performance ends. She plays with historical materialism—taking "the mode of production as the defining structure of political economy" and arguing "that sexuality must be understood as part of that mode of production" (273)—

and then, in a cynical, parodic move, turns Marxism on its head when she attributes to it a "remanufacturing" of the "distinction between the material and the cultural . . . that jettisons sexuality from the sphere of fundamental political structure!" (274). In other words, she turns Marxism into a masquerade, erasing its complex dialectical understanding of the relation of culture to the material base.

One defense of Butler is that hers is a purely kynical performative. For Sloterdijk the kynical is the resistance to cynicism; it is the provocative resistance of "pantomimic, wily . . . individualism" (218) and involves the cheeky, irreverent actions of a defiant body. But as a viable political strategy, the kynical is indeterminate. As Andreas Huyssen points out, "the kynic can no longer be distinguished from the cynic. Is Sloterdijk displaying kynical strategies or cynical attitudes? It is anybody's guess" ("Foreword" xxi). Butler's cynico-kynical critique translates globalization into the question of the state and, in doing so, displaces class, labor, and value by discussing the fluidity of the boundaries of the state, the contingency of the nation, and (liberal) human rights (Butler and Spivak, *Who Sings the Nation State*). The burning issue is not the appropriation of global surplus labor but the singing of "The Star-Spangled Banner" in Spanish.

Cynical reason critiques class as a metaphysical fiction without any objective grounding because the objective itself is considered to be a fiction of the will to truth. In order to show this, it textualizes class by claiming, first, that like all concepts, class is merely a trope without any authority over the reality of a referent (de Man, *Allegories* 135–59), and, second, that class is not a difference between the bourgeoisie and the proletariat (because such a betweenness presupposes stable identities for the two terms of the opposition) but a difference within itself. The differences that, according to a materialist theory of class, exist between owners and workers is displaced onto a difference within each group. Each class is more at odds with itself than with another class. In other words, there is more difference within the proletariat, in this culturalist (linguistic) view, than there is between the proletariat and the bourgeoisie. The proletariat, in this kynical script, is a parody of itself because it is more a sign in playful oscillation than an economic category with a stable referent.

In spite of all its linguistic aggressiveness, however, Butler's cynico-kynicism is within the conventional codes of philosophy. These codes are brought to the breaking point in the more recent writings of Slavoj Žižek, who writes mostly about the same traditional texts as Butler, Derrida and other cynics. But Žižek's interpretations take cynicism to a higher and more intense level. I call this level *hypercynicism,* which is a response to the increasing class contradictions of capitalism—contradictions that can no longer be effectively contained by the interpretive strategies of cynics such as Derrida, Butler, and Gallop. In order to understand his cynical practices, one has to first analyze Žižek's position in the contemporary Left and the place of his hypercynicism in the order of new cynicisms. Cynicism is not a personal attitude but a historical condition; it is a response to the more complex processes in the material base of an increasingly more global capitalism. Through cynicism, kynicism, and hypercynicism—cultural manipulations with knowing smiles—capitalism discursively "solves" its material class contradictions.

Capitalism needs legitimization by the Left as much as it needs justification by the Right. In order for capitalism to maintain its self-representation as a regime of democratic equality, it has to have, if not a consensus, at least a cultural commonsense that assumes that although capitalism is not perfect, other social and economic regimes are worse. In establishing such a commonsense, Left critics have played and continue to play a significant role because any support they show is interpreted as a concession to and affirmation of opponents and, as such, carries much more cultural authority than the expected Right-wing relegitimization and defense of capitalism.

The problem, however, is the "Left" that capitalism has relied on since the end of the cold war—namely, the liberal Left, the New Left, neomarxism, and most significant, postmarxism—have all lost their analytical credibility and cultural authority to varying degrees. Their analyses explain little of historical and social significance and tend to repeat familiar liberal themes in ever more seductive idioms that are aimed at shocking the bourgeoisie rather than advancing knowledge of the social. The writings of Left authors continue to give rhetorical pleasure to their readers: the more they have avoided confronting the class realities of the times, the more linguistically subtle and pleasing these texts have become. They have turned into sophisticated entertainment rather than effective work toward transformation of existing social relations. In a short note on Žižek's *Sublime Object of Ideology,* for example, a reviewer called it "the best intellectual high since *Anti-Oedipus*" (*Voice Literary Supplement,* December 1990, 13). Nowadays, one reads such Left writers as Derrida, Laclau, Mouffe, Butler, Badiou, and Agamben mostly for amusement and finds humor in their making what they seem to think of as "'world shattering' statements," to use the words of Marx and Engels in their critique of Hegelian Left adventurism (*German Ideology*). The most familiar examples of this textually rich but conceptually blank analysis are Michael Hardt and Antonio Negri's *Empire* and its sequel *Multitude*, in which the analysis of the contemporary situation has turned out to be as funny and seductive, but ultimately vacuous, as the political analyses in *Vanity Fair*. The most radical acts of postmarxists today seem to have become annotations of the theories of democracy in Nazi writers such as Carl Schmitt (Mouffe, *Return of the Political*; Derrida, *Politics of Friendship*; Agamben, *State of Exception*) or retreats to the liberalism of Hannah Arendt (Butler, "I Merely Belong to Them").

Capitalism now needs a different Left: one that can produce less overtly trivial analyses, an analytically believable Left that can act under the banner of the revolution and evoke a seemingly materialist Marxism and Leninism as its guiding principle. It needs a Left that can write in the idioms of dialectical and historical materialism because the jargons of identity, multiculturalism, queer theory, ludic feminism, and cultural antiracism have lost their cultural cover and are now seen as what they have always been: liberal platitudes deployed to normalize existing social relations. These discourses simply cannot explain the complex material differences that overwhelm the everyday and instead, through a sleight of tropes, substitute discussions of cultural differences for the class contradictions that cause them. Capitalism now needs a robust neomaterialist Left that can engage class and at the same time defuse it as a social problem. It requires a Left that can offer a new, believable legitimacy to capital in a world that is more than ever before torn by class antagonism, yet can do so without in any serious way challenging capitalism's fundamental principle, namely, taking the surplus labor of the workers of the world.

Derrida's later work was aimed at producing such a Left, but his writings were too firmly rooted in the textual order to be useful. As Geoffrey Bennington notes, "At the 1995 'Applied Derrida' conference in Luton, . . . in a general discussion with Derrida, an irritated participant demanded that Derrida say 'what he really thought' about Marx; when politely pointed by Derrida to *Specters of Marx*, the now angry participant replied that he'd read that, but wanted to know what Derrida *really thought* about Marx" ("Derrida and Politics" 210, emphasis in original). In spite of Bennington's seeming intention to discredit the questioner, the question remains, which means capitalism needs more complex strategies than Derrida was able to muster. In the age of neoimperialism, deconstruction is an evasion.

Žižek is the theorist of this neomaterialist Left. Žižek's writings, especially the more recent texts, are responses to the new needs of transnational capitalism and are infused by lessons learned from Derrida's failure.

These are subtle two-track texts of confirmation by deletion: on one track revolutionary language is evoked ("A Leninist Gesture Today"), and on the other all concepts that support and explain revolution (class, the labor theory of value, democratic centralism, and so on) are eviscerated.

Žižek's first task as the messiah (without messianism) of this new, seemingly materialist Left has been to break the "false idols" by clearing away the debris of the new Left, the neo-Left, and the post-Left. Žižek, therefore, has fought social movements (for example, in his arguments against Judith Butler in *Contingency, Hegemony, Universality*, where he reads her gender theories as a version of liberalism) and, perhaps more significant, has conducted a discursive war against the postmarxism of Ernesto Laclau. In his treatment the "post-politics" of the mainstream Left, Žižek sets up a new analytics that echoes (classical) Marxist concepts in its nomenclature but is strangely void of their explanatory power. It is a Marxism beyond Marxism not in its Negrian sense (Negri, *Marx Beyond Marx*), but a beyond of excess and unrepresentability that finds its theoretical ground in the Lacanian Real, which is itself a Hegelian narrative related by Kojeve ("Dialectic of the Real").

It is by appealing to the Lacanian Real, for example, that Žižek reduces class to sheer spectrality, hollowing it out, removing all its historical and material content. Class binaries—the opposition between the bourgeoisie and the proletariat—are unraveled, according to him, and class as a revolutionary analytical concept (that is, as a relation to ownership of the means of production) is thus brought to ruin because of the spontaneous emergence of "a third element which does not 'fit' this opposition, (*lumpenproletariat,* etc.)" ("Class Struggle or Postmodernism" 132). For Žižek, in other words, *lumpenproletariat* is an ontoepistemological excess (not a historical outcome of the social division of labor) whose presence breaks the class binary and turns the concept of class into an errant trope. He does not overtly dismiss class and, in fact, uses it as a point of difference with respect to Ernesto Laclau, who aims at a more straightforward deconstruction of classes ("Deconstructing Classes" 296–301). But this is hypercynicism at its most subtly aggressive: Žižek makes class an impossibility, specifically, the impossibility of the Real to be realized on the symbolic level (in the Lacanian sense). To be more clear, what matters to him is not actual historical class relations but that "the very constitution of social reality involves the 'primordial repression' of an antagonism," which means that for him the question of class is not a question of "'reality' but the 'repressed' real of antagonism." He therefore insists on the "interpretation of social antagonism (class struggle) as Real, not as (part of) objective social reality" ("Spectre"

25). Class struggle is thus dissolved into an ahistorical Real of "social antagonism," which Žižek describes as a "constant," the "non-symbolizable traumatic kernel that found expression in the very distortions of reality, in the fantasized displacements of the 'actual' . . . in the guise of spectral apparitions" (26). His cynico-kynical miming, what he calls "this 'return to Marx,'" entails "a radical displacement of the Marxian theoretical edifice: a gap emerges in the very heart of historical materialism" (28). This kynical gap, of course, is the dissolution of class struggle into "spectrality." "Class struggle," Žižek declares, "is none other than the name for the unfathomable limit that cannot be objectivized" (22).

Žižek's emptying class of its material reality (while asserting the existence of class against the ludic Left) is the main unsaid in his theory of transnational globalization and his opposition to internationalism. If language theorists such as Derrida and Laclau critique class with an ironic smile by pointing to the slippages of its referent, Žižek's critique of class is carried out in a space of panic. It is the panic of "enlightened" persons who do not want to be "taken for suckers," as Sloterdijk says (*Critique* 5), and who develop, as a mode of survival, a "permanent doubt about their own activities" (5). This is the reality of the unhappy consciousness that knows but cannot act on what it knows. In his reading of class, Žižek parodies Marx and turns a materialist ideology critique—which is a cultural element of class struggle, as Marx argues in *A Contribution to the Critique of Political Economy*—upside down, making it into a Hegelian idealism. Consequently, he dissolves class struggle into the surplus of the Real, a surplus that can not be contained in any representation (the symbolic). The outcome of Žižek's neomaterialism is that the binary theory of class is quietly converted into a Weberian plurality, and class antagonism is dissolved into life chances in the market. Revolutionary class struggles, which develop at the point of production, are dissipated by the codes of an idealist psychoanalysis into the pleasures of consumption (market). A politics without class is a cynical politics.

Not only is class gutted in Žižek's neomaterialism, but materialism itself is dematerialized, and dialectics is reduced to a kynical différance at the same time Žižek promotes his own version of the social by announcing that "Derridean fashion" is "fading away" (*Parallax View* 11). After Derrida and with a gesture to the subtractive theory of Alain Badiou, Žižek cynically rewrites dialectical materialism—in the name of what he calls a "rehabilitation," which apparently makes him a social healer and cultural conciliator (4)—as a difference-within, a self-difference that he calls a "parallax gap" (4), namely, the "inherent 'tension,' gap, noncoincidence, of the One itself" that separates one from one (7). The

parallax gap diffuses social class antagonism into a containable immanent rift and makes impossible any knowledge of totality; the one that
is always missing makes totality an incomplete project (shades of Laclau
and Mouffe, *Hegemony and Socialist Strategy* 122–27). The parallax gap,
to put it differently, dismantles dialectical materialism as the analytics
of an antagonism of opposites that ends in a totality and reconstructs
it as a permanent, transhistorical rift within. In resignifying dialectical
materialism, Žižek renders impossible any grasping of class as a conflict
of opposites by turning each term of the opposition into a heterogeneous
entity that is at variance with itself. Each term emerges from this refur-
bished dialectics as the sublime of the heterogeneous; each one has no
common ground with anyone, not even itself.

   Žižek's remanufactured dialectical materialism is a machine for normalizing. By translating opposites into self-heterogeneous entities, he
naturalizes estranged labor and its self-alienation (Marx, *Manuscripts of
1844* 270–82) and thus provides the basis for the subjectivity of the (self-)
competing entrepreneur as the irreducible singular without any common
ground with anyone. His valorization of the incommensurable (which was
popularized by poststructuralism) pulverizes the ontology of collectivity
and turns dialectical materialism into the applied bourgeois science of
the singular, which not only treats alienated labor as the mark of self-
sovereignty but also crushes collectivity and demolishes "independent
objectively existing, reality" (*Parallax View* 6). The singular, the heterogeneous, and the unrepresentable (the Real), not class struggle, become
the dynamics of history in Žižek's cynically rehabilitated dialectical
materialism. He, of course, claims that dialectical materialism not only
is not demolished by the "insurmountable parallax gap" that prevents its
sublation (4) but, on the contrary, is itself a performative parallax fissure
(*Parallax View* 124–44). He believes that through the parallax gap dialectical materialism's "subversive core" becomes available to us (4). With
this the circle of his kynico-cynical interpretation closes upon itself. We
are, in other words, back again in the discursive militancies of resistance,
subversion, and negation that he has repeatedly mocked in the practices
of cultural studies and the acts of the "gang of democracy-to-come" (11).
In Žižek's hypercynical refurbishing, dialectical materialism has nothing
to do with dialectics or materialism: it is yet another expression of what
Lenin calls "objective idealism" (*Materialism and Empirio-Criticism* 23),
and it recalls Derrida's notion of différance (*Margins* 1–27), the bourgeois
militant's "difference" with a fist, a concept without referent deployed
to produce a neomaterialist Left friend for global capitalism.

For the neomaterialist Left, Žižek also invents a new theory of ideology *(Parallax View* 365–66). Ideology, for him, is not the social relation that regards the exchange of labor power for wages as fair. Rather, it is a fantasy that covers up the constitutive lack in the subject (*Sublime Object* 124–28). This is why he is critical of both poststructuralist theories and (post)Althusserian theories of ideology. He believes that they only take into account the imaginary and symbolic orders and ignore the order of the Real, thus bypassing the grounding lack of the subject: "'Beyond interpellation' is the square of desire, fantasy, lack in the Other and drive pulsating around some unbearable surplus-enjoyment" (124).

The role of "ideology critique" for Žižek is not demystification of the class interests that "lurk in ambush" in all representations (Marx and Engels, *Manifesto* 58) but a stripping away of the fantasies that cover up the lack in the subject. Ideology critique brings the subject back to a recognition of its founding lack (*Sublime Object, Tarrying with the Negative, Parallax View*). According to Žižek, it is the practice of self-clarification—making the subject aware of fantasies about its own presence and fullness.

Ideology, in this sense, is a fantasy that fills the lack in the subject and "offers us the social reality itself as an escape from some traumatic real kernel" (*Sublime Object* 45). Žižek thus legitimates capitalism by naturalizing the alienation of labor as an inherent lack of the subject, which is, he says, the effect of the impossibility of the Real in excess of all representations. Such a view of ideology is based on Žižek's notion that "there are no 'objective' relations of production" (*Contingency* 320), and therefore classes are not "positive" entities (132) but only constitute an impossible antagonism. He recognizes social contradictions, but he immediately converts them into uncanny and unrepresentable fissures that are beyond the social and its symbolic order. In other words, the "classic critical-ideological procedure" has become "impossible—or, more precisely, vain" (*Sublime Object* 29) because false consciousness is no longer external to knowing; it is now seen as constitutive of knowing. The subject of cynical reason "is quite aware of the distance between the ideological mask and the social reality, but he none the less insists upon the mask" (29). The cynical subject's mode of intelligibility is "lying in the guise of truth" (8). This allows Žižek to claim that "the extra-ideological point of reference that authorizes" a critique of ideology "is not 'reality' but the 'repressed' real of antagonism" ("Spectre" 25)—not the materiality of class struggle but the unfathomable, idealist constant of a "non-symbolizable traumatic kernel." As he does with class and materialism, he continues to cynically defend the concept of ideology, but only as what he defines as a kynical strategy of containment: a hypercynical reversal of ideology into a ludic figure.

Žižek's militant neomaterialism, however, finds its most telling articulation in his theory of globalization. In his more recent writings, he has deployed a theory of globalization to represent actually existing capitalism as the transcendent order of the social and, in effect, scaring people into thinking that any disturbance of that order will inevitably bring chaos to the everyday. His theory of globalization is a cynical interpretation of a cynical interpretation: a reading of Hardt and Negri's *Empire*—a work that exemplifies in Lenin's words, the writings of "bourgeois scholars and publicists [who] usually come out in defense of imperialism in a somewhat veiled form, and obscure its complete domination and its profound roots; they strive to concentrate attention on partial and secondary details and do their very best to distract attention from the main issue by means of ridiculous schemes for 'reforms'" (Lenin, *Imperialism* 287).

Žižek first remarks on *Empire* in a short affirmative footnote in *Contingency, Hegemony, Universality* (329); he then elaborates on this, repeating his observations in several other texts, notably in *Rethinking Marxism, Welcome to the Desert of the Real, The Parallax View*, and *Conversations with* Žižek. His remarks about *Empire* are part of his attack on Ernest Laclau's postmarxist theories of class, hegemony, and subjectivity and on the conclusions he draws about capitalism. I focus on his expanded riff on global capitalism in *Revolution at the Gates* (specifically the note on 330–32, as well as "Afterword: Lenin's Choice," 165–336). It is a "middle" instance of his argument concerning globalization—one in which he has already developed his main points but his cynical treatment has not yet taken over and displaced his focus on globalization. In reading globalization through his interpretation of *Empire*, Žižek has the ironic double task of affirming that work (against Laclau's postmarxism) while also confining it in order to advance his own neomaterialist Left.

He begins his reading of *Empire* by praising it for its theory of globalization as an "ambiguous de-territorialization" *(Revolution at the Gates* 331). A triumphant capitalism, in Žižek's reading of Hardt and Negri, is said to have permeated all spheres of social life. It has done so not by means of the old hierarchies of oppression, such as patriarchy, but by the proliferation of hybrid identities. Capitalism is thus seen as unleashing a revolutionary potential over which it eventually loses control, forcing capitalism to encounter its own limits. Žižek's narration of Hardt and Negri's views resembles Marx's theories. The similarities, however, are only on the surface; the idea of the end of capitalism in these narratives is purely cultural. Žižek (along with Hardt and Negri) has already dismantled all concepts (for example, class, dialectics, and the labor theory of value) that provide a historical materialist account of capitalism and globalization. Their simulation of Marxism, however, gives Žižek the cultural authority, in the name of neomaterialism, to put forth a veiled defense of transnational globalization by attacking the antiglobalization Left for its reformist "welfarism." It opposes globalization, according to Žižek, because it wants to "rescue (what there is left to rescue of) the Welfare State" (331). Not only is the Left mired in a nostalgic politics (recall Butler's "left conservatism"), but it is, Žižek maintains, also culturally Luddite: it is "imbued with a profoundly conservative mistrust of . . . digitalization" (331). In the present historical situation, however, Žižek's critique, made in the name of a revolutionary project, is more of a Hayekian view than a Marxist theory, and his ecstasy concerning the digital is yet another concession to antilabor theories of knowledge capitalism and to populist digitalists such as Alvin Toffler (*Powershift*).

Žižek then proceeds to make sure that globalization is always and ultimately transnationalism—which is actually corporate welfarism—and never becomes internationalism. He does this through a reading of the three "rights" that Hardt and Negri place at the end of *Empire* (393–413) as axes of radical organizing for a new joyful communism (411–13). I focus on their first right and the way Žižek treats it, because my subject is his hypercynical legitimization of transnational capitalism and not *Empire.* It is here, in his critique of this right, that Žižek's cynico-kynistic logic of social theory, which he represents as dialectical materialism, becomes especially visible.

The first right articulated in *Empire* (396–400) is "the right to global citizenship." Critiquing this right, Žižek writes: "Theoretically this right, of course, should be approved; however, if this demand is to be taken . . . seriously . . . then it would mean the abolition of state borders—under present conditions, such a step will trigger an influx of cheap labor from India, China, and Africa towards the USA and Western Europe, which would in turn result in a populist revolt against immigrants, a revolt of such violent proportions that people like Haider would look like models of multicultural tolerance" (*Revolution at the Gates* 331).

In formal terms, then, Žižek supports the right of global citizenship. I put aside the point that rights are essentially based on a constitutional liberalism, the very liberalism that he calls "pre-marxist" at the end of his critique of *Empire* (*Revolution at the Gates* 332), which he has found to be largely naïve. In critiquing this right, he is actually defending transnationalism, because this right will allow labor free movement across borders and thus make labor more expensive. With the right to global citizenship, labor will be able to move to places where wages are higher. The consequence of his argument against this movement is to trap labor in specific localities where capital will have unrestricted access to it. In Žižek's theory, labor should be stationary; only capital should be given the right of free movement across borders, so that it can go wherever wages are lowest.

In order to legitimate capital's freedom of movement but restrict labor's movement ("immigration"), Žižek resorts to well-tested Right-wing panic tactics. If labor is given the right to free movement, he argues, the fascist Right will create mayhem and devastation, and the workers themselves will become targets of Haider-type hatred. Žižek's new "revolutionary" declaration revives an old claim: it is in the interests of the workers to confine their movements and submit to exploitation by capitalism. In other words, labor should be kept in restricted zones, in labor "Bantustans." Globalization is a form of labor apartheid: the transnational segregation of labor and capital in which labor is the prey of capital.

The movement of workers across national borders breaks up this apartheid and establishes an internationalism based on class; it puts an end to nation and nationality and stops the politics of identity. This is not the international of the unrepresentable Real. Neither is it what is envisioned by Derrida as an international of "links of affinity, suffering, and hope" (*Specters of Marx* 85), nor is it based on the synthetic spirituality of a "joyous life including all being and nature, the animals, sister moon, brother sun, the birds of the field and exploited humans, together against the will of power and corruption" as manufactured in *Empire* (413). It is globalization as the international class collectivity grounded in the dialectics of human labor and nature. The time of internationalism is now, not the time "to come" of Žižekian materialist theology (*Parallax View* 122).

8. Reading Ideology:
Marx, de Man, and Critique

Reading, Critique, and "Uncritical Reading"

Jean-Paul Sartre opens his *Search for a Method* by declaring, "A Philosophy is first of all a particular way in which the 'rising' class becomes conscious of itself" (3–4). Reading, regardless of its immediate subject and empirical object, is always and in the end philosophy in a different mode. For reasons that will soon become clear, however, it is more common today to say the reverse, namely, that philosophy is a form of reading as writing. All readings, to expand on Sartre's point, are ways in which classes become aware of themselves and represent their material interests as the meanings of texts of culture. Reading is class struggle in the sphere of culture—the "dominant material relations," to use Marx and Engels' phrase, grasped as meanings. Like class struggle, it involves an unsurpassable binary that I mark as "materialist" and "tropological": reading as a struggle for freedom from necessity and reading as unconcealing the "rhetorical and tropological dimension of language" (de Man, *Resistance to Theory* 17), which is the theory of reading in normal cultural critique. For some critics, such as Roland Barthes, it leads to unexplainable ecstasies about the heterogeneity of the text and the waywardness of its signs.

Normal contemporary cultural critique—meaning "normal' as in "normal science" (Kuhn, *Structure* 10–34)—is tropological. It assumes that reading is an account of a text's self-difference and the way a text undoes its own assertions through its tropes, thus becoming a nonreferential allegory of (the difficulties of) its own reading (de Man, *Allegories* 17, 72, 77, 142, 242). Reading, for normal critique, is a writerly resignification of the text as it playfully puts itself out of joint and becomes corporeal "pleasure in pieces, language in pieces, culture in pieces" (Barthes, *Pleasure* 51). Contemporary cultural critique, to use a different idiom, has remade reading into a form of scopophilia in relation to the "linguistic sensuality" of the text (54) by turning it into objects of bliss and the reader into its voyeuristic subject as the text unravels itself and shifts its "value . . . to the sumptuous rank of signifier" (65). To move to a somewhat different but ultimately related perspective, reading bears witness to a text as it "deconstructs it-self" (Derrida, "Letter to a Japanese Friend" 274).

Dominant cultural critique marginalizes the idea of reading as a materialist practice whose trajectories of interpretation are determined not by the desire of the reader or by the tropics of the text itself but by class relations. It regards such a materialist reading to be an extension of the metaphysics of mimesis (Derrida, *Dissemination*, "Economimesis"), which seeks presence (social Truth) in the text by discovering a fixed reference for it in its outside. But "the outside is the inside" (Derrida, *Grammatology* 44) and, therefore, all references to the outside are regarded as optical illusions produced by bad readings. The text reads itself, theorizes itself, and puts its own claim to Truth in question (de Man, *Allegories* 245). It is not a reflection of presence; presence is a construct of the text.

However, the common practice in cultural critique of reading-as-différance (the difference of a text from itself) and the consequent demolishing of materialist reading—as a misguided logocentric epistemology—lost most of its interpretive confidence and ethical authority after the launching of imperialist wars in Afghanistan and Iraq. This was because it was unable to read imperialism in any other way than through the idioms of "supplementation," "difference," and "undecidability" as annotated by liberal pieties. Nor could it grasp Abu Ghraib (which was the scene of a class confrontation) in any terms other than the rhetoric of representation and the play of wayward signifiers, which turned representation into a scene of incoherence and self-canceling claims as in, for example, Donald Rumsfeld's language (Butler, *Precarious Life* 50–100). Imperialism, in other words, was "explained" by the errancy of tropes. Lacking any substantive analysis of the war or 9/11 and their historical and material conditions, or of the international relations of labor and capital, Derrida, in his contribution to *Philosophy in a Time of Terror*, falls back on the familiar deconstructive formula that states that (a) the trouble with the world is "representation," in which terrorism is constructed as the binary good/evil, and (b) redemption lies in the deconstruction of this binary and replacing it with what he had previously called "affinity, suffering, and hope" in his discussion of a world to come, that is, the "New International" (Derrida, *Specters of Marx* 85). In these readings, the world emerges in the form of assemblages of signifiers of remembrance and traveling affects.

After 9/11, materialist reading (reading as class practice) had to be marginalized in more credible terms. Consequently, in recent forms of cultural critique, materialist reading is purged, not as a logocentric will to presence but through a new populist rhetoric that depicts it as an elitist practice of "demystification" that "goes by the name of critique" (Warner, "Uncritical Reading" 17). Critique, according to Warner, is violence against "actual reading" (13), against authentic reading by people. In Warner's narrative the ostensible subject of criticism is what he calls "critical reading," by which he means reading practices inherited from the Enlightenment and grounded in reason. This is, of course, the broad theoretical frame of mainstream cultural critique, which is even more rigorous in its mistrust of reason and the Enlightenment: "Critique is . . . the handbook of reason that has grown up in Enlightenment" (Foucault, "What Is Enlightenment?" 308). The object of Warner's criticism is therefore not tropological reading, which marks the text with its contingencies, indeterminacies, and fissures and points to its postrational rhetoric, but materialist reading, which shows how the logic of the social relations of production determine both critical and uncritical readings of cultural texts.

In his criticism of materialist critique, Warner strategically puts aside textualism's old story line—"There is nothing outside of the text" (Derrida, *Grammatology* 158)—and its corollary that everything exists within representation, because these claims have lost credibility in the age of empire. He deploys other strategies to marginalize materialist reading.

Materialist reading is a causal analysis of the way things are and why they are that way, which ultimately is a question of the relationship of the forces and relations of production. Its reading is always global in its reach and explanations, which involve analysis of the structures of class relations and indicate that there is no such thing as a "cultural logic"— that all cultural writings, affects, and interpretations have one and only one logic, which is the logic of production. Warner first reduces materialist reading to a parochial hermeneutics of reason that, according to him, is practiced by the subject of self-reflexivity ("Uncritical Reading"

16–17). Materialist critique, however, is an analysis of social relations and their material conditions and not a formalist protocol of ahistorical reason. He then contrasts this form of reading, which, he implies, is an elitist interpretation favoring demystification as a sign of its rational (paranoid?) knowingness, with "actual" reading that he claims is viewed by elitist critique as "uncritical" (15).

After 9/11 the rhetoric of the "materiality of text" becomes a "slogan," and the argument that materialist critical reading is a logocentric quest for presence and decidability in normative thinking loses its persuasiveness. Warner replaces these catchphrases with new idioms that marginalize critique as exclusive, self-important, and dismissive of others as "uncritical."

The antimaterialism of mainstream cultural critique, in other words, is updated and rewritten by Warner as a post-9/11 anti-elitism that is not free from the reverberations of patriotism, localism, and Americanism. "Actual" (uncritical) reading, unlike elitist critique, according to Warner, is not aloof, cold, humorless, and charged with negative affects but is full of joy, affective attachment, reverie, and (American) spontaneity and, like American thought, is individualistic and anti-totality ("Uncritical Reading" 17–18). "Uncritical reading," in Warner's narrative, overflows with spirituality and religious feeling (18).

In place of a materialist reading, Warner, by his rereading of Sedgwick's writings (for example, *Touching Feeling* 123–51), valorizes readings that are unlike aloof and rational critique but that instead practice styles that share "a rhetoric of attachment, investment, and fantasy" ("Uncritical Reading" 17). Uncritical reading is "local, detailed, and unsystematized" (17). Warner displaces materialist critique with "reparative reading" (17). Instead of the reader as self-agent, Warner privileges affective readers who, like women in Egypt's mosque movement, for example, "aspire to be slaves of God" (18). In place of "critical reflection," which is often taken as the only form of subjectivity, they "cultivate piety" (18).

Warner reduces materialist critical reading to a convention (21–32) and then in a populist rhetoric demands the right of counter-convention. What he mystifies as "actual reading" is the circuit of received affects and opinions, since what he regards to be the lived experience of readers "like yourselves" (15) "is not . . . given by a pure reality, but is the spontaneous 'lived experience' of ideology in its peculiar relationship to the real" (Althusser, *Lenin and Philosophy* 223).

Warner's "uncritical reading" is a faith-based reading constructed after 9/11, but its arguments and its antireason theory (like Sedgwick's views, on which he relies) are grounded in the philosophical and theoretical assumptions of the tropological readings of Derrida and de Man and later Barbara Johnson, Judith Butler, and others. I thus focus on analyzing the conceptual grounds and some of the arguments offered by theorists of tropological readings rather than on the translation of their views into the populist rhetoric of uncritical reading. Warner's uncritical reading, contrary to his claims, is not a break from current practices. Rather, it updates them to fit the cultural climate of the United States after 9/11. His reading is solidly grounded in Paul de Man's hermeneutics, which privileges rhetoric (as postreason desire) over grammar (reason) and, unlike Derrida's discourse, is more practical (American) than philosophical (de Man, *Resistance to Theory*). Warner updates de Man's antireason and antimaterialist interpretive strategies by suturing them to Sedgwick's more affective "reparative reading" and, by means of a populist American New Age rhetoric produces a quasi-theoretical and deeply affective reading manner whose anti-intellectualism (already latent in de Man's opposition to theory) appeals to readers "like yourselves" ("Uncritical Reading" 15). The object of criticism in Warner is not the "critical," as in critical reading, but critique, or demystification. His uncritical reading is a uniquely American project of valorizing not "uncritical" but "un-critique-al" reading: it is critically un-critique-al.

Reading the Unreadable

In *The Ethics of Reading*, J. Hillis Miller writes that he "would even dare to promise the millennium [of universal justice and peace] would come if all men and women become good readers in de Man's sense" (58). Miller describes de Manian reading as recognition of "the 'impossible' task of reading unreadability" (59). But this still leaves the question, how does reading the unreadable lead to "universal justice and peace," if at all, and why is this the task of reading? Miller's comments, however, point to the importance that has been given to reading in cultural critique and the way it has been represented as a factor in cultural change.

In practice, there are as many ways of reading as there are readers. Each individual act of reading, however, is itself affected by a particular logic. Contemporary readings are shaped, I have suggested, by two contesting analytics: the tropological and the materialist. Tropological reading is antimimetic and grounded in its questioning of the correspondence between language and reality. It situates what is traditionally called the "meaning" of the text in the text itself.

The materialist theory of reading understands meaning primarily as a social relation. By *materialist*, as I have discussed in previous chapters,

I do not mean the material or materiality of language, which is the sense in which it is used in tropological readings. These regard language itself to be material, meaning the sensuousness of the signifier and the resistance of language to the conceptualization of its meaning as a "message" or other forms of fixed meanings. The materiality of language, in other words, is an allusion to its corporeal undecidability and sensible tropics that cannot be reduced to mere intelligibility.

Contemporary cultural critique has evolved and is evolving around these two modes of reading. In his essay "Cultural Studies and Its Theoretical Legacies," Stuart Hall gives a genealogy of cultural studies within these contesting ways of reading. "What I mean," Hall writes, "is certainly not that . . . cultural studies . . . wasn't, from the beginning, profoundly influenced by the questions that marxism as a theoretical project put on the agenda: . . . the global reach and history-making capacities of capital; the question of class; . . . and exploitation; . . . and the production of critical knowledge as a practice" (265).

Today the Marxist roots of cultural critique are largely obscured by the "linguistic turn" that has instituted tropological reading as the canonic protocol of reading. This linguistic turn, as I have argued elsewhere, has its roots in material changes that took place in the relation of labor and capital during the transformation of Keynesian economics into neoliberal economic policies in the 1960s and the beginnings of the modern phase of globalization. Stuart Hall calls the effects of the linguistic turn a "necessary delay or detour through theory." But by *theory* he is referring specifically to what he describes as "the discovery of discursivity, of textuality" and the embrace of "the crucial importance of language and linguistic metaphor to any study of culture" ("Cultural Studies" 270–71).

This textual-discursive form of reading is what has now become the canonic protocol of reading in cultural critique. As Hall writes, "The metaphor of the discursive, of textuality, instantiates a necessary delay, a displacement, which I think is always implied in the concept of culture" ("Cultural Studies" 271). But after 9/11 and within the realities of the new imperialism, which have put the material disparities of the global South and North on full display, contemporary cultural critique increasingly finds itself facing the limits of the linguistic turn that has shaped its work for the last several decades. Theses limits are so obvious that they cannot be ignored by even the staunchest supporters of ludic critique. In a recent essay, for example, Lawrence Grossberg asks for a shift away from "textual" cultural studies and its immanent critique. What is required, he says, "is a (re)turn to a more classical British cultural studies emphasis on 'political economy'" (quoted in G. Hall, "Politics" 66). The influence of the textual turn and ludic critique is so deep (because of the rooted class interests they legitimate) that Grossberg's call for a return to a materialist mode of cultural studies is itself written in terms of textualist cultural studies. It is telling that he completes his statement by adding that it is "a 'new' or significantly rethought political economy in which politics, the state, and economies are thought of as inescapably cultural" (66). Not only is culture itself now assumed to be an autonomous zone that is self-producing, but it is also seen as producing other social relations and spheres of social life including the economic. His call for "return" is, in effect, a coming back to where things stand now but in a different language. Any materialist understanding of the economic as an articulation of the social relations of production is marginalized, and instead the economic is understood as what Angela McRobbie calls the "microeconomies" of cultural production.

In contemporary cultural critique, politics, too, is translated into an indeterminate discourse without set references or oppositionality. In one of his last essays, printed in *Le Monde Diplomatique,* Derrida calls for a politics based on "something more sophisticated than simplistic binary oppositions," By "binary opposition" he seems to mean the opposition that, at its root, is the effect of antagonisms between what Marx and Engels call the "Bourgeoisie and Proletariat" (Marx and Engels, *Manifesto*). Politics, for Derrida, is a self-reflexive activity that keeps the space of the political open by resisting taking sides, which he equates with closure. The political is that which is nonclosural and has no fixed referent and therefore does not become, for example, about wage labor or gender. Politics is an ethics of the undecidable. If one is committed in advance (for instance, as a socialist) and thus knows what politics is, one is carrying out a program and not doing politics. This is the ground of his theory of "democracy-to-come" (*Politics of Friendship*).

A version of this idea of politics is taken up by Gary Hall, who claims that "politics cannot simply be calculated in advance; but . . . like Derrida's texts . . . [it] 'performatively' transform[s] and so 'create[s]' the 'context' in which [it] can be read" ("Politics of Secrecy" 75). He calls for a "new cultural studies," a more political one based on "a careful 'deconstructive' reading" (74) that opens cultural studies "to the incalculable, to the other, to singularity and to chance" in order for "cultural studies to be political in each singular situation" (78), that is, not to have a "theory" but to work as a situational ethics. Such a politics denies any knowledge in advance; it is an encounter with the uncertain (Hall and Birchall, *New Cultural Studies*). This is an alienated politics that expresses itself as norm-breaking cultural politics. It is the politics of and on behalf of a class that has lost its bearings in history and instead of moving to the future seeks enclaves of discursive actions in the present. Politics is a struggle for freedom from necessity (Marx, *Gotha Programme*), which means one has to know in advance what needs to be done. Theory is a necessary part of politics. Cultural politics, on the other hand, seeks the joyful unconcealment of the uncertain, the nomadic, and the ecstatic surprises of the cultural unforeseen as a way out of the endemic melancholic estrangement of the everyday.

For all their differences, textual and materialist readings share a necessary critique of experiential reading, which finds transparency in experience and an unproblematic correspondence between language and reality. They are both critical practices that, in different ways, demystify the seeming naturalness of experience and the way it means. Tropological readings, such as those by Paul de Man, of course, disclaim demystification because it is seen as presupposing a position of external critique from which one might be closer to the plenitude of Truth. They prefer instead to bear witness to the text's self-disarticulation though its own rhetorical work. Nonetheless, both the tropological and the materialist are modes of reading as demystifying and denaturalizing.

More specifically, de Man says, "It would be unfortunate to confuse the materiality of the signifier with the materiality of what is signified" (*Resistance to Theory* 11). In fact, for him such confusion, as I discuss more fully below, is the very definition of ideology: "What we call ideology," he writes "is precisely the confusion of linguistic with natural reality, of reference with phenomenalism" (11). This does not mean, he contends, that "the referential function of language is being denied"; instead, "what is in question is its authority as a model for natural or phenomenal cognition" (11). For a materialist reading, however, this seeming naturalness of reference is not linguistic but an effect of the material conditions of life under capitalism, in which the opacities of production are inverted into the seeming transparencies of exchange in the market. The market represents the social hieroglyphic of the unequal exchange of wages for labor power as a clear exchange of equals. Tropological reading attributes the seeming clarity produced by this inversion in the market to the closure of reference in language rather than to the transposition of the material relations of labor and capital. Tropological reading thus turns opacity into a fetish, dehistoricizing it as a permanent condition of the confusion of language and reality.

Ideology as Trope

"The materiality of the signifier," or as de Man also says, the "materiality of the letter" (*Resistance to Theory* 11, 89), is the interpretive dynamic of his reading. The materiality of the signifier is not only the phenomenal matter of sound or sign but also the irreducible and immaterial difference of an ungraspable excess. De Man describes it in *The Resistance to Theory* as the "the disjunction between grammar and meaning." What is "being named here," he writes, "is the materiality of the letter, the independence, or way in which the letter can disrupt the ostensibly stable meaning of a sentence and introduce in it a slippage by means of which that meaning disappears, evanesces, and by means of which all control over that meaning is lost" (89). The materiality of the signifier disrupts not only the referential function of language but also any stable logic in the disjunction between meaning and grammar. It frees what de Man calls the "vertiginous possibilities of referential aberration" (*Allegories* 10), disrupting the hegemony of fixed ideas and dislodging power from its ossification in received beliefs.

"Reading," de Man says, is thus "a negative process in which the grammatical cognition is undone, at all times, by its rhetorical [that is, its tropological] displacement" (*Resistance to Theory* 17). He makes this quite clear in his discussion of difference. In reading a cultural text, the television characters Archie Bunker and his wife, de Man illustrates the "tension between grammar and rhetoric" that produces the "contingent errors" by which "meaning disappears":

> [A]sked by his wife whether he wants to have his bowling shoes laced over or laced under, Archie answers with a question: "What's the difference?" Being a reader of sublime simplicity, his wife replies by patiently explaining the difference between lacing over and lacing under, whatever this may be, but provokes only ire. "What's the difference" did not ask for difference but means instead "I don't give a damn what the difference is." The same grammatical pattern engenders two meanings that are mutually exclusive: the literal meaning asks for the concept (difference) whose existence is denied by the figurative meaning. (*Allegories* 9)

De Man notes that "as long as we are talking about bowling shoes, the consequences are relatively trivial," but if we are dealing with a "debunker of the arche (or origin)" such as Jacques Derrida, "who asks the question 'What is the Difference,'" then we are "confronted" with the "difference between grammar and rhetoric" in which "we cannot even authoritatively decide whether a question asks or doesn't ask" (10).

To return to Archie Bunker, his anger, de Man writes, "reveals his despair when confronted with a structure of linguistic meaning that he cannot control and holds the discouraging prospect of an infinity of similar confusions" (10). This impossibility of deciding between incompatible meanings, this slippage between concept and metaphor, grammar and rhetoric, reason and desire is, for de Man, the operation of the materiality of the letter and produces the "unreadability" of reading—the inability to secure any stable meaning or fix a secure referent for the signifier. This is why he warns readers not to "confuse the materiality of the signifier with the materiality of what is signified" (*Resistance to Theory* 11). For Warminski, de Man's material inscription of the letter is "a radical materialism" ("Introduction" 7) that displaces ideology critique and shows how ideology and politics form a "tropological system" that can be "disarticulated" by "critical-linguistic analysis, a reading, of rhetoric" (12). In fact, de Man specifies that politics is linguistic. In *Allegories of Reading,* he says that "the political destiny of man is structured like and derived from a linguistic model that exists independently of nature and independently of the subject," but it is a model of language that "is not conceived as a transcendental principle but as the possibility of contingent error" (*Allegories* 156). He goes on to say that the "the foundation of civil society" is "conceptual language," and this "is also, it appears, a lie superimposed upon an error" (155). In other words, our understanding of the political and of civil society is textual; it is achieved through language.

In order to explore the consequences of these questions for cultural critique, it is necessary to go back to de Man's theory of ideology and examine some of its assumptions more carefully. I focus on the passage in *The Resistance to Theory* to which I have already referred: "What we call ideology is precisely the confusion of linguistic with natural reality, of reference with phenomenalism. It follows that, more than any other mode of inquiry, including economics, the linguistics of literariness is a powerful and indispensable tool in the unmasking of ideological aberrations, as well as a determining factor in accounting for their occurrence" (11).

I leave aside the uses of "unmasking," "aberrations," and "determining," which contradict de Man's claim about language and its undecidable truth (unmasking is, by any account, the promise of a decidable truth). What I am interested in is the way de Man dissolves determinate social structures into linguistic indeterminacy as a resistance to sedimented meanings and how this subversion turns out to be an affirmation of capitalism. In other words, I am concerned with the way in which, by subverting what he calls "phenomenalism," he demolishes materialism-as-economic and puts in its place materiality-as-language and, in doing so, contributes to emptying ideology of all its class contents.

He starts his reading of ideology at a distance from ideology by arguing that literary "theory" comes into being when "literary texts" are read locally as the functioning of language and not in terms of such external frames as history (*Resistance to Theory* 7). The immanent reading of literary texts as language produces "literariness" (9), which is, he contends, the resistance of the rhetoric of the text to its grammar (14); it is freedom from regulation and determination. Literariness is the residue that exceeds the representation of a text as being "about" anything but itself (including and especially the aesthetic). Literariness, in de Man's narrative, is the marker of language's freedom from mimesis and the materiality of its autonomy from the restraints of reference (10). The "literary," in other words, is the negative knowledge that puts in question the "reliability of linguistic utterance" (10) and obliterates the assumption that language is transparent. Ideology is produced by the certainty about the transparency, reliability, and decidability of language and the a priori confidence that language is referential and functions according to the principle of a phenomenal world (11). Ideology, de Man contends, is a form of the metaphysics of mimesis; it is a mistaking of language for reality, a phenomenalism that takes the referent to be reality instead of recognizing it as language. To put it differently, ideology is a piece of language, and, therefore, the most effective way to unmask it, for de Man, is to read it as language—to restore it to its linguisticity, which is obscured by phenomenalism.

Reading ideology by carefully teasing out the local working of language reveals it to be a structure of tropes and thus a form of writing, a literary event. Although the working of tropes is most explicit in literature, it becomes clear that they are constitutive of any "verbal event" when "it is read textually" (*Resistance to Theory* 17). As the site of tropes, ideology is, thus, a literariness that frees itself from any reference to its outside.

With a certain interpretive excitement, de Man declares that this is not "what generally passes as a 'critique of ideology'" (*Resistance to Theory* 121), which he considers to be a determination of ideology from its outside. Ideology unravels itself from the "inside," by itself, and unfolds its phenomenalism as language-at-work. Thus the claims for ideology as representation (truth or falsehood) are constructed by rhetoric and not by an outside power such as class relations. Ideology unravels itself from within because "the text knows in an absolute way what it's doing," de Man says, and, thus, "deconstructs itself." It is "self-deconstructive" rather than "being deconstructed . . . from the outside of the text" (118).

It is not clear, however, how de Man's reading, which differentiates itself from the familiar "ideology critique," produces a different critical understanding because it takes place within the same textual and tropological order in which ideology is made and is subject to the same tropological fate as ideology. How does it mark the unraveling of ideology from within without itself being unraveled from within? In other words, if one reads de Man's reading of ideology reflexively, subjecting it to the same terms of reading by which he reads ideology, his reading also emerges as ideology. It is not simply ideology that collapses on itself, but its reading does so, as well. If ideology as language deconstructs itself, so does its reading, which is also language. How, in other words, does "the linguistics of literariness" act as a "powerful and indispensable tool in the unmasking of ideological aberrations" without being unmasked itself (from within) as an "ideological aberration"? In his theory, critique and ideology are parts of the same tropological system (Warminski, "Introduction" 10). What makes the difference?

This question has interested many of de Man's readers. What saves his reading of ideology from falling into ideology—the substitution of one trope (critical consciousness) for another (false consciousness) within the same system—and thus not be "possessed" by the very system it attempts to foreclose? In answer, one of de Man's most perceptive readers, Andrzej Warminski, argues that the difference is in de Man's radical materiality ("Ending Up/Taking Back [with Two Postscripts on de Man's Historical Materialism]"). Yet, he suggests, one cannot understand de Man's materiality without understanding the working of "rhetoric" in his writings, because it is rhetoric that makes all the difference in his project and distinguishes it from mere ideology critique (Warminski, "Introduction" 9, 10). In order to understand de Man's difference (given that critique and ideology, in this view, are verbal events in the same tropological order) we need a "different activity" (11), according to Warminski: one that begins "to account for the putting into place of the tropological system itself, its inaugural grounding or foundation on the basis of principles that, wherever they come from, cannot come from within the tropological system itself" (11). The activity that takes place is the return of "factors and functions of language," which de Man discusses, for example, in *The Resistance to Theory* (13) and that "resist the phenomenalization made possible (and necessary) by tropes and their system" ("Introduction" 11). The "factors and functions of language" that "lie at the bottom of all tropological systems as their material condition of possibility" produce an excess in the troplogical order that prevents it from closure. "They leave marks and traces 'within' (or 'without'?) these tropological systems, marks and traces that may not be accessible to the knowing, conscious-ness, or science of 'critical critics' but that nevertheless remain legible in the texts of these systems: in their inability to close themselves off, for instance, which always produces an excess (or lack) of tropology, a residue or remainder of trope and figure irreducible to them" (11).

In order to secure de Man's reading of ideology as different from the "critique of ideology" and demonstrate its different materiality, Warmin-ski must do what de Man has warned against in all his writings: he must go outside the "verbal event" (tropological system) to deconstruct it and secure the nontropic materiality of the inside. Warminski must ground de Man's rhetoric in the nonrhetorical (its outside) at the same time that both de Man and he prohibit thinking of ideology as anything but an inside that cannot be determined by an outside, an inside determined by its own textuality and not by an outside such as class (as in classical Marxism). By insisting on the inside, de Man argues that ideology falls apart in its own terms; there is no need for a revolution to put an end to ideology. Leave it alone, and it undoes itself. In other words, de Man's theory of reading is a political theory of preserving the system by promising reform and discrediting revolution—the outside. But the "verbal event," the tropological, cannot deconstruct its own phenomenalization (from the inside); it cannot "deconstruct itself," as de Man claims (*Resistance to Theory* 118). Therefore, its phenomenalization has to be deconstructed from the outside by the factors and functions of language.

It is, of course, true that within de Man's theory the "trope" has a tendency to totalize (*Resistance to Theory* 89) because it always attempts to put itself in place of reality as, for example, in Schiller's reading of Kant (*Aesthetic Ideology* 147). Yet these phenomenalizing tendencies are seen as deconstructed by the trope itself and, as de Man shows in his reading of Benjamin, are resisted by the tropic acting out of "the discrep-ancy between symbol and meaning" (89). Tropological structures, which are self-knowing, deconstruct the verbal event because "the figurative structure is not one linguistic mode among others but it characterizes language as such" (*Allegories* 105). The tropological, the rhetorical, and the figurative, de Man says, always deconstruct themselves.

If de Man's theory is to be taken seriously in terms of its reading of ideology, then the trope as a verbal event must be self-deconstructive and self-(de)determining. What de Man calls the "epistemological examina-tion of tropes" (*Aesthetic Ideology* 132) must be conducted from within the tropological system itself, according to his own theory (*Resistance to Theory* 118). The point is that the tropological system is a verbal system, and because all verbal orders are tropic and figurative, it should know itself "in an absolute way" and deconstruct itself (118). To have to go to its outside to deconstruct the trope's totalization (phenomenalization) is to reveal that de Man's theory of ideology is an interpretive metaphysics, an ideology.

It turns out that de Man's theory of reading, which is grounded in a text's absolute knowledge of its own working (118), is not so much a theory of "literariness" (*Resistance to Theory* 9) as a political exegesis aimed at repressing the outside of ideology, that is, getting class out of literary and cultural critique. It suspends the outside of ideology as an economic phenomenon but restores it as a linguistic one. It is not the outside that is being questioned but the outside-as-economic. In short, de Man's theory of ideology is not a theory of reading but a political semiotics that represents itself as literariness, as rhetoric. It sees no "problem" in going outside to detotalize tropes but insists that there *is* no outside to ideology and that ideology is a self-deconstructing text since it is, above all, a "verbal event." To put it differently, his theory is the rewriting of the materialism of labor as the matter of language—dispersing the represented in the indeterminacy of representation.

There are other problems in de Man's and Warminski's reading of ideology that further unfold the contradictions (class interests) of de Man's theory of ideology.

It is important to return to a key passage by Warminski to examine the way he obscures the contradictions that arise from the binary logic of inside/outside. Following de Man, he places the "factors and functions of language"—which, he says, "resist the phenomenalization made . . . by tropes"—"at the bottom of all tropological systems" ("Introduction" 11). In other words, they are not quite outside but are somewhere on the inside. This "bottom" to "top" relation of the "factors and functions of language" to "tropological systems" foregrounds the central contradiction in this reading because it duplicates the architecture of base/superstructure that de Man and Warminski critique as deterministic in their reading of ideology in classical Marxism. It seems that neither has any interpretive problem with determinism as such: he objects to determinism only when the "bottom" is economic (base), shaping the 'top' cultural texts (superstructure). In order to save de Man's ideology theory from falling back into ideology and to represent the class interests that it legitimates as the order of language itself, Warminski resorts to linguistic determinism.

It is clear that to say that the "factors and functions of language" determine the working of tropes (resist their totalization) is to essentialize the very elements that are supposed to resist essentialization.

By placing the factors and functions of language, as Warminski does, "at the bottom" is a move to "solve" the problem of inside/outside within the doctrine that "The Outside is the Inside" (Derrida, *Grammatology* 44). In his renarration of de Man, he puts these factors and functions, —which are not from "within the tropological system" and are not on the outside but at the bottom (11), in proximity to the inside. But what makes the relation of the factors and functions and the "tropological system" one of inside/outside is not their topographies. It is what the former are said to be doing, namely, resisting the phenomenalization of tropes not from within them but by producing a remainder from their outside that is irreducible to figurality (11) and, consequently, produces "materiality." Contrary to what is axiomatic to de Man's theory of textuality, figures do not deconstruct themselves but have to be deconstructed. It is here that not only Warminski's reading of de Man's reading of ideology but, more important, de Man's entire theory of rhetoric and reading falls apart: a "verbal event," contrary to the internal logic of his theory (*Resistance to Theory* 118), does not deconstruct itself from within. It is deconstructed from its outside, whether this outside is at the bottom, on the side, or even inside the inside, because the outside is not topography. It is history. The inside is always in the outside, which is in history.

Warminski's reading, however, has the value of demonstrating that what he and de Man claim to be materialism (de Man, "Kant's Materialism") is nothing but an objective idealism. It is a type of literariness obtained by declaring, in the manner of all idealisms, language's autonomy: "Language is the immediate actuality of thought. Just as philosophers have given thought an independent existence, so they were bound to make language into an independent realm" (Marx and Engels, *German Ideology* 447).

The construction of ideology in de Man's writings matters because the contestations about ideology in cultural critique are about the very formation and social role of culture.

If in All Ideology

The materialist reading of ideology is radically different from its tropological interpretation. After the appearance of Althusser's groundbreaking essay "Ideology and Ideological State Apparatuses" it has become routine to marginalize the classical Marxist theory of ideology as "false consciousness" and then dismiss it as an essentially idealist or positivist concept, perhaps a residue of Hegelianism in Marx. The basis of this (post)Althusserian interpretation is *The German Ideology*, and I closely read one of its crucial passages below. But the theoretical underpinning of this passage, which is implied in *The German Ideology* (35–93, 455–57), is spelled out in detail in *Capital*, and the materialist basis of ideology is made very clear. "False consciousness" is not, to simplify a very complex matter, about epistemology (false/true); it is about class relations and the way consciousness is determined not by ideas but by the social relations of production.

In chapter 6 of *Capital* (vol. 1), "The Sale and Purchase of Labour-Power," to which I have referred several times in other chapters, Marx argues that the exchange of wages for labor power is an unfair exchange that is accepted as fair. It is unfair not because of moral issues—namely, the capitalist is paying the worker less than the market value of her labor power. It is unfair because labor power is a commodity unlike any other, one "whose use-value possesses the peculiar property of being a source of value, whose actual consumption is therefore itself an objectification [*Vergegenstandichung*] of labour, hence a creation of value" (1: 270). Labor power, in other words, is that unique commodity that when used, produces value (what Marx calls "surplus" value) and is appropriated by capital. The wage laborer not only earns her wages but also produces a surplus that is the secret of the "working day," which is silently divided into two parts: a "necessary labour-time and surplus labour-time" (1: 341), and the worker is paid only for the "necessary labour-time" of her working day. Accepting wages as equal to labor power is the direct effect of the ways the actual material relations of labor and capital are inverted so that capital rather than labor is represented as the source of wealth. This class relation, which is the unsaid of the unequal exchange of wages for labor, is constitutive of ideology, which renders as fair the unfair material relation between workers and owners in all class societies. Ideology is the cultural (religious, spiritual, legal, and pedagogical) explanation of material practices. What makes this cultural explanation of the material necessary, Marx argues, is that

> it is not enough that the conditions of labour are concentrated at one pole of society in the shape of capital, while at the other pole are grouped masses of men who have nothing to sell but their labour-power. Nor is it enough that they are compelled to sell themselves voluntarily. The advance of capitalist production develops a working class which by education, tradition and habit, looks upon the requirements of that mode of production as self-evident natural laws. The organization of the capitalist process of production, once it is fully developed, breaks down all resistance. The constant generation of a relative surplus population keeps the law of supply and demand of labour, and therefore wages, within

narrow limits which correspond to capital's valorization requirements. The silent compulsion of economic relations sets the seal on the domination of the capitalist over the worker. Direct extra-economic force is still of course used, but only in exceptional cases. In the ordinary run of things, the worker can be left to the "natural laws of production," *i.e.*, it is possible to rely on his dependence on capital, which springs from the conditions of production themselves, and is guaranteed in perpetuity by them. (*Capital* 1: 899)

What are some of the consequences of de Man's and Marx's theories of ideology for cultural critique? To explore this question, I focus on the well-known passage on the "camera obscura" in Marx and Engels' *German Ideology*. But first let us recall that in *The Resistance to Theory*, de Man reproaches critics of literary theory for being "very poor readers of Marx's *German Ideology*" (11).

Marx and Engels' text reads:

The production of ideas, of conceptions, of consciousness, is *at first directly* interwoven with the material activity and the material intercourse of men, the language of real life. Conceiving, thinking, the mental intercourse of men, appear at this stage as the direct efflux of their material behaviour. The same applies to mental production as expressed in the language of politics, laws, morality, religion, metaphysics, etc., of a people. Men are the producers of their conceptions, ideas, etc.—real, active men, as they are conditioned by a definite development of their productive forces and of the intercourse corresponding to these, up to its furthest forms. Consciousness can never be anything else than conscious existence, and the existence of men is their actual life-process. *If* in all ideology men and their circumstances appear upside-down as in a camera obscura, this phenomenon arises just as much from their historical life-process as the inversion of objects on the retina does from their physical life-process. (emphasis in original)

In "Phenomenality and Materiality in Kant" de Man writes that "we have come upon a passage that, under the guise of being a philosophical argument, is in fact determined by linguistic structures that are not within the author's control" (*Aesthetic Ideology* 87). He goes on to say that "the bottom line, in Kant as well as Hegel, is the prosaic materiality of the letter, and no degree of obfuscation or ideology can transform this materiality into the phenomenal cognition" (90). A tropological reading would demonstrate the way the materiality of the letter disrupts the cognition and critical argument being made and exposes the contradictions and disjunctions that break up the theoretical system of historical materialism and disarticulate its concept of ideology.

I focus my discussion on the famous last sentence:, "If in all ideology men and their circumstances appear upside-down as in a camera obscura, this phenomenon arises just as much from their historical life-process as the inversion of objects on the retina does from their physical life-process."

I start with the "prosaic materiality" of the signifier *if*. This seemingly marginal grammatical sign is the "hinge" on which hangs the logic as well as the contradictions of the passage. Here the linguistic properties of *if* destabilize any fixed meaning for the argument. Does *if* indicate the conditional or the subjunctive? If it is conditional, what is the condition? It can be read as setting up the condition of objective reality for the ideological inversion, asserting that it is just as real as the physical process of inversion on the retina. If the *if* alludes to the subjunctive, however, the meaning is quite opposite because the subjunctive indicates unreal states; it refers to conditions contrary to fact. But even this difference is disarticulated. The purpose of the conditional is to provide the inversion with the literalness and objectivity of the physical phenomena of the retina, but it does so through a metaphor of the camera obscura and thus succumbs to what de Man, in his reading of Rousseau, calls metaphorical error or blindness. The metaphor, he says, "refers to a condition of permanent suspense between a literal world in which appearance and nature coincide and a figural world in which this correspondence is no longer *a priori* posited. Metaphor is error because it believes or feigns to believe in its own referential meaning" (*Allegories* 151). In short, the figural undoes the literal; there is no adequation to reality. If that is not enough disruption of meaning, the *if* can also be read as referring to a different condition: Which ideology? A specific ideology, "German Ideology," all ideology, all ideology at the time Marx and Engels were writing, ideology for the reader, a universal, a particular ideology?. The referent slides away, and we can no longer find any correspondence between the signifier and its reference. The very subject, ideology, has dissolved into a vertiginous series.

Already we see how destabilizing the "prosaic materiality of the letter" can be and how it unsettles any reading of the text that seeks to fix its meaning. I have not even introduced the issue of translation, for the English *if* is a translation of the German *wenn*, which not only has the signified of *if*—conditional—but also a further destabilizing series of signifieds involving the temporal: when, whenever, as soon as, and so on. "This errancy of language which never reaches the mark, which is always displaced in relation to what it meant to reach" is a "permanent disjunction," de Man says, that "inhabits all language" (*Resistance to Theory* 92). The significance of de Man's critical-linguistic reading is to disarticulate and disrupt the ideological or metaphysical closure imposed on the open play of language in cultural texts. It disrupts the ideological fixities in language that have solidified into certainties in support of power.

But is it enough to destabilize meanings? What kind of *freedom* is at play in the seemingly free play of signifiers? More important, what kind of knowledge does this critical-linguistic analysis produce when it rewrites all concepts as tropes and reads the entire social series in linguistic terms? What are the consequences for cultural critique if it concludes, as de Man seems to do, that "the complex relationship between Rousseau's and Marx's economic determinism could and should only be approached from this point of view," which finds that "the economic foundation of political theory in Rousseau is not rooted in a theory of needs and appetites, and interests that could lead to ethical principles of right and wrong; it is the correlative of linguistic conceptualization" (*Allegories* 158)?

But is de Man not simply substituting a linguistic determinism for what he considers economic determinism? It is, I argue, a linguistic determinism that is blind to its own limits. The materiality of the letter is premised on the independence, the irreducible autonomy of the signifier. The seeming openness of language is itself a closed system, cut off from the larger social totality. In fact, it denies totality, seeing it as the beginning of totalization and totalitarianism. Instead, it reads the social totality itself as a play of differences, denying its existence outside "linguistic conceptualization." Ernesto Laclau takes this deconstructive logic so far as to declare that "society does not 'exist' insofar as objectivity, as a system of differences that establishes the being of entities, always shows the traces of its ultimate arbitrariness" (*New Reflections* 183).

In the Way in Which a Society Gains Its Livelihood, It Writes Its Texts

I want to turn now to a historical materialist reading. Unlike de Man's insistence that, like language, texts are about themselves and thus form a self-referential series, a materialist reading sees texts as always meaning something other than themselves. Texts are articulations of social relations. Language is not simply an autonomous system of formal relations, as de Saussure claims. In *The German Ideology,* Marx and Engels argue that "language . . . is practical, real consciousness that exists for other men as well, and only therefore does it exist for me: language, like consciousness, only arises from the need, the necessity, of intercourse with other men. Where there exists a relationship, it exists for me. . . .

Consciousness is, therefore, from the very beginning a social product, and remains so long as men exist at all" (44).

Like consciousness, language is always directed toward the other: it is for the other that it has meaning. This is another way of saying that texts are the effects not of the working of tropes but of the social relations of production that actually activate tropes. Tropes mean different things in different classes and in different periods of history. In other words, their play is historically and socially conditioned. In his *Marxism and the Philosophy of Language*, Voloshinov annotates Marx's argument by saying that in social struggles, the "Sign becomes an arena of the class struggle" (23). A text, in other words, is not merely a "galaxy of signifiers," as Roland Barthes claims (*S/Z* 5), whose meanings are primarily effects of a formal system ("language") that absorbs the social into the semiotic. Instead, social conflicts stubbornly make the semiotic a site of class struggle. The indeterminacy of the sign is the result of ongoing class struggles that put fixed meanings in jeopardy. Meanings are never stable and fixed because they are social relations, and social relations are effects of class conflicts and contradictions. This determination of language and its meanings by class is obscured by what I call a *mid-analytic* interpretation: an analytical foreshortening that isolates language from its material conditions. By *material conditions* I do not mean the materiality of language—the body of its medium, the matter of the signifier—but its relation to the social division of labor. Constituted by language (which is always for the other), texts, whether literature or popular media, always mean something other than themselves for a someone other than themselves. Texts do not narrate allegories of their own unreadability to themselves; they are not self-sovereign but always an effect of the relations between labor and capital. In the ways in which a society gains its livelihood, it writes its texts.

Contrary to Kantian aesthetics, which de Man, Lyotard, and Barthes, among many other recent writers, rearticulate with different degrees of formal distancing from Kant, there is no cultural "purposive purposelessness," a "purposiveness without purpose" ("Zweckmässigkeit ohne Zweck"), as Kant writes in his *Critique of Judgment* (secs. 5–8, 17). Or, to be more precise, all instances of cultural "purposiveness without purpose" are culturally purposive; their purpose is to have no purpose and to teach a general cultural skepticism about the purpose— the "determinacy"—of language and to teach against adopting decided positions that may lead to a definite purpose, such as social change. But the free play of language in the textual is free only within certain limits set by the social conditions in which it is produced.

Texts form part of the cultural superstructure through which, as Marx writes in his "Preface to a Contribution to the Critique of Political Economy," people fight out the social conflicts over material priorities. As such, all texts of culture are participants and so are overtly or covertly partisans in social struggles not only for freedom of meanings but also for freedom from necessity. There are no neutral texts in culture, and the Kantian idea of a "purposiveness without purpose," which seems to propose such a neutrality, is itself part of this conflict and social struggle. As participants in this struggle, texts of culture teach the reader how to understand the social world and to take sides in the great contestations over the surplus of social labor.

This is not to say that we can directly read off a particular text what specific interventions it makes into social struggles. The relation of the textual to the social is not direct; its mediations have to be teased out through critique. Tropological reading, of course, recognizes only one mediation, which is no meditation at all, and that is a text's self-reference: a text mediating between its difference from itself, which is another way of saying that difference is its self-mediation. Texts, in this reading, do not mediate between culture and its materialist base; culture is itself a text that is always in difference from itself, a language in constant oscillation and play. But a materialist reading reveals the social contradictions. It does not simply open up texts to vertiginous meanings and unsettle them. It marks the cultural fissures and exposes the material causes of discursive fissures, namely, the fundamental contradictions in the social division of labor.

The Meaning of If Is Not in If

I want to examine the work of a materialist reading, first, by returning to the passage about the "camera obscura" and then by reading a popular cultural text.

The signifier *if* is marking a fissure in this passage. Again, the sentence begins:

> If in all ideology men and their circumstances appear upside-down as in a camera obscura,

The rupture marked by *if* is not merely a textual tension. *The meaning of if is not in if. It is in its outside: it is a break that articulates social relations.* It marks the conditions of an inversion of circumstances as they appear in ideology. Recall the problem of translation. The English *if* is a translation of the German *wenn*, which has a series of signifieds involving not only the conditional but also the temporal: "when," "whenever," "as soon as." So if we consider the multiple signifieds and their relations, a possible condition for this break is the condition of a temporal relation. The temporal does not simply mark the natural; it is also an index of social processes of transformation (of labor), that is, the historical. In short the sign *if* or *when* is marking a historical relation, and it does so in relation to the opening sentences of the paragraph that include the temporal markers "at first" and "at this stage." To quote the beginning of the passage again:

> The production of ideas, of conceptions, of consciousness, is *at first* directly interwoven with the material activity and the material intercourse of men, the language of real life. Conceiving, thinking, the mental intercourse of men, appear *at this stage* as the direct efflux of their material behaviour.

The ideological inversions in which ideas, consciousness, and language appear autonomous and cut off from real, material processes are themselves an effect of "historical life processes," of the labor and class relations of production. There is still an "unsaid" in the text, to use Pierre Macherey's term. What is the condition "when" the inversion occurs? The text is establishing not only the material relations for language and consciousness in which "consciousness is a social product" but also their historicity: when the relations of production change, so do the forms of consciousness. The stage "at first," when ideas appear as a direct relation, is the stage of direct exploitation of labor and appropriation of its products that we find in feudalism and ancient class societies. But with the emergence of a new mode of production—capitalism, which is based not on the direct appropriation of use value but in the production of commodities for exchange—new social forms and new forms of consciousness develop in which the material relations appear upside-down. In short, the inversion of consciousness, or false consciousness, is a result of the way the realities of the working day at the point of production are reversed in the market during the process of distribution. The market inverts the truth of production and represents *trade*, not *labor*, as the source of social wealth.

If is the space of a social fissure marking the inverted relation of production and market. *If* or *when* signals the break in class relations when, under the pressure of commodity exchange in capitalism, people lose direct knowledge of their own exploitation, and labor relations appear upside down. *If* signals the fundamental class conflict between capital and labor.

From the perspective of a materialist theory, de Man's theory of reading obscures the material class antagonisms by turning social conflicts
into tropes. In foregrounding the linguistic fissures of reading, it deflects
awareness away from the social fissures. Contrary to hegemonic cultural
critique, a linguistic reading does not open the text, it closes it. It imposes a
textual closure and obscures the social crisis found in the text. In contrast,
a materialist reading activates the social fissures of which the linguistic
fissure is only a symptom and exposes the class contradictions in the text.
To further demonstrate this critical surfacing of social contradictions in
cultural texts, I want to briefly look at a popular text, in part because the
popular has been such a privileged object in cultural studies.

Women's Romances and Their Ideology

Women's romances are the most widely read of all popular print works,
and are the most marginalized by critics. These texts so saturate the market, appearing everywhere from grocery-store shelves to best-seller lists,
their very ordinariness renders them culturally invisible and critically
neglected. This neglect, however, covers over the considerable textual,
social, and ideological complexity by which romance novels shape the
popular imaginary in order to reconcile readers with the class contradictions of capitalism and to normalize the inversion of production in the
market. Although these novels represent themselves as narratives of a
natural intimacy between men and women, they construct that intimacy
in such a way that the reader not only accepts the contradictions of capitalism but concedes that they are natural and normal. The resolution
of tensions in romances, in other words, is a cultural lesson for solving
problems in such a way that the existing social division of labor and property relations are left intact and are seen as normal a results of a natural
evolution of history: the way things are is the way they ought to be.

I focus on two sentences from Elizabeth Lowell's *Pearl Cove.* About
one-third of the way into the narrative, the widowed heroine voices her
desire in the following way: "She didn't have to marry in order to enjoy
passion. She was free" (134). These two short sentences are set off as
a single paragraph ending with and foregrounding the signifier "free,"
whose meaning is not in the sentence but is understood in terms of the
dominant social relations. The immediate meaning of "free" is "choice,"
the most privileged marker of individual freedom in commodity culture: "The choice was hers," the narrator proclaims. Another meaning
is to be free from commitment. It marks the individual as free from social or ethical responsibility, as free from the other: "she was a woman

who answered only to herself" but also was free to take "risks" ("the risk was hers"). This of course, is the idea of "free love," the desire for unconstrained sexual passion and its conflicting cultural construction of "love" and intimacy, in which the freedom of desire can only occur within the safe space of mutual commitment in marriage. Freedom, in other words, is only realizable within unfreedom. In romances the free expression of desire requires the protected, risk-free space of the hero's commitment to marriage: "I want it all," the heroine says, "protection and sex and babies . . . and love" (407). She also wants the multimillion-dollar treasure they have been hunting: the pearl necklace called the Black Trinity. These contradictions are effects of alienated labor, which is obscured in the freedom of desire.

The "deep desire" in romance, to put it differently, is the desire for nonalienated relations, for use value. It is the dream that love and marriage do not form an exchange relation: exchange of sex for security, of love for property. It is a fantasy that defies the long history of bourgeois marriage, which is a property relation. At the conclusion of *Pearl Cove*, the heroine declares, "I want it all, Archer, the Black Trinity. The baby. You. . . . I'm afraid of losing you. Every time I think about it, I'm back in Rio and night is coming down—and I'm holding you to your promise. Protection and sex. And babies" (406–7). This refrain, "I'm back in Rio and night is coming down," is the marker of economic necessity throughout the novel. It refers to the time when, as young woman, the heroine flees her missionary home in the Amazon rain forest and is standing on the street corner, hungry and destitute, having to "freely" choose her fate, looking one way at the prostitutes on the street and the other way at marriage. "Her choice," the heroine reminded herself. "She paid her way out of the rain forest with her virginity" (115). This is not free choice but the silent compulsion of economic need. This first marriage is represented as "wrong," both because it is an exchange relation—sex for security—and also because it is to the "wrong man," the wrong brother, the ruthless one who failed to protect and who squandered wealth and property. In contrast, the second marriage, the "right" one, is to the hero, the wealthy, propertied protector who is an exemplary model of the owning class. Though represented as the outcome of a pure, free passion—a pure use value—this marriage is just as much an economic exchange, is just as much an exchange of sex for security, of love for property.

There is no escape from commodification in capitalism. The inversion of ideology, as we see with wage labor, is to represent commodity relations as if they were free and natural choices, not compulsory practices that can only be fulfilled by the exchange of commodities. Thus we see that no matter how much romances valorize the fantasy of "free" desire and the dream of noncommodified intimacy, the narratives simultaneously work against this desire. *"Free" does not mean "being free" but rather "freely" accepting "unfree" conditions.* To read "free" in terms of the materiality of the letter is to absorb the class contradictions of capital into the self-displacing language of the novel—its vertiginous excess of meanings. By assuming that meanings are products of an autonomous system of differences, such reading produces pleasure in the reader but blocks social knowledge.

The "free" in Lowell's novels is a social fantasy of escape from alienated labor. In his "Contribution to the Critique of Hegel's Philosophy of Right," Marx writes that social fantasies express a real yearning for "true reality," a reality in which one is not alienated from oneself and others. Fantasies are illusions that promise to cure alienation. By providing an "illusory happiness," however, romances obscure the struggles for "real happiness."

Reading is an intervention in cultural intelligibilities that is made not in order to produce more linguistic fantasies but to put an end to social illusions. The call for readers to "abandon their illusions about their condition" is, as Marx says, "a call to abandon a condition which requires illusions" ("Critique of Hegel's Philosophy of Right" 244).

Coda: Reclaiming Totality

Theodor Adorno's proclamation "The whole is the false" (*Minima Moralia* 50) is the theoretical dogma of contemporary cultural critique, which claims that totality is the negation of difference. But totality, in fact, is the very condition of difference. Only in "relation to society *as a whole*" (Lukács, *History and Class Consciousness* 50) is difference freed from being merely a bourgeois fantasy and becomes material reality. Difference is always difference in totality, which becomes possible only after freedom from necessity (Marx, *Gotha Programme*) puts an end to class fragmentations and makes totality the everyday consciousness. Without it, difference is the alienated concrete of wage labor.

Through the rhapsodies of "culture in pieces" (Barthes, *Pleasure* 51), the sentimentalism about the "materiality of the letter" (de Man, *Resistance to Theory* 89), and the ecstasies over "différance" (Derrida, *Margins* 1–27), contemporary cultural critique has fought a "war on totality" in a bid to become the uncanny "witness to the unrepresentable" (Lyotard, *Postmodern Condition* 82). It has displaced the stubborn material totality of class with subtle theosophical talk about "links of affinity, suffering, and hope" (Derrida, *Specters of Marx* 85).

Consequently, contemporary cultural critique has turned culture into zones of nomadic meanings and floating singularities. It celebrates this disconnectedness as an affirmation of the heterogeneity of the corporeal concrete as a resistance to abstract unconcerned totality, as the secret of the subject's difference (Derrida and Ferraris, *Taste for the Secret*). But this is all the estranged difference of the "working day." To put it another way, the fetishizing of the singular in canonic cultural critique is an attempt to represent the prevailing alienation of labor under capitalism as an unexplainable spirituality of difference.

If cultural critique is going to matter and become more than delightful entertainment for the cynical, it must abandon the mythologies of singularity and become materialist. It must become an explanation of totality and understand the singular in the collective. Difference is honored only when the subject is freed from needs. Under all other conditions, difference is merely another name for the boundless rule of the entrepreneur in the free market where use value is obscured by exchange relations and human labor is traded. Materialist critique is a critique for totality. It is not diverted by the profusion of details, textures, and heterogeneities that capitalism manufactures in order to obscure the material logic of the exchange of human labor for a wage.

Cultural critique becomes critique-al only when it becomes a critique for collectivity and joins the cultural struggles for social freedom from necessity, because beyond it "begins that development of human energy which is an end itself": the "true realm of freedom" (Marx, *Capital* 3: 959).

BIBLIOGRAPHY

Abrams, M. H. *Doing Things with Texts.* New York: Norton, 1997.

Adorno, Theodor W. *The Culture Industry.* London: Routledge, 2001.

———. *Minima Moralia.* London: NLB, 1974.

———. *Negative Dialectics.* New York: Continuum, 1973.

Agamben, Giorgio. *Means without End.* Minneapolis: University of Minnesota Press, 2000.

———. *State of Exception.* Chicago: University of Chicago Press, 2005.

Alliott, Catherine. *A Married Man.* New York: Ballantine. 2002.

Althusser, Louis. *For Marx.* London: NLB, 1977.

———. *Lenin and Philosophy.* New York: Monthly Review Press, 1971.

Appadurai, Arjun. *Modernity at Large.* Minneapolis: University of Minnesota Press, 1996.

Aristotle. *Metaphysics. Basic Works of Aristotle.* Ed. R. McKeon. New York: Random House, 1941. 689–934.

Auerbach, Erich. *Mimesis.* Princeton: Princeton University Press, 1953.

Bacon, Francis. *The New Organon.* Indianapolis: Bobbs-Merrill, 1960.

Badiou, Alain. *Deleuze.* Minneapolis: University of Minnesota Press, 2000.

———. *Saint Paul.* Stanford: Stanford University Press, 2003.

Bakhtin, Mikhail. *Essays and Dialogues on His Work.* Ed. G. Morson. Chicago: University of Chicago Press, 1986.

Balzac, Honoré. *The Peasants.* New York: Howard Fertig, 2004.

Barthes, Roland. *The Pleasure of the Text.* New York: Hill and Wang, 1975.

———. "Reality Effect." *The Rustle of Language.* New York: Hill and Wang, 1986. 141–48.

———. *S/Z.* New York: Hill and Wang, 1974.

Bataille, Georges. *The Accursed Share.* Vol 1. New York: Zone, 1988.

Baudrillard, Jean. *The Mirror of Production.* St. Louis: Telos, 1975.

———. *Simulacra and Simulation.* Ann Arbor: University of Michigan Press, 1994.

Bennington, Geoffrey. "Derrida and Politics." *Jacques Derrida and the Humanities.* Ed. Tom Cohen. Cambridge: Cambridge University Press, 2001. 193–212.

Bergson, Henri. *Creative Evolution.* New York: University Press of America, 1983.

Berkeley, George. *A Treatise Concerning the Principles of Human Knowledge. Berkeley's Philosophical Writings.* Ed. D. Armstrong. New York: Collier Books, 1965. 42–128.

Bhabha, Homi, ed. *Nation and Narration.* London: Routledge, 1990.

Brenner, Robert. "Agrarian Class Structure and Economic Development in Pre-Industrial Europe." *The Brenner Debate.* Ed. T. Aston and C. Philpin. Cambridge: Cambridge University Press, 1985. 10–63.

———. "The Agrarian Roots of European Capitalism." *The Brenner Debate.* Ed. T. Aston and C. Philpin. Cambridge: Cambridge University Press, 1985. 213–327.

Bridger, Sue, Rebecca Kay, and Kathryn Pinnick. *No More Heroines? Russia, Women and the Market.* London: Routledge, 1996.

Broyelle, Claudia. *Women's Liberation in China.* December 19, 1998. http://www.blythe.org/mlm/misc/women/wom_ch_toc.htm.

Bukharin, Nikolai. *Imperialism and World Economy.* New York: Monthly Review Press, 1929.

Butler, Judith. *Bodies That Matter: On the Discursive Limits of "Sex."* New York: Routledge, 1993.

———. *Gender Trouble.* 10th anniv. ed. New York: Routledge, 1999.

———. "I Merely Belong to Them." *London Review of Books,* May 10, 2007, 15–17.

———. "Merely Cultural." *Social Text* 15.3–4 (1997): 265–77.

———. *Precarious Life: The Powers of Mourning and Violence.* New York: Verso, 2004.

———. *Undoing Gender.* New York: Routledge, 2004.

———. "What Is Critique?" *The Political.* Ed. D. Ingram. Oxford: Blackwell, 2002. 212–26.

Butler, Judith, Ernesto Laclau, and Reinaldo Laddaga. "The Uses of Equality." *Diacritics* 27.1 (Spring 1997): 2–12.

Butler, Judith, Ernesto Laclau, and Slavoj Žižek. *Contingency, Hegemony, Universality: Contemporary Dialogues on the Left.* London: Verso, 2000.

Butler, Judith, and Gayatri Chakravorty Spivak. *Who Sings the Nation State? Language, Politics, Belonging.* New York: Palgrave, 2007.

Campbell, Kirsten. *Jacques Lacan and Feminist Epistemology.* New York: Routledge, 2004.

Campbell, Rosie, and Maggie O'Neill, eds. *Sex Work Now.* London: Willan, 2006.

Canclini, Nestor Garcia. *Consumers and Citizens.* Minneapolis: University of Minnesota Press, 2001.

Carroll, Michael. "A Comment on 'Pedagogy of the Distressed.'" *College English* 53.5 (September 1991): 599–601.

Chanda, Nayan. *Bound Together.* New Haven: Yale University Press, 2007.

Chow, Rey. "How (the) Inscrutable Chinese Led to Globalized Theory." *PMLA* 116.1 (2001): 69–74.

Clegg, Sue. "Theories of Racism." *International Socialism* 37 (1988): 93–117.

Clements, Barbara Evans. *Bolshevik Feminist: The Life of Aleksandra Kollontai.* Bloomington: Indiana University Press, 1979.

Copjec, Joan. *Read My Desire.* Cambridge: MIT Press, 1996.

Cornell, Drucilla. *At the Heart of Freedom.* Princeton: Princeton University Press, 1998.

Coward, Rosalind, and John Ellis. *Language and Materialism.* London: Routledge, 1977.

Bibliography 199

de Certeau, Michel. *The Practice of Everyday Life.* Berkeley: University of California Press, 1984.

de Lauretis, Teresa. *The Practice of Love.* Bloomington: Indiana University Press, 1994.

Deleuze, Gilles, and Felix Guattari. *Anti-Oedipus.* Minneapolis: University of Minnesota Press, 1983.

———. *A Thousand Plateaus.* Minneapolis: University of Minnesota Press, 1987.

de Man, Paul. *Aesthetic Ideology.* Minneapolis: University of Minnesota Press, 1996.

———. *Allegories of Reading.* New Haven: Yale University Press, 1979.

———. *The Resistance to Theory.* Minneapolis: University of Minnesota Press, 1986.

Derrida, Jacques. *Archive Fever.* Chicago: University of Chicago Press, 1996.

———. "Deconstruction and the Other." *Dialogues with Contemporary Continental Thinkers.* Ed. Richard Kearney. Manchester: Manchester University Press, 1984.

———. "Différance." *Margins of Philosophy.* 1–28.

———. *Dissemination.* Chicago: University of Chicago Press, 1981.

———. "Letter to a Japanese Friend." *A Derrida Reader: Between the Blinds.* Ed. Peggy Kamuf. New York: Columbia University Press, 1991. 269–76.

———. *Limited Inc.* Evanston: Northwestern University Press, 1988.

———. *Margins of Philosophy.* Chicago: University of Chicago Press, 1982.

———. *Of Grammatology.* Baltimore: Johns Hopkins University Press, 1976.

———. *Of Hospitality.* Stanford: Stanford University Press, 2000.

———. *Paper Machine.* Stanford: Stanford University Press, 2005.

———. "Politics and Friendship." *The Althusserian Legacy.* Ed. E. A. Kaplan and M. Sprinker. London: Verso, 1993. 183–231.

———. *Politics of Friendship.* London: Verso, 1997.

———. *Positions.* Chicago: University of Chicago Press, 1981.

———. *Specters of Marx.* New York: Routledge, 1994.

———. "Typewriter Ribbon." *Material Events.* Ed. T. Cohen et al. Minneapolis: University of Minnesota Press, 2001. 277–360.

———. *Writing and Difference.* Chicago: University of Chicago Press, 1978.

Derrida, Jacques, and Maurizio Ferraris. *A Taste for the Secret.* Cambridge: Polity, 2001.

Derrida, Jacques, Jürgen Habermas, and Giovanna Borradori. *Philosophy in a Time of Terror.* Chicago: University of Chicago Press, 2003.

de Saussure, Ferdinand. *Course in General Linguistics.* New York: McGraw-Hill, 1966.

Descartes, René. *Discourse on Method and the Meditations.* Harmondsworth: Penguin, 1968.

Dickstein, Morris. *A Mirror in the Roadway.* Princeton: Princeton University Press, 2007.

Dimock, Wai Chee. "Literature for the Planet." *PMLA* 116.1 (2001): 173–88.

Donoghue, Denis. *Speaking of Beauty.* New Haven: Yale University Press, 2004.

du Gay, Paul, and Michael Pryke. "Cultural Economy." *Cultural Economy.* Ed. Paul du Gay and Michael Pryke. London: Sage, 2002. 1–19.

Dziech, Billie Wright, and Linda Weiner. *The Lecherous Professor: Sexual Harass-ment on Campus.* 2d ed. Urbana: Illinois University Press, 1990.

Ebert, Teresa L. *Ludic Feminism and After: Postmodernism, Desire and Labor in Late Capitalism.* Ann Arbor: University of Michigan Press, 1996.

Ebert, Teresa L., and Mas'ud Zavarzadeh. *Class in Culture.* Boulder: Paradigm, 2008.

————. *Hypohumanities.* Forthcoming.

Engels, Frederick. *Anti-Dühring. Collected Works.* Vol. 25. New York: Interna-tional, 1987. 5–309.

————. *The Condition of the Working-Class in England. Collected Works.* Vol. 4. New York: International, 1976. 295–596.

————. "Letter to Joseph Bloch." *Selected Correspondence.* K. Marx and F. Engels. 3d rev. ed. Moscow: Progress, 1975. 394–96.

————. *The Origin of the Family, Private Property, and the State. Collected Works.* Vol. 26. New York: International, 1990. 129–276.

————. "Outline of a Critique of Political Economy." *Collected Works.* Vol. 3. New York: International, 1975. 418–43.

Ferguson, Adam. *An Essay on the History of Civil Society.* New ed. Cambridge: Cambridge University Press, 1996.

Ferriss, Suzanne, and Mallory Young, eds. *Chick Lit: The New Woman's Fiction.* New York: Routledge, 2006.

Fielding, Helen. *Bridget Jones's Diary.* New York: Penguin, 1996.

Fish, Stanley. "Theory's Hope." *Critical Inquiry* 30.2 (2004): 374–78.

————. *The Trouble with Principle.* Cambridge: Harvard University Press, 1999.

Fiske, John. *Reading the Popular.* New York: Routledge, 1989.

Foucault, Michel. "Governmentality." *Power: Essential Work of Michel Foucault.* Vol. 3. Ed. J. Faubion. New York: New Press, 2000. 201–22.

————. *Herculine Barbin.* New York: Pantheon, 1980.

————. *History of Sexuality.* Vol. 1. New York: Vintage, 1980.

————. *Language, Counter-Memory, Practice.* Ed. Donald E. Bouchard. Ithaca: Cornell University Press, 1977.

————. "Nietzsche, Genealogy, History." *Language, Counter-Memory, Practice.* Ed. Donald E. Bouchard. Ithaca: Cornell University Press, 1977. 139–64.

————. *Power/Knowledge.* Ed. Colin Gordon. New York: Pantheon, 1980.

————. "What Is Critique?" *The Political.* Ed. D. Ingram. Oxford: Blackwell, 2002. 191–211.

————. "What Is Enlightenment?" *The Foucault Reader.* Ed. Paul Rabinow. New York: Pantheon, 1984. 32–50.

Frank, Thomas. *One Market under God.* New York: Anchor, 2001.

Frankel, Valerie. *The Accidental Virgin.* New York: Avon, 2003.

Freire, Paulo. *Pedagogy of the Oppressed.* New York: Continuum, 1990.

Friedman, Thomas L. *The World Is Flat 3.0: A Brief History of the Twenty-first Century.* Further updated and expanded. New York: Farrar, Straus and Giroux, 2007.

Fussell, Paul. *Class.* New York: Ballantine, 1983.

Gallop, Jane. *Anecdotal Theory.* Durham: Duke University Press, 2002.

————. *Around 1981: Academic Feminist Literary Theory.* New York: Routledge, 1992.

————, ed. *Pedagogy: The Question of Impersonation.* Bloomington: Indiana University Press, 1995.

————. "The Teacher's Breasts." *Anecdotal Theory.* Durham: Duke University Press, 2002.

Gallop, Jane, Marianne Hirsch, and Nancy Miller. "Criticizing Feminist Criticism." *Conflicts in Feminism.* Ed. Marianne Hirsch and Evelyn Fox Keller. New York: Routledge, 1990. 349–69.

Garber, Marjorie. *Symptoms of Culture.* New York: Routledge, 1998.

————. *Vice Versa.* New York: Simon and Schuster, 1995.

Gates, Bill. *The Road Ahead.* Rev. ed. New York: Penguin, 1996.

Geertz, Clifford. *The Interpretation of Cultures.* New York: Basic, 1977.

German, Lindsey. *A Question of Class.* London: Bookmarks, 1996.

Gibson-Graham, J. K. *The End of Capitalism (As We Knew It).* Minneapolis: University of Minnesota Press, 2006.

————. *A Postcapitalist Politics.* Minneapolis: University of Minnesota Press, 2006.

Gitlin, Todd. *The Intellectuals and the Flag.* New York: Columbia University Press, 2007.

"Globalizing Literary Studies." Special Issue, *PMLA* 116.1 (2001).

Gray, Francine du Plessix. *Soviet Women.* New York: Anchor-Doubleday, 1990.

Green, Jane. *Jemima J.* New York: Broadway, 2001.

————. *Mr. Maybe.* New York: Broadway, 2001.

Greenblatt, Stephen. "Racial Memory and Literary History." *PMLA* 116.1 (2001): 48–63.

Grosz, Elizabeth. *Architecture from the Outside.* Cambridge: MIT Press, 2001.

————. *Volatile Bodies.* Bloomington: Indiana University Press, 1994.

Halberstam, Judith, and Ira Livingston, eds. *Posthuman Bodies.* Bloomington: Indiana University Press, 1995.

Hall, Gary. "The Politics of Secrecy." *Cultural Studies* 21.1 (2007): 59–81.

Hall, Gary, and Clare Birchall, eds. *New Cultural Studies.* Athens: University of Georgia Press, 2006.

Hall, Stuart. "The Centrality of Culture." *Media and Cultural Regulation.* Ed. Kenneth Thompson. London: Sage, 1997. 207–38.

————. "Cultural Studies and Its Theoretical Legacies." *Stuart Hall.* Ed. D. Morley and K. Chen. London: Routledge, 1996. 262–75.

Haraway, Donna. *Simians, Cyborgs, and Women.* New York: Routledge, 1991.

Hardt, Michael. "Folly of Our Masters of the Universe." *Guardian* (U.K.), December 18, 2002.

Hardt, Michael, and Antonio Negri. *Empire.* Cambridge: Harvard University Press, 2000.

————. *Labor of Dionysus.* Minneapolis: University of Minnesota Press, 1994.

————. *Multitude.* New York: Penguin, 2004.

Harman, Chris. "From Feudalism to Capitalism." *Marxism and History.* London: Bookmarks, 1998. 55–117.

Harman, Chris, and Robert Brenner. "The Origins of Capitalism." *International Socialism* 111 (Summer 2006): 82–106.

Hayek, F. A. *The Fatal Conceit.* Ed. W. Bartley. Chicago: University of Chicago Press, 1988.

Hayles, N. Katherine. *How We Became Posthuman.* Chicago: University of Chicago Press, 1999.

———. *My Mother Was a Computer.* Chicago: University of Chicago Press, 2005.

Healey, Dorothy, and Maurice Isserman. *Dorothy Healey Remembers: A Life in the American Communist Party.* New York: Oxford University Press, 1990.

Hegel, G. W. F. *On Art, Religion, Philosophy.* Ed. J. Gray. New York: Harper and Row, 1970.

———. *Phenomenology of Spirit.* Oxford: Oxford University Press, 1977.

Heidegger, Martin. *Poetry, Language, Thought.* New York: Harper and Row, 1971.

Heng, Geraldine. "Pleasure, Resistance, and a Feminist Aesthetics of Reading." *The Cambridge Companion to Feminist Literary Theory.* Ed. Ellen Rooney. Cambridge: Cambridge University Press, 2006. 53–72.

Hessen, B. *The Social and Economic Roots of Newton's* Principia. New York: Howard Fertig, 1971.

hooks, bell. "Eros, Eroticism, and the Pedagogical Process." *Teaching to Transgress.* New York: Routledge, 1994. 191–99.

———. "Good Sex: Passionate Pedagogy." *Teaching Community.* New York: Routledge, 2003. 139–56.

Hume, David. Enquiries Concerning Human Understanding *and* Concerning the Principles of Morals. 3d Ed. Oxford: Oxford University Press, 1975.

Huyssen, Andreas. Foreword to *Critique of Cynical Reason, by* P. Sloterdijk. Minneapolis: University of Minnesota Press, 1987. ix–xxv.

Irigaray, Luce. *This Sex Which Is Not One.* Ithaca: Cornell University Press, 1985.

Jameson, Fredric. *Archaeologies of the Future.* London: Verso, 2007.

———. Introduction to *Marxist Esthetics,* by Henri Arvon. Ithaca: Cornell University Press, 1973. vii–xxiv.

———. "Marxism and Dualism in Deleuze." *South Atlantic Quarterly* 96.3 (1997): 393–416.

———. *Postmodernism, or, the Cultural Logic of Late Capitalism.* Durham: Duke University Press, 1991.

———. *A Singular Modernity.* London: Verso, 2002.

Kant, Immanuel. *Critique of Judgment.* New York: Hafner-Macmillan, 1951.

———. *Critique of Pure Reason.* New York: St. Martin's, 1965.

———. "What Is Enlightenment?" Foundations of the Metaphysics of Morals *and* What Is Enlightenment? Indianapolis: Bobbs-Merrill, 1959. 85–92.

Kautsky, Karl. "Imperialism and the War." 1914. http://marxists.org/archive/kautsky/1914/09/war.htm.

Kellner, Douglas. *Media Spectacle.* New York: Routledge, 2003.

Kempadoo, Kamala, and Jo Doezema, eds. *Global Sex Workers.* New York: Routledge, 1998.

Keyes, Marian. *Last Chance Saloon.* New York: Perennial, 2003.

———. *Lucy Sullivan Is Getting Married.* New York: Avon: 1996.

Kinsella, Sophie. *Confessions of a Shopaholic.* New York: Delta, 2001.

———. *Shopaholic Takes Manhattan.* New York: Delta, 2002.

Kipnis, Laura. *Against Love: A Polemic*. New York: Vintage, 2003.
———. *The Female Thing*. New York: Vintage, 2006.
Kojeve, Alexandre. "The Dialectic of the Real and Phenomenological Method in Hegel." *Introduction to the Reading of Hegel*. Ithaca: Cornell University Press, 1980. 169–260.
Kollontai. Alexandra. *Selected Writings of Alexandra Kollontai*. Ed. Alix Holt. New York: Norton, 1977.
Krentz, Jayne A., ed. *Dangerous Men and Adventurous Women: Romance Writers on the Appeal of the Romance*. Philadelphia: University of Pennsylvania Press, 1992.
———. *Flash*. New York: Pocket, 1998.
Kristof, Nicholas D. Review of *Golden Arches East*, edited by J. Watson. *New York Times*. March 22, 1998.
Kuhn, Thomas. *The Structure of Scientific Revolutions*. 2d ed. Chicago: University of Chicago Press, 1970.
Kwitney, Alisa. *The Dominant Blonde*. New York: Avon, 2002.
Lacan, Jacques. *Ecrits*. Trans. Bruce Fink. New York: Norton, 2002.
———. *The Four Fundamental Concepts of Psycho-Analysis*. Ed. J.-A. Miller. New York: Norton, 1981.
———. "God and the *Jouissance* of ~~The~~ Woman: A Love Letter." *Feminine Sexuality*. Ed. J. Mitchell and J. Rose. New York: Norton, 1985. 137–48.
Laclau, Ernesto. "Beyond Emancipation." *Emancipation(s)*. London: Verso, 1996. 1–19.
———. "Deconstructing Classes." *Contingency, Hegemony, Universality*. J. Butler, E. Laclau, and S. Žižek. London: Verso, 2000. 296–301.
———. *New Reflections on the Revolutions of Our Time*. London: Verso, 1990.
———. "Why Do Empty Signifiers Matter to Politics?" *Emancipation(s)*. London: Verso. 36–46.
Laclau, Ernesto, and Chantal Mouffe. *Hegemony and Socialist Strategy*. London: Verso, 1985.
Lacoue-Labarthe, Philippe. *Typography: Mimesis, Philosophy, Politics*. Stanford: Stanford University Press, 1989.
Lapidus, Gail. *Women in Soviet Society*. Berkeley: University of California Press, 1978.
Larrain, Jorge. *Marxism and Ideology*. Atlantic Highlands: Humanities, 1983.
Lash, Scott, and John Urry. *Economies of Signs and Space*. London: Sage, 1994.
Leacock, Eleanor Burke. "Introduction." *The Origin of the Family, Private Property and the State*. Frederick Engels. New York: International, 1972. 7–66.
Lefevre, Wolfgang. "Science as Labor." *Perspectives on Science*. 13.2 (2005): 194–225.
Lenin, V. I. "Conspectus of Hegel's Book *The Science of Logic*." *Collected Works*. Vol. 38. Moscow: Progress, 1976. 85–238.
———. "A Great Beginning." *Collected Works*. *Vol.* 29. Moscow: Progress, 1965. 410–34.
———. *Imperialism, the Highest Stage of Capitalism*. *Collected Works*. Vol. 22. Moscow: Progress, 1964. 185–304.
———. *Materialism and Empirio-Criticism*. *Collected Works*. Vol. 14. Moscow: Progress. 1962. 17–361.

————. "Once Again on the Trade Unions." *Collected Works.* Vol. 32. Moscow: Progress, 1965. 70–107.

————. *On the Emancipation of Women.* Moscow: Progress, 1974.

————. "On the Question of Dialectics." *Collected Works.* Vol. 38. Moscow: Progress, 1976. 353–61.

————. *Philosophical Notebooks. Collected Works.* Vol. 38. Moscow: Progress, 1976.

————. "Soviet Power and the Status of Women." *Collected Works.* Vol. 30. Moscow: Progress, 1965. 120–23.

————. *The State and Revolution. Collected Works.* Vol. 25. Moscow: Progress, 1964. 383–492.

————. *What Is to Be Done? Collected Works.* Vol. 5. Moscow: Foreign Languages Publishing, 1961. 347–529.

Lenoir, Timothy, ed. *Inscribing Science.* Stanford: Stanford University Press, 1998.

Lévi-Strauss, Claude. *The Raw and the Cooked.* New York: Harper and Row, 1975.

————. *The Savage Mind.* Chicago: University of Chicago Press, 1966.

Livingston, Robert Eric. "Glocal Knowledges." *PMLA* 116.1 (2001): 145–57.

Locke, John. *An Essay Concerning Human Understanding.* Ed. A. Woozley. New York: New American Library, 1964.

————. "Second Treatise." *Two Treatises of Government.* Ed. I. Shapiro. New Haven: Yale University Press, 2003. 100–209.

Lowell, Elizabeth. *Amber Beach.* 1997. New York: Avon, 1998.

————. *Death Is Forever.* New York: Avon, 2004. Reissue and retitling of Ann Maxwell [pseud.], *The Diamond Tiger* (1992, 1999).

————. *Jade Island.* 1998. New York: Avon, 1999.

————. "Love Conquers All." *Dangerous Men and Adventurous Women.* Ed. Jayne Ann Krentz. 89–97.

————. *Midnight in Ruby Bayou.* New York: Avon, 2001.

————. *Pearl Cove.* 1999. New York: Avon, 2000.

————. *Running Scared.* New York: Avon, 2002.

Lukács, Georg. *History and Class Consciousness.* Cambridge: MIT Press, 1983.

————. *Realism in Our Time.* New York: Harper and Row, 1971.

————. *Studies in European Realism.* New York: Grosset and Dunlap, 1964.

Lyotard, Jean-François. *The Differend.* Minneapolis: University of Minnesota Press, 1988.

————. *Just Gaming.* Minneapolis: University of Minnesota Press, 1988.

————. *The Postmodern Condition.* Minneapolis: University of Minnesota Press, 1984.

Mabry, Rochelle A. "About a Girl: Female Subjectivity and Sexuality in Contemporary 'Chick' Culture." *Chick Lit.* Ed. S. Ferris and M. Young. New York: Routledge, 2006. 191–206.

MacCabe, Colin. *Tracking the Signifier.* Minneapolis: University of Minnesota Press, 1985.

Machel, Samora. "Women's Liberation Is Essential for the Revolution." *Revolutionary Thought in the 20th Century.* Ed. Ben Turok. London: Zed, 1980. 157–67.

Mandel, Ernest. *An Introduction to Marxist Economic Theory.* New York: Path-finder, 1983.

Marcuse, Herbert. *The Aesthetic Dimension.* Boston: Beacon, 1978.

———. *Negations.* Boston: Beacon, 1968.

Margolis, Sue. *Apocalipstick.* New York: Dell, 2003.

Marks, Elaine. "In Defense of Modern Languages and Literatures, Masterpieces, Nihilism, and Dead European Writers." *MLA Newsletter* (Fall 1993): 2–3.

———. "Memory, Desire, and Pleasure in the Classroom." *MLA Newsletter* (Winter 1993): 3–4.

Marvell, Andrew. "The Garden." *The Complete Poems.* London: Penguin, 2005. 100–102.

Marx, Karl. *Capital.* Vol. 1. New York: Penguin, 1976.

———. *Capital.* Vol. 3. New York: Penguin, 1981.

———. "A Contribution to the Critique of Hegel's Philosophy of Right. Introduction." *Early Writings.* New York: Vintage, 1975. 243–58.

———. *A Contribution to the Critique of Political Economy.* New York: International, 1970.

———. *Critique of the Gotha Programme.* New York: International, 1966.

———. *Early Writings.* Ed. Lucio Colletti. New York: Vintage, 1975.

———. *Economic and Philosophic Manuscripts of 1844. Collected Works.* Vol. 3. New York: International, 1975. 229–443.

———. *Grundrisse.* London: Penguin, 1973.

———. *The Poverty of Philosophy. Collected Works.* Vol. 6. New York: International, 1976. 105–212.

———. "Theses on Feuerbach." *Collected Works.* Vol. 5. New York: International, 1976. 3–8.

———. Wage-Labour and Capital *and* Value, Price and Profit. New York: International, 1976.

Marx, Karl, and Frederick Engels. *The German Ideology. Collected Works.* Vol. 5. New York: International, 1976. 19–539.

———. *Manifesto of the Communist Party.* Moscow: Progress, 1977.

———. *Selected Correspondence.* 3rd ed. Moscow: Progress, 1975.

McNally, David. "Language, History, and Class Struggle." *In Defense of History.* Ed. E. Wood and J. Foster. New York: Monthly Review Press, 1997. 26–42.

Menzel, Peter, and Faith D'Aluisio. *Robo Sapiens.* Cambridge: MIT Press, 2001.

Micklethwait, John, and Adrian Wooldridge. *A Future Perfect.* New York: Random House, 2003.

Miller, J. Hillis. *The Ethics of Reading.* New York: Columbia University Press, 1987.

Mouffe, Chantal. *The Return of the Political.* London: Verso, 2006.

Munoz, Ana, and Alan Woods. "Marxism and the Emancipation of Women." *In Defense of Marxism.* March 3, 2000. http://www.marxist.com/Theory/ .Marxism and women.html.

Nagle, Jill, ed. *Whores and Other Feminists.* New York: Routledge, 1997.

Navarro, Vicente. *Dangerous to Your Health.* New York: Monthly Review Press, 1993.

Naylor, Clare. *Dog Handling.* New York: Ballantine, 2002.

————. *Love: A User's Guide.* New York: Ballantine, 1997.

Negri, Antonio. *Marx Beyond Marx.* South Hadley, Mass.: Bergin and Garvey, 1984.

Nietzsche, Friedrich. *Beyond Good and Evil.* Harmondsworth: Penguin, 1973.

————. The Birth of Tragedy *and* The Case of Wagner. New York: Vintage, 1967.

————. *The Gay Science.* New York: Vintage, 1974.

————. *Human, All Too Human.* Lincoln: University of Nebraska Press, 1984.

————. On the Genealogy of Morals *and* Ecce Homo. New York: Vintage, 1969.

————. *Thus Spoke Zarathustra.* Harmondsworth: Penguin, 1969.

————. Twilight of the Idols *and* The Anti-Christ. Harmondsworth: Penguin, 1973.

————. *The Will to Power.* New York: Vintage, 1967.

1917 Collective, The. "Capitalism and Homophobia." *The Material Queer.* Ed. Donald Morton. Boulder: Westview, 1996. 369–79.

Ohmae, Kenichi. *The End of the Nation State.* New York: Simon and Schuster, 1996.

Olivera, Oscar. *¡Cochabamba! Water War in Bolivia.* Boston: South End, 2004.

Penley, Constance. "Crackers and Whackers." *White Trash.* Ed. M. Wray and A. Newitz. New York: Routledge. 1997. 89–112.

Petras, James, and Henry Veltmeyer. *Globalization Unmasked.* London: Zed, 2001.

Pirenne, Henri. *Medieval Cities.* Princeton: Princeton University Press, 1969.

Probyn, Elspeth. *Carnal Appetites.* New York: Routledge, 2000.

Proust, Marcel. *Swann's Way.* New York: Vintage, 1970.

Readings, Bill. *The University in Ruins.* Cambridge: Harvard University Press, 1996.

Reich, Wilhelm. *The Sexual Revolution.* New York: Pocket Books, 1975.

Reiche, Reimut. *Sexuality and Class Struggle.* New York: Praeger, 1971.

Ritzer, George. *Enchanting a Disenchanted World.* 2d ed. London: Pine Forge, 2004.

Robertson, Roland. *Globalization: Social Theory and Global Culture.* London: Sage, 1992.

"Romance Writers of America's 2005 Market Research Study on Romance Readers." https://www.rwanational.org/eweb/docs/05MarketResearch.pdf.

Ronell, Avital. *Crack Wars.* Urbana: University of Illinois Press, 2004.

————. "On the Misery of Theory without Poetry." *PMLA* 120.1 (2005): 16–32.

————. *The Telephone Book.* Lincoln: University of Nebraska Press, 1989.

Rorty, Richard. *Contingency, Irony, and Solidarity.* Cambridge: Cambridge University Press, 1989.

————. *Philosophy as Cultural Politics.* Cambridge: Cambridge University Press, 2007.

Ross, Andrew, ed. *Science Wars.* Durham: Duke University Press, 1996.

Rousseau, Jean-Jacques. "Discourse on Political Economy." *Rousseau's Political Writings.* Ed. A. Ritter and J. Bondanella. New York: Norton, 1988. 58–83.

————. *On the Social Contract. Rousseau's Political Writings.* Ed. A. Ritter and J. Bondanella. New York: Norton, 1988. 84–173.

Rule, Sheila. "Reagan Gets Red Carpet from British." *New York Times,* June 14, 1989.

"Russian Revolutions: Sex in Russia." *Nightline* (ABC News), March 17, 2000. http://abcnews.go.com/onair/nightline/transcripts/nl000317__trans.html.

Salaman, Graeme. "Culturing Production." *Production of Culture/ Cultures of Production.* Ed. P. du Gay. London: Sage, 1997. 235–79.

Sanbonmatsu, John. *The Postmodern Prince.* New York: Monthly Review Press, 2003.

Sartre, Jean-Paul. *Being and Nothingness.* New York: Washington Square, 1956.

———. *Search for a Method.* New York: Vintage, 1968.

Scheper-Hughes, Nancy. *Death without Weeping.* Berkeley: University of California Press, 1992.

Schor, Naomi. *Reading in Detail.* New York: Methuen, 1987.

Sedgwick, Eve Kosofsky. *Touching Feeling.* Durham: Duke University Press, 2003.

Showalter, Elaine. "The Professor Wore Prada." *Vogue,* December 1997: 80, 86, 92.

Shumway, David. "Cultural Studies and Questions of Pleasure and Value." *The Aesthetics of Cultural Studies.* Ed. M. Berube. Oxford: Blackwell, 2005. 103–16.

Sloterdijk, Peter. *Critique of Cynical Reason.* Minneapolis: University of Minnesota Press, 1988.

Spivak, Gayatri Chakravorty. *A Critique of Postcolonial Reason.* Cambridge: Harvard University Press, 1999.

———. *Outside in the Teaching Machine.* New York: Routledge, 1993.

Stade, Ronald, and Gurdun Dahl. "Globalization, Creolization, and Cultural Complexity." *Global Networks* 3.3 (July 2003): 201–6.

Stiglitz, Joseph. "Globalism's Discontents". *American Prospect,* January 2002, 1–14.

———. *Globalization and Its Discontents.* New York: Norton, 2002.

———. *Making Globalization Work.* New York: Norton, 2007.

Sweezy, Paul, et al. *The Transition from Feudalism to Capitalism.* Atlantic Highlands, N.J.: Humanities: 1976.

Tabellini, Guido. "Culture and Institutions: Economic Development in the Regions of Europe." Working Paper no. 292, Innocenzo Gasparini Institute for Economic Research, Bocconi University, 2005. http://ideas.repec.org/p/igi/igierp/292.html.

Talbot, Margaret. "A Most Dangerous Method." *Lingua Franca* (January-February 1994): 1, 24–40.

Taussig, Michael. *Mimesis and Alterity.* New York: Routledge, 1993.

Thompson, E. P. "The Long Revolution." *New Left Review* 1 (1961): 24–39.

Toffler, Alvin. *Powershift.* New York: Bantam, 1991.

Tompkins, Jane. "Pedagogy of the Distressed." *College English* 52.6 (October 1990): 653–60; "Comments and Response." *College English* 53.5 (September 1991): 599–605, 53.6 (October 1991): 714–17.

Trotsky, Leon. "From the Old Family to the New." *Women and the Family.* New York: Pathfinder, 1970. 19–28.

———. *The Revolution Betrayed.* New York: Pathfinder, 1972.

Voloshinov, V. N. *Marxism and the Philosophy of Language.* Cambridge: Harvard University Press, 1973.

Wacquant, Loïc. "Critical Thought as Solvent to Doxa." 2006. http://transform.eipcp.net/transversal/0806/wacquant/en.

Wallerstein, Immanuel. *The Capitalist World Economy*. Cambridge: Cambridge University Press, 1979.

————. *Historical Capitalism*. London: Verso, 1983.

Warminski, Andrzej. "Ending Up/Taking Back (with Two Postscripts on Paul de Man's Historical Materialism." *Critical Encounters*. Ed. Cathy Caruth and Deborah Esch. New Brunswick: Rutgers University Press, 1995. 11–41.

————. "Introduction: Allegories of Reference." *Aesthetic Ideology, by Paul* de Man. Minneapolis: University of Minnesota Press, 1996. 1–33.

Warner, Michael. "Uncritical Reading." *Polemic*. Ed. Jane Gallop. New York: Routledge, 2004. 13–38.

Waters, Malcolm. *Globalization*. 2d ed. London: Routledge, 2001.

Watt, Ian. *The Rise of the Novel*. Berkeley: University of California Press, 1965.

Weber, Max. "Class, Status Party." *Max Weber*. Ed. H. Gerth and C. Wright Mills. New York: Oxford University Press, 1946. 180–95.

————. *The Protestant Ethic and the "Spirit" of Capitalism*. New York: Routledge, 1992.

Weinberg, Steven. "Two Cheers for Reductionism." *Dreams of a Final Theory*. New York: Pantheon, 1992. 51–64.

Weiner, Jennifer. *Good in Bed*. New York: Washington Square, 2001.

"What Is Chick Lit, You Ask?" http://www.chicklit.us/whatiscl.htm (accessed July 2006).

Whelehan, Imelda. *Helen Fielding's* Bridget Jones's Diary. New York: Continuum, 2002.

Williams, Raymond. *Problems in Materialism and Culture*. London: Verso, 1980.

Wood, Ellen Meiksins. *The Origin of Capitalism: A Longer View*. London: Verso, 2002.

World Social Forum. "Charter of Principles." http://www.forumsocialmundial .org.br/main.php?id_menu=4&cd_language=2.

Wright, Elizabeth. *Lacan and Postfeminism*. London: Totem, 2001.

Yates, Michael. *Cheap Motels and a Hot Plate*. New York: Monthly Review Press, 2007.

Yergin, Daniel, and Joseph Stanislaw. *The Commanding Heights*. Rev ed. New York: Free Press, 2002.

Young, Iris Marion. "Breasted Experience." *Throwing Like a Girl and Other Essays in Feminist Philosophy and Social Theory*. Bloomington: Indiana University Press, 1990. 189–209.

Yudice, George. *The Expediency of Culture*. Durham: Duke University Press, 2003.

Zavarzadeh, Mas'ud. "The Pedagogy of Totality." *Journal of Advanced Composition Theory* 23.1 (2003): 1–54.

————. "Postality." *Post-Ality*. Ed. M. Zavarzadeh et al. Washington, D.C.: Maisonneuve, 1995. 1–75.

Zilsel, Edgar. *The Social Origins of Modern Science*. New York: Springer, 2003.

Žižek, Slavoj. "Class Struggle or Postmodernism?" *Contingency, Hegemony, Universality*, by Judith Butler, Ernesto Laclau, and Slavoj Žižek. London: Verso, 2000. 90–135.

———. *Did Somebody Say Totalitarianism?* London: Verso, 2001.

———. "Have Michael Hardt and Antonio Negri Rewritten the Communist Manifesto for the Twenty-first Century?" *Rethinking Marxism* 13.3 (2001): 190–98.

———. *Iraq: The Borrowed Kettle.* London: Verso, 2005.

———. "Kate's Choice, Or, the Materialism of Henry James." *The Parallax View.* Cambridge: MIT Press, 2006. 124–44.

———. "A Leninist Gesture Today: Against the Populist Temptation." *Lenin Reloaded.* Ed. Sebastian Budgen, Stathis Kouvelakis, and Slavoj Žižek. Durham: Duke University Press, 2007. 74–99.

———. *Organs without Bodies.* New York: Routledge, 2003.

———. *The Parallax View.* Cambridge: MIT Press, 2006.

———. "A Plea for Return to *Différance* (with a Minor 'Pro Domo Sua')." *Critical Inquiry* 32.2 (2006): 226–49.

———. *The Puppet and the Dwarf.* Cambridge: MIT Press, 2003.

———. *Revolution at the Gates.* London: Verso, 2002.

———. "Spectre of Ideology." *Mapping Ideology.* Ed. Slavoj Žižek. London: Verso, 1994. 1–33.

———. *The Sublime Object of Ideology.* London: Verso, 1989.

———. *Tarrying with the Negative.* Durham: Duke University Press, 1993.

———. *Welcome to the Desert of the Real.* London: Verso, 2002.

Žižek, Slavoj, and Glyn Daly. *Conversations with Žižek.* Cambridge: Polity, 2004.

INDEX

abstract, x, 4, 7, 13–14, 17, 40–42, 45, 60

Adorno, Theodor W., 29, 90, 100–101, 195

Agamben, Giorgio, 19, 160–61

Alliott, Catherine, 104

Althusser, Louis, 42, 52, 107, 183

Appadurai, Arjun, 135

Aristotle, 31

Auerbach, Erich, 29, 32–33

Bacon, Francis, 12

Badiou, Alain, 58, 163

Bakhtin, Mikhail, xv

Balzac, Honoré, 41–43

Barber, Benjamin R., 143

Barthes, Roland, 6, 32, 169–70, 188, 195

Baudrillard, Jean, 40, 137

Bell, Daniel, 143

Bergson, Henri, 48, 72, 74

Berkeley, George, 13, 63

Bhabha, Homi, 144

body: body without organs, 57; conceptuality, 25; concrete, 3, 7; corporeality, 51, 56; flat-ing, 51–54; materiality, 46–48; social production, 86

Bourdieu, Pierre, 98

Brenner, Robert, 9

Broyelle, Claudia, 131

Butler, Judith, 7, 74, 88–89, 125, 157–59, 162

Canclini, Nestor Garcia, 147

chick lit, 102–4; capitalism, 111–13; cynicism, 105, 108, 116; first-person, 108; ideology, 107; romance, 104

Chow, Rey, 140

Cixous, Hélène, 129

class: definition, 101–2; desire, 70–74; love, 118–33; mimesis, 27–33; pedagogy, 69; reading, 44; Žižek, 162

Clegg, Sue, 84

concrete, 3, 14, 29, 32–33, 41–42, 45, 60

Cornell, Drucilla, 126

de Certeau, Michel, 30, 47, 100

Deleuze, Gilles, 52–53, 56–59, 70–74, 99, 117

de Man, Paul, 7, 27, 34, 37, 169–91, 195

Derrida, Jacques, 17–18, 20, 53, 72, 88–89, 170–71, 175, 195–96; globalization, 133–36; mimesis, 27–28, 31–33

de Saussure, Ferdinand, 84, 96, 100, 125, 187

Descartes, René, 74

detailism, 33

Dimock, Wai Chee, 139

Ebert, Teresa L., 60, 70, 102, 139, 141

Engels, Frederick, 21, 40, 54, 105, 146

Feuerbach, Ludwig, 24–25, 88

Fish, Stanley, 6, 23

Fiske, John, 48, 100, 147

Foucault, Michel, 17, 22, 33, 49–50, 56, 77, 88–89, 131, 145

Frank, Thomas, 147, 152

Frankel, Valerie, 106, 115
Freire, Paulo, 82–83
Freud, Sigmund, 99
Friedman, Thomas L., 52–54, 134–35, 143

Gallop, Jane, 75–79, 81, 95, 125
Gates, Bill, 59
Geertz, Clifford, 33
Gibson-Graham, J. K., 4–6, 76, 103, 120, 125, 153
globalization: internationalism, 148; interpretive imaginary, 134; structure of feeling, 140; surplus labor, 149–50; transnationalism, 134
Green, Jane, 103, 105, 108, 111, 114
Greenblatt, Stephen, 136, 141
Grossberg, Lawrence, 174–75
Grosz, Elizabeth, ix, 46–63, 84–86, 125
Guattari, Felix, xi, 49, 52–53, 56–59, 70–74, 85, 96, 99, 117, 125, 145

Hall, Gary, 175
Hall, Stuart, 21, 100, 137, 174
Haraway, Donna, 137
Hardt, Michael, xii, 60, 143, 151–54, 161, 167
Harman, Chris, 9
Hayek, F. A., 145
Hayles, N. Katherine, 61–62
Hegel, G. W. F., xv, 3, 13, 26, 74, 116, 155, 157
Heidegger, Martin, 13, 40
hooks, bell, 75, 79–81
Horkheimer, Max, 29, 87, 90
Howard, Linda, 104
Hume, David, 11–13, 16

ideology, 34, 172; de Man, 177–83; materialist, 187–91
Irigaray, Luce, 86, 89–90, 129

Jameson, Fredric, 25, 43, 52, 64–65, 90, 138, 147

Kant, Immanuel, 3, 12, 45, 74, 181, 183, 185, 188

Kautsky, Karl, 153
Keyes, Marian, 104
Kinsella, Sophie, 116
Kipnis, Laura, 130–31
Kojeve, Alexandre, 162
Kollontai, Alexandra, 118–33
Krentz, Jayne Ann, 110
Kristof, Nicholas D., 135
Kuhn, Thomas, 134
Kwitney, Alisa, 114, 117

Lacan, Jacques, 30, 69–74, 106
Laclau, Ernesto, 160, 162–66, 187
Lacoue-Labarthe, Philippe, 40
Lapidus, Gail, 122–23
Larrain, Jorge, 63–64
Lash, Scott, 138, 142
Lenin, V. I., 44–45, 54–55, 63, 122–23, 146, 153–56
Lévi-Strauss, Claude, 18, 20
Livingston, Robert Eric, 139–40
Locke, John, 11, 13
love: corny, 106; finicky signifier, 113; red, 118–33; for suckers, 104, 116
Lowell, Elizabeth, 99, 104, 106–7, 116, 191, 193
Lukács, Georg, xi, 4, 30, 39–42, 44, 195
Lyotard, Jean-François, 8, 17, 19, 40, 52, 148, 188, 195

Mabry, Rochelle A., 108
Machel, Samora, 75
Macherey, Pierre, 190
Mallarmé, Stéphane, 28, 31
Margolis, Sue, 111
Marks, Elaine, 74–75
Marx, Karl, 10, 25, 40–45, 63, 76, 87, 97, 147, 169–93, 196; concrete, 66; consciousness, 7; essence and appearance, 30–31; labor power and wages, 21–22, 92–93, 101, 128–29, 150–51; needs and wants, 70–73; ruling ideas, 91
materialism, 12, 24; delectable, 3, 25, 46–47; dialectical, 164; historical, 25; neo-materialism, 163; objectivity, 157; without materiality, 24

McLuhan, Marshall, 40, 137, 143
McNally, David, 23
McRobbie, Angela, 100, 175
meaning, 39–40
Miller, J. Hillis, 44, 173
Mouffe, Chantal, 17, 160–61

Nagle, Jill, 126
Naylor, Clare, 102, 104
Negri, Antonio, 60, 143, 151–54,
    167–68
Nietzsche, Friedrich, xiii–xv, 14–17,
    19–20, 39, 49, 55–56, 145

Ohmae, Kenichi, 141

Paglia, Camille, 81
Pirenne, Henri, 9
Probyn, Elspeth, 46, 70, 130,
Proust, Marcel, 34–39, 41, 43–44

Readings, Bill, 141
Reiche, Reimut, 131
Ritzer, George, 148
Robards, Karen, 104
Roberts, Nora, 104
Robertson, Roland, 135, 143
Roiphe, Katie, 81
romance: class, 100; consumption,
    103; corny love, 106; cultural
    capital, 98; desiring production, 99;
    fantasy, 100; ideology, 102; prop-
    erty, 107
Ronell, Avital, 7, 47
Rorty, Richard, xiv, 23, 143
Rousseau, Jean-Jacques, 3, 14, 39,
    186–87

Sartre, Jean-Paul, 3, 169
Scheper-Hughes, Nancy, 95–96
Sedgwick, Eve Kosofsky, 3, 47, 86,
    125, 172–73
Showalter, Elaine, 47–48
Sloterdijk, Peter, 105, 107, 116, 157,
    159, 163

Spivak, Gayatri Chakravorty, 6, 140,
    159
state: class, 144; Lenin, 146, 153;
    nation-state, 143–45, 153; post-
    state, 148
Stiglitz, Joseph, 134
surplus labor: desire, 99; globaliza-
    tion, 149–50; language, 39
Sweezy, Paul, 9

Tabellini, Guido, 137
Taussig, Michael, 29
Thompson, E. P., 147
Toffler, Alvin, 147
Tompkins, Jane, 82–83, 87
totality, 4, 195–96
Trotsky, Leon, 119, 122–24
Turkle, Sherry, 137

Urry, John, 138, 142

Voloshinov, V. N., 188

Wacquant, Loïc, 87
Wallerstein, Immanuel, 9, 143,
    148–49
Warminski, Andrzej, 178, 180–83
Warner, Michael, 13, 171–73
Waters, Malcolm, 138, 144, 147–48,
    154
Watt, Ian, 33
Weber, Max, 65, 137, 143
Weiner, Jennifer, 104–5, 115
Williams, Raymond, 147
Wolf, Naomi, 81
Wood, Ellen Meiksins, 9

Young, Iris Marion, 86, 120

Zavarzadeh, Mas'ud, 60, 139, 141
Žižek, Slavoj, 13, 19, 65, 72, 102, 105,
    107, 116, 155–68

TERESA L. EBERT is the author of *Ludic Feminism and After: Postmodernism, Desire, and Labor in Late Capitalism* and coauthor of *Class in Culture*. She has published numerous essays and articles in such journals as *Cultural Critique, College English, Science and Society, Rethinking Marxism, Genders, Poetics Today, Language and Style, Journal of Advanced Composition Theory, American Journal of Semiotics, American Quarterly, and Women's Review of Books*. Her long essay "Quango-ing the University: The End(s) of Critique-al Humanities" appeared in *Cultural Logic*. She is the coeditor of *Post-ality: Marxism and Postmodernism* and *Marxism, Queer Theory, Gender*. She is also the coauthor of a new book, *Hypohumanities*.

The University of Illinois Press
is a founding member of the
Association of American University Presses.

Composed in 9.5/12.5 Trump Mediaeval
by Jim Proefrock
at the University of Illinois Press
Manufactured by Cushing-Malloy, Inc.

University of Illinois Press
1325 South Oak Street
Champaign, IL 61820-6903
www.press.uillinois.edu